THE DAY WE BOMBED SWITZERLAND

THE DAY WE BOMBED SWITZERLAND

Flying with the US Eighth Army Air Force in World War II

JACKSON GRANHOLM

Airlife
CLASSIC

Copyright © 2000 Jackson Granholm

First published in the UK in 2000
by **Airlife Publishing Ltd**

This edition published 2002

British Library Cataloguing-in-Publication Data
A catalogue record for this book
is available from the British Library

ISBN 1 84037 371 7

Printed in England by Livesey Ltd., Shrewsbury (01743) 235651

Distributed in North America by
STACKPOLE BOOKS
5067 Ritter Road, Mechanicsburg, PA 17055
www.stackpolebooks.com

For a complete list of all Airlife titles please contact:

Airlife Publishing Ltd
101 Longden Road, Shrewsbury, SY3 9EB, England
E-mail: sales@airlifebooks.com
Website: www.airlifebooks.com

FOREWORD

World War II, like all wars was fought by the young. I was one of those young.

In no other time nor place could I have done the things and met the people that I did in the U.S. Eighth Army Air Force.

The Eighth was the greatest air force in history. Over three hundred thousand Americans served with the Eighth during the three years it was stationed in Europe. Over twenty-six thousand died in that military service, most of them combat aircrewmen.

The American Military Cemetery at Cambridge is the resting place of many who died in European skies. The scattered, burned, exploded, and drowned remains of many more lie in forests, fields and waters from the North Sea to the Mediterranean.

In spite of this vast carnage – this returning of emigrant blood to be spilled upon the motherlands – the *esprit de corps* of the Eighth Air Force was unmatched. Everyone who flew in that Air Force knew he was with the finest military outfit of the War, the world, and all history.

This was especially true of people of Second Air Division; their numbers were fewer. They flew the ugly bombers. To compensate, they went about their deadly work with special and aggressive pride.

My times with Second Air Division were unique and unforgettable.

Friends of those war days are etched forever in memory. The days of World War II ended long ago. But the history of those days is worth retelling.

Many kind people helped in this modest retelling of my days with the Eighth. Foremost among them was a dear friend, Charles Davis, writer, actor, and director. It was Charles who urged me to write this book, insisting that it must be created.

Many others shared with me photos and details from their memories, and facts from their related experiences. Among them were the following:

A. Rohl Barnes	Lawrence Fick
Carl C. Barthel	Carsie E. Foley
Paul Betzold	Dominic Giordano
Charles H. Booth	Dores Gniewkowski
Charles Breeding	Irving Goldman
Louis Brumble	Teague Gray Harris, Jr
George Chimples	Robert Hayzlett
James H. Doolittle	Brownie Harvath
Wilbur B. Eaton	Allen F. Herzberg

James A. Hogg   Frederick O'Neill
James H. Isbell   Weldon Sheltraw
Donald C. Jamison   Maurice Speer
Leon W. Johnson   James M. Stewart
Myron Keilman   Fred Vacek
Albert Kemp   Valin Woodward
Tony North   Theodore Zelasko

To these dear people gratitude and deep thanks. With their help I was able to round out many facts that had remained ragged in my own mind.

JACKSON W. GRANHOLM
Roseburg, Oregon
2000

PREFACE

William Tecumseh Sherman said, 'War is Hell!' So it is. However, it's many other things as well. This book shares with the reader a broad spectrum of emotions: humour, fear, frustration, sorrow, and triumph. These are the stories of young men, far from home, doing what they felt had to be done. Their adventures bonded them to one another for life. Where would we be without their efforts? I've enjoyed learning about the men, and you will too.

We must honour and respect all who served. Appreciation for their sacrifice, whether it was life, limb, or health, must always be with us. None who served were left untouched, nor were their families.

My father, Charles Giesen, was a pilot in the 458th Bomb Group, flying out of Horsham St Faith. The story about him recalls the 23rd mission of himself and his crew. From that mission he did not return. I was too young to know him, but after reading this story he was suddenly *real* for me. Here was a man with fears and doubts just like me, and I loved him. I wish I had been there to hold him and tell him so. I gained tremendous insight into the daily lives of these airmen. It's a wonder any of them survived.

I've had occasion to meet some of these men, write to them, and talk to them. I've come to the conclusion that they were good back then, but they are *wonderful* now. There is an elegance to these caring old warriors that you do not find in the average man.

Always remembering,

Linda Giesen Lord
New Iberia, Louisiana

CONTENTS

Lieutenant Jackson Granholm at Blythe, California in 1944.

CHAPTER 1

HANDWRITING ON THE WALL

World War II was the foremost event of the Twentieth Century. It may have been the foremost happening of all human history.

Fifty million people died as a direct result of that war. While I was involved in its latter years, as a military combatant, I was a fortunate survivor. Looking back at those days, over time, I see them as an adventure I would not want to have missed, but an adventure I would not care to repeat.

In June the Class of 1939 graduated from Puyallup Junior–Senior High School in the State of Washington; I was a member of that Class.

Like many of my fellow graduates, I was glad to leave. Much of my time at school had been happy and filled with exciting activities, but there were times which dragged with boredom. I needed to get out into the real world, to become an adult, and to do all those things that were possible, presumably, for those of us freed from academia.

But events in the real world were disturbing. News came to us in those days primarily by radio and newspaper. In our high school classes devoted to current events, we sometimes listened to the broadcast speeches of Adolf Hitler. While we understood little of the shouted phrases of this German dictator, his tone was enough to provoke uneasiness.

Hitler, as he built the German military machine to unprecedented might, grew ever more threatening to his European neighbours. In 1936 when we were freshmen at Puyallup, Hitler marched three battalions of his newly-expanded army into the Rhineland, a part of Germany purportedly exempt from military occupation.

In March of 1938 when we were juniors, Hitler declared union of Austria with Germany and marched his troops into Vienna. Later that year, loudly proclaiming that Czechoslovakia mistreated the people of the Sudetenland, the German-speaking Czech border area, Hitler demanded its immediate annexation. This demand provoked the Munich meeting with British Prime Minister Neville Chamberlain and French Premier Edouard Daladier – the result was a craven assent to Hitler's demands. Such action convinced even us, far away American high school students, that Prime Minister Chamberlain was too easily deceived.

In March, shortly before our graduation, the Germans occupied all of Czechoslovakia, sending the people of that nation back into worse oppression than they had endured from the Austro-Hungarian Empire for hundreds of years. In the same month the Germans marched into and occupied the port city of Memel in Lithuania. This, the only good harbour of this tiny Baltic nation, had been a German port before World War I when the Russian czars dominated the rest of Lithuania. Through all of these events the British and French governments, self-appointed champions of human rights and fair play in Europe, did nothing other than begin half-hearted attempts to strengthen their own inadequate military capabilities.

On the other side of the world the Japanese Empire had occupied Manchuria in 1931. This Chinese province, home state of a long line of ruling Chinese emperors, became a captive province of Japan with a member of the one-time Chinese imperial family as its satrap. In 1937 an incident involving the Japanese guard of the embassy at Peking (now Beijing) touched off a general Japanese attack on China. By the time of our graduation, much of China's most fertile land was under Japanese occupation and Chinese people in the occupied areas were being treated worse than animals.

We looked forward to a new and broader life as graduates. We were ready to go forth and conquer the world with our successful careers. That these careers were largely undefined was of little concern to us. With the broad and positive knowledge of youth, complemented by endless days of accomplishment ahead, we were filled with self-confidence. Yet, we knew there was a manifest chance that our new-found freedom might be short-lived. The world seemed headed for conflict that might involve all peoples and all nations. That prospect was not a happy one.

In 1939 the United States was still suffering from the effects of the great economic depression which had started ten years earlier. One of the toughest assignments for a high school graduate was to find a job. Actually, I didn't particularly want a job, I wanted a pay cheque. However, luck was with me, and I got a job as a mechanic at the local cannery, a place where almost everyone in town looked for work, at least in the summer-time.

In September of 1939, after our too-brief summer of freedom from high school, Hitler's troops fell upon Western Poland. The military campaign was over in less than a month, and the Polish people became captive slaves, victims of an overwhelming evil.

In mid-September troops of the Soviet Union invaded eastern Poland. Negotiations which Germany and the Soviets had concluded prior to the attacks on Poland included an agreement to divide the country. Poland had been a Russian province in the time of the czars. With the attack on Poland the governments of Britain and France declared war on Germany. They didn't take any positive military action, but they did declare war.

The Soviet Union issued ultimatums to the small Baltic countries of Lithuania, Latvia, and Estonia. Yielding in the face of overwhelming force, these states were invaded by Russian troops. Their people became slaves once again, as they had been in czarist days. Lithuania, which had been a big and powerful European state in mediaeval times, was reduced to utter powerlessness.

Things were different in Finland. The czars of Russia, capturing Finland from the ruling Swedes, had been also dukes of Finland in imperial times, but the Finns won their freedom in 1917, driving out the Bolsheviks who intended to keep the country within the new Soviet Union.

At the end of November in 1939, following Finnish rejection of their territorial demands, the Soviets sent forty divisions against Finland.

Though the Finnish military force numbered less than twenty per cent of the masses the Russians threw against them, the Finns resisted superbly. Finally, faced by overwhelming numbers of Russians, they gave up the territory which Stalin wanted. The number of Finnish war casualties – 25,000 – looked small in comparison to the total of more than 200,000 Russians who died. The Russians were happy when this brief northern war ended. In the spring of 1940 Germany launched a surprise attack upon both Denmark and Norway, which ended in German occupation of both countries.

Events in Europe and Asia disturbed the tranquillity of our young lives, but still the United States remained officially uninvolved in the growing conflict. I got a better-paying job operating a turret lathe at a brass foundry – I was probably inept at the work, but the pay was helpful.

In May of 1940 Hitler began his primary attack on Western Europe. German troops poured into Luxembourg, Belgium, and The Netherlands. A rapid German drive to Abbeville on the French coast trapped the British forces next to the sea in western Belgium and northern France. In a series of apparent miracles, aided by one of Hitler's more foolish decisions, the majority of the surrounded British escaped through the port of Dunkirk to return to their homeland, minus most of their equipment. In June of 1940, France surrendered. To all intents and purposes, effective French government on the continent of Europe ended.

To those of us who had graduated in the class of 1939, it seemed as though fate was inexorably moving this War towards including the United States in the active conflict. I had enrolled in the University of Washington in Seattle. The studies were tough and the environment was certainly not like that of Puyallup Junior–Senior High School, but I was a drama major, and got a job on the stage crew of the campus Showboat Theatre, which was a fun job, and exciting.

Later I left the University in order to recoup my finances for a while. I was hired by the Boeing Company to operate a turret lathe in the machine shop on the graveyard shift. Things were beginning to boom at Boeing as federal orders for B-17 bombers came in. Somebody in Washington D.C. apparently thought it might be useful if the United States had some air power.

One night, during lunch hour for the machine shop people of the Boeing graveyard shift, we were gathered together by our foreman who led us across the plant into the giant aircraft assembly bay. We were taken into an area shrouded off with huge hanging sheets of canvas and were permitted to look at a new Boeing product to which we had unknowingly contributed. There on the assembly floor stood the XB-29, the first of a new line of huge bombers; it made the B-17 look small, though there was a manifest family resemblance. The most remarkable difference was in the aeroplane's nose section; it appeared to be a gigantic greenhouse, shaped like the front of a dirigible. The B-29 was indeed an impressive weapon, the first big bomber with a pressurised crew cabin. It would take a while, however, to get it into production.

In early July 1940, Hitler sent his own air force, the *Luftwaffe*, across the English Channel to attack Great Britain in force. These attacks began with bomber raids that were minuscule compared with what would come later. Formations of thirty or so Heinkels attacked port cities such as Dover, Plymouth, and Portsmouth. However, the results were disappointing.

In August Hitler gave Air *Reichsmarschal* Göring a jab in the butt with his directive to 'overpower the English' quickly. As a result the *Luftwaffe* took a new approach to dumping bombs on England. German aircraft began to attack airfields and aircraft factories in addition to other targets. These attacks inflicted serious damage on the Royal Air Force and its ability to fight back. But Hitler, ever impatient, did not see the British hurrying to surrender to him. Therefore in September, he changed horses again. The primary target, he decreed, would be the city of London.

Big formations of Heinkel, Junkers and Dornier bombers, supported by Messerschmitt fighters, pounded London daily. On 15 September over 200 German bombers headed for London. Nearly sixty of them were shot down by R.A.F. fighters.

In October more and more of the German aerial attacks were sent across the Channel at night. The bombing was considerably less accurate than during the day, but the losses were fewer. By November all German aerial attacks on England were by night, and they tailed off to be more inconvenient than dangerous. To those of us in the then neutral world of the United States, this was a convincing demonstration of the key role that air power was destined to play in this great War.

In the skies of Great Britain Hitler met his first obvious defeat. While the score was close, the British had clearly exacted unacceptable losses in terms of German aeroplanes and people.

Far away Puyallup High School made its own contribution to this air war over England and Scotland. My friend and high school chemistry lab partner, Doug Kelley, had joined the Royal Canadian Air Force. Kelley saved his money for flying lessons while he was in high school, and flew a night-fighter all through the Battle of Britain. Knowing what a tough cookie and a wild man Kelley was, I felt sorry for the German air-crews.

At the end of 1940, Hitler had enough. Massive German air attacks on Great Britain ceased for the rest of the war. The expected German invasion of the British Isles never came. Hitler then turned his unwelcome attentions eastward. The Germans, with inept and unwilling help from their Italian allies, conquered Albania, Yugoslavia, and Greece. Hungary and Romania became their quasi-enthusiastic partners.

The German military then attacked the Soviet Union. On the day of the summer solstice in 1941 Germany set in motion a well-co-ordinated attack all along the Russian border. The resulting *blitzkrieg* was as successful as had been previous efforts in the west. By the end of the year the Germans had driven far inside Soviet territory.

On 7 December 1941 the Japanese launched their infamous attack upon Pearl Harbor. The United States was in the war, whether we wanted to be or not. Clearly I was one of the class of 1939 fated to be eligible as cannon fodder. I was two and a half years past my high school graduation, and twenty years old; I was also registered for the draft, and scared. However, my workplace at the turret lathe in the Boeing machine shop made me, probably, exempt from military service for as long as I cared to be – it could have been worse.

About a quarter of our classmates in Puyallup were kids of Japanese ancestry. Typically their parents were farmers – hard working people who kept immaculate farms growing lettuce and other similar produce. The kids all had to go to Japanese school after public school sessions and most of them hated it. An opportunity to become trans-Pacific bilingual was a pain in the butt to them. Shortly after the Pearl Harbor attack all the Puyallup Valley people of Japanese parentage were rounded up. They were put into a temporary camp on the parking lot of the Western Washington fair-ground. Our classmates were all behind a tall fence with barbed wire at the top. We didn't know why – these people were not some kind of oriental spies. They were our friends, neighbours and classmates. We took little gifts, candy bars and similar cheap items, to the fair-ground stockade and tried to find people we knew and hand them the loot through the fence. My girlfriend was a leader in this effort, and she usually managed to drag me along. All through high school my locker partner had been Hareo Kajimura. I was seldom able to find him in the great crowd of people behind the fence. One day we went to the fair-ground, and all our classmates with Japanese ancestry were gone. They were moved somewhere east of the Cascade Mountains, so the rumour had it.

The war's effects were immediately noticeable to those of us on the Boeing graveyard shift. We had to begin driving to work in the dark without head-lights turned on. The whole City of Seattle was blacked out at night, as were all the surrounding cities and communities, because there were rumours that we could expect the Japanese to bomb at any time. Such rumours were never substantiated.

In Puyallup, my hometown, as in other places throughout the land, men stood in the streets and climbed into trucks as National Guard units of Washington State were called to active duty. I watched friends and acquaintances, most of them upper-class men from high school days, depart from our quiet home. Some of them would never be seen at home again.

The National Guard of Washington State soon disappeared from the local armouries. All these men were called to active duty.

To replace its part-time and volunteer troops the State of Washington formed a new organisation, the Washington State Guard, in which I enlisted. This gave the opportunity and obligation to show up one night a week at the Tacoma armoury. I had a sort of nondescript uniform with a crow patch sewed to the shoulder – the crow is the state bird of Washington. We spent a lot of time practising close-order drill on the armoury floor – I got to be pretty good at it. More interesting were our basement practices with real rifles and live ammunition in the basement shooting gallery. To my own surprise, I proved to be very good indeed at using a rifle and hitting the target square on. It was to be, fortunately, an ability that I never had to use except in practice.

The Washington State Guard was a diverse organisation – it had such people such as myself, young and just out of high school, and others who were middle-aged patriots, too old to be accepted as volunteers into the regular military. Among those I remember of these more senior gentlemen were Frank Giusti who ran the biggest beer tavern in Tacoma, and Pierce County Superior Court Judge Rossellini who was later to become a member of the Washington State Supreme Court. These gentlemen, devoted guardsmen of Washington, demonstrated that Americans of Italian ancestry had no particular love for Mussolini's friendship with Hitler.

When America was precipitated into World War II we were not much of an air power. At the time of Pearl Harbor the American Army had about a thousand aeroplanes purportedly fit for combat, and some of these bordered on laughable.

The news from the war fronts was not good. Having destroyed the battleship strength of the U.S. Navy at Pearl, the Japanese romped through the Pacific with nothing in sight to stop them. The Japanese air force dominated in their take-over of the Philippines. Is it possible, I wondered, that we could lose this war?

CHAPTER 2

OFF TO WIN THE WAR

With the entry of the United States of America into World War II things went into super-high gear at Seattle Plant 2 of the Boeing Company. John Stewart Detlie, architect and motion picture art director, a man I was later to know very well, designed a great cloth tent which covered the entire vast expanse of the plant. The scheme was that, from the air, the plant should look like a modest residential neighbourhood. The fact that there was a long aircraft runway alongside it may not have fooled everyone. But still we went to work under the giant tent.

I was busy at my turret lathe each night, and had learned to sleep in the daytime, with goof-off hours devoted to tennis games and similar scholarly pursuits. Meanwhile the American military got its drubbing in the Pacific theatre, the Japanese took the Philippines and thousands of Americans went off into captivity. Many of them did not survive. One from Puyallup, fellow high school student Albert Tresch, was a captive in the Bataan death march. But Albert survived, we were to learn much later.

The American flyers in the Pacific began to do a bit better under their tough commander, General George Kenney. Particularly in the battle of the Bismarck Sea they turned in a spectacular performance which helped to make General MacArthur's fight into New Guinea an ultimate success.

Generals Ira Eaker and Carl Spaatz were sent to England to supervise the build-up of American air forces there. The British thought the American intent to bomb Europe by daylight was doomed to fail, but there were some interesting successes among the failures.

The War was in all of our thoughts constantly and the daily news was frequently disturbing. I kept wishing that we could crank out more B-17 bombers and send them all over Japan. The United States put into action a plan to have every company possibly qualified building combat aircraft and new plants were built from scratch in a hurry.

Finally I felt compelled to face my own role, my proper part to play, in this escalating War. I was young, able and single, with a bit of job experience. I had a high school certificate from Puyallup High School and a few quarters of study at the University of Washington. I had no wife, no children, and no family-supporting duties. My nightly operation of the Boeing turret lathe was adequate, but could have been learned by a milkmaid in a week or so. Clearly, I belonged in the military with the rest of the able-bodied young men. There I might make a useful contribution.

I debated what to do. Back in grade school days, and in junior high, I had seen, along with my friends, the movies of World War I airmen. That ultimate villain, Jack Holt, in his tri-winged Fokker, would chase the utterly good and honourable Richard Barthelmess in his SPAD. Though their lives were short, these men of the sky were totally heroic.

By now it was manifest that one of the keystones of the United States' War effort was to be mass production of military aircraft – many people would be needed to fly them. Our high school friend, Doug Kelley, had made a wise and proper choice to be off and flying with the Royal Canadian Air Force. Now, along with many another American volunteer, he had been transferred into the U.S. Army Air Corps.

The ultimate in heroic news came to us in May of 1942. Lieutenant-Colonel Jimmy Doolittle, famous for his civilian flying exploits and awards, led an attack of B-25 bombers over Tokyo, the Japanese capital. The twin-engined B-25s were brought within range on a Navy aircraft carrier, and while there were a number of big glitches in the Doolittle raid, its ultimate effect was magnificent. This mission sent Doolittle on his spectacular wartime rise from Lieutenant-Colonel to Lieutenant-General.

Should I have stayed home? Flying in the United States Army Air Force was the thing to do in World War II – it was the greatest show on earth. If I hadn't gone I'd have missed the chance to earn my wings and my crushed cap, and to look like a flyboy. I wouldn't have flown all those scary missions five miles up over Nazi Germany. I wouldn't have met all those crazy people, like Max Sokarl. And I'd have missed the day the Second Air Division bombed Switzerland.

So I went to the Army recruiting office that sunny morning in Seattle; 28 July 1942 was the fateful day. I stood with a group of young men and together we swore our allegiance to the Government and Constitution of the United States of America. When the ceremony finished we were aviation cadets in the Army of the United States.

It was the following winter before I got notice to show up for active duty. By then I suspected, and half hoped, that the Federal Government had forgotten me, or lost my papers, but the notice did come. It told me to be standing in the railroad station in Portland, Oregon, on an appointed evening a couple of weeks later. I said goodbye to my mother and my girlfriend in Tacoma, thinking that I might never see them again, and went bravely off into the afternoon on the Northern Pacific Railroad.

I got to Portland in time to spend about four boring hours at the station. There was not much sense in going out for a walk in the rain, so I had two milk shakes and five coffees, and looked at all the passengers waiting to go somewhere. At the appointed hour, those of us there for our common purpose were greeted by a tired-looking sergeant. He took the roll, ushered us all onto the train, and put us to bed like a fairy-godmother. The train hauled out on time, southbound.

I woke at five in the morning and opened the shade to peer out through the dirty Pullman window. We were making a great loop around Mount Shasta. The snow-covered volcano glistened in the dark and I couldn't go back to sleep. I'd never been to California before.

When I was a child, growing up near Tacoma, I used to wonder if I would live long enough to go to Seattle, the big city that I had heard about, but never seen. Now that I was older, I had been to Seattle, worked there, and gone to the University. I had even been to Portland, but I had never been as far away as Vancouver, B.C. or Spokane. Now I was off to see the world at Government expense. By breakfast time our train was into the great Central Valley of California. Though it was winter, the countryside looked spring-like, quite different from western Washington in February. By lunchtime we were almost at Sacramento, and by suppertime we were south of Fresno.

Next morning I woke again at five a.m. The train was winding slowly through Tehachapi Pass. There had been a bad freight derailment a few days previously. As we came out of a tunnel I could see a great cab-front articu-lated steam engine upside-down in the canyon below, freight cars piled around it – a memorable sight. We rolled out onto the floor of the high desert and stopped for a time in the big railroad yard at Mojave. The dawn was grey, and a grey wind was blowing dust to the horizons. Mojave looked like the anus of the universe, I had never seen a more depressing place. But by mid-morning we were in the San Fernando Valley, rolling past orange groves, and in a short time we pulled into Union Station in downtown Los Angeles.

I got off the train wearing my big winter overcoat. The patio of Union Station was like fairyland. Flowers were blooming, pretty girls wore delicate spring dresses, palm trees grew here and there, the sunshine was warm and brilliant. It was all true – everything I'd ever heard about Southern California. It was balmy summertime forever and ever.

The following day there was pouring rain, followed by rain every day for a month.

Our sergeant took us by bus to the Pacific Electric Station. There we boarded a Big Red Car for Santa Ana. After an hour's ride or so, we got off the red car and were herded into an Army truck which deposited us at the Santa Ana Aviation Cadet Center on the site of the Orange County Fair Grounds. As we walked in with our suitcases and civilian garb, cadet heads poked out of every barracks window, chanting a common refrain: 'You'll be sorry!'

Santa Ana was a place of mud, endless testing, and school. We took tests in co-ordination, physical aptitude, mental ability, and so forth. Flight surgeons examined every part we had, and poked endless series of inoculation needles into us. We learned such essential military skills as bed-making and close-order drill. We also learned potentially more useful skills such as the shapes of Japanese battleships and how to fire a Thompson submachine-gun. Certainly we were busy enough at Santa Ana. We were rousted from the sack before dawn each morning, and kept on the steady run till about eight thirty p.m. every day. At that time we fell gratefully into bed to rest up for the next day's ordeal.

Through all of this we were kept as prisoners on the base. The theory was that one or more of us might have arrived carrying bubonic plague, or some such disease, and we might be a hazard to the world at large if let loose on the weekend streets. One cadet got into bad trouble during this period. He contracted a case of gonorrhoea which seemed to be clear evidence that he had engaged in unauthorised absence from the base. However, he insisted that he had acquired the infection while engaging in a romantic interlude with a female civilian employee in the phone booth at the back of the area P.X. (post exchange), so the fortunate fellow was washed out of the cadet programme and sent off to gunnery school instead of being court-martialled for desertion.

After a month or so we were let out in public briefly each weekend to the alleged delight of the young female population of Southern California. But I had an aunt and uncle in Long Beach, and brief weekends sharing their domestic tranquility and wonderful hospitality was a good antidote for the homesickness that was the common lot of inmates of the Santa Ana Cadet Center.

Getting to Long Beach from Santa Ana presented another problem, however. On a cadet's pay of $75 per month, the fare of Pacific Electric red cars could eat up a proportionate amount of funds, and while it was O.K. for standard G.I.s, aviation cadets were forbidden to hitchhike – it was not considered to be dignified. I developed a particularly effective method of standing on the highway at the red car stop in Costa Mesa looking forlorn and was very gracious in accepting the offered ride when someone with an automobile stopped on his way north.

While we were allowed out at weekends, we had to be back at the base each Sunday afternoon in time for the gigantic parade. The public was invited to this event to watch all the embryo flyboys in their quasi-officer uniforms march by in good order. Because I was tall, I got to carry the guidon banner of our squadron. This was an easy job, since I was not required to line up on anyone else. It was essential, however, to have good arm muscles to hold the stupid banner staff out horizontally while colonel whatsisname gave his customary speech from the reviewing stand, telling the public in attendance how glorious we were.

One cadet (whose name should be carved in stone for posterity) became famous on his return to Santa Ana for Sunday parade. This enterprising fellow had acquired a sexy Hollywood girlfriend who regularly drove him back to the base in her bright-red convertible. How sexy she really was was amply demonstrated one sunny afternoon when they arrived back at the base early. Apparently needing one more attempt at romance, the cadet and his Hollywood girlfriend engaged in vigorous social callisthenics in the convertible, right in the middle of the base parking lot. There they were within full view of thousands of envious cadets who were pushing and shoving each other for a better view out of the upstairs barracks windows.

Cadets at Santa Ana were often picked on by having some high-ranking sergeant come around regularly demanding stated donations to buy 'grass seed' to help beautify the base. Everyone kicked in the demanded amount from our munificent $75-per-month pay, but, while I was there, I never saw any grass planted in the Santa Ana mud. Much later, when I was away from it all, I read an article in the newspaper, which reported that colonel whatsisname had been sent off to the federal slammer for having run a super scam operation at the Santa Ana Cadet Center. Allegedly everyone who stepped into the place was ripped off, including all the civilian suppliers, one of whom had blown the whistle – so the newspaper reported.

But not all was grim gloom at Santa Ana. As cadets we were expected to run our own little paramilitary organisations. Each barracks was organised into a squadron and we had our own cadet officers and discipline system, modelled somewhat after that of West Point. It grew to be a standard procedure to throw a bucket of water down the stairs on the unlucky cadet officer who was assigned to the evening bed check.

At Santa Ana, for the first time, I met young men from all over the United States. I was vaguely aware that there were regional differences in culture, but the diversity thereof had not previously been so obvious. In the cadet programme I heard modes of speech and expression that I had not imagined to exist. One of my barracks mates from Mississippi made astoundingly colourful use of expletive, blasphemy, and obscenity in his day-to-day speech. He might, for instance, glance casually at his wrist-watch and remark in offhand fashion, 'Well I be goddam if it ain't two shit-eatin' thirty o' half-assed clock.'

We took turns at various idiotic military jobs. I was assigned to stay up all night as corporal of the guard, a regular cadet duty performed with unloaded rifles. About two hours into the shift a heating boiler blew up in some building in the area, and I spent the rest of the night being quizzed by the base fire chief and the provost marshal, and signing interminable military forms which explained why the event was nobody's fault.

After a while we had completed our Santa Ana ground school classes. Our squadron, let out for the weekend in our dressy uniforms, held a big party at Earl Carroll's theatre restaurant in Hollywood. We all blew the rest of our pay on the event.

The big party at Earl Carroll's was a fitting end to our days at Santa Ana. Our time as ground-based cadets was over, and now we were all going off to a flight school somewhere to be turned into proper fliers.

Reassignment orders came cranking out of military mimeographs and we each went off in a different direction to more specialised schools. I was sent to the primary flight school at Eagle Field. This was a private airport, appropriated for the duration, and located out in the tules south of the small town of Dos Palos, California.

As was customary, we travelled by train. The group of us assigned to Eagle Field spent two days in a railroad coach rattling up the San Joaquin Valley, being put off on sidings so the more important traffic of wartime freight could pass. It was early on a hot, dry morning when we pulled into the railroad station at South Dos Palos – the place looked like the back gate of Hell.

Dos Palos was an agricultural area, but situated in the western nowhere of California's great Central Valley. Interstate 5 and the California Aqueduct were decades in the future, and there was nothing much between the town and the Coast Range mountains but arid land and creosote bush.

We were lined up in our customary trim formation, trying to stand at stiff attention while carrying our military duffle bags. The formation was essential so we could be herded into trucks and buses for our brief trip to the airfield. We went south along a dusty road, crossed the irrigation canal, then turned west to the main gate of Eagle Field.

The place was painted in psychedelic colours – bright in the California sun.

There were two big hangars. Little aeroplanes with yellow wings were parked all over the place. Here and there were various administrative buildings and small barracks – apparently all built of cardboard and chewing gum with a bit of gingerbread thrown in.

The military chickenshit continued at Dos Palos, much as it had at Santa Ana. We had regular stand-up inspections, bed checks, etc. often carried out by sergeants and corporals. Eagle Field had a dearth of commissioned officers. At one inspection I was precipitated into unseemly laughter by the stupid expression on the face of the cadet standing at attention opposite me. For this horrifying breach of military decorum I was sentenced to spend the afternoon marching on the ramp, wearing gas mask and back pack, and carrying a heavy, though unloaded, rifle.

At Eagle Field we buckled down to a busy life of ground school and pilot training. I was assigned to the care of a civilian instructor named Loyal E. Oesau. He was a friendly person who seemed less than enthralled with the job of risking his life daily, trying to teach inept greenhorns the correct operation of an aeroplane.

Our aeroplanes were Ryan PT-17 primary trainers. They were little, low-wing monoplanes built in San Diego. Each had a hot-rod five-cylinder radial engine as power plant. Compared to Boeing-built Stearman biplanes which most primary cadets flew, the little Ryans were beautiful. Stearmans looked like rejects left over from World War I. The Ryans were two-seaters – fore-and-aft open cockpit jobs. We flew with leather jackets, goggles and flying helmets, just like the Red Baron over Verdun.

As time went on, Oesau permitted me to fly solo. I had learned to take off, land, turn, spin and recover, and all those other important things. I was looking forward to barrel rolls and Immelmann turns, but I was among the less adept of Loyal Oesau's students and while I scored well in ground school, my piloting of an aeroplane resembled the work of a grandma driving a bread truck. Oesau turned me over to a high-ranking second lieutenant who put me through a series of flying tests. The lieutenant was not favourably impressed. He washed me out of pilot training and I became a cadet with clipped wings.

Having nothing else to do while awaiting the fates decreed by the output of the military mimeographs, I volunteered to help out as a junior assistant clerk in the base headquarters. There I met the base commander – a non-flying captain. He seemed to enjoy his job of commanding a primary school out in the tules, and he was wonderful as long as nothing upset him. Unfortunately, he was always upset. I continually got on his shit list by the simple expedient of standing there looking in the right direction at the wrong time.

At last the orders came down from God, ordering me to report, on the week following, back to the Cadet Center at Santa Ana! I figured it was a short stop on the way to gunnery school.

Our crusty captain proved to be a good guy after all. While I was on his current list of bad cadets confined to base, having dipped the pen in the wrong ink, I summoned up remarkable courage: remembering a World War I event in which my father, a Navy C.P.O., while confined to the brig had asked his captain for shore leave, I asked mine for two days off to go to San Francisco. He granted the request.

A friendly truck driver gave me a ride all the way to the big city. I had never been to San Francisco before, and I spent my time looking in wonderment. I rode the cables end to end. The O'Farrell and Hyde line still ran at that time, and the California Street Cable went almost to Golden Gate Park. The San Francisco weather was magnificent, so I enjoyed my brief time back in civilisation.

The day following my return to Eagle Field I was driven to the railroad station in Dos Palos. Along with another washed-out cadet, I was sent off on the night train to Los Angeles. When I got back to Santa Ana, I would learn my future fate at the merciless hands of the American military.

Shack Time.

CHAPTER 3

NAVIGATION SCHOOL

I anticipated being sent from Santa Ana directly to aerial gunnery school. Aerial gunnery school students were regular G.I.s, so that assignment would mean giving up my exalted status and low pay as an aviation cadet. I would have to turn in my treasured uniform with the blue band and frontal wings on the dress hat.

But my thinking scores had apparently been good enough to send me from Santa Ana to the Navigation school at San Marcos, Texas. The Government's decision to turn me into an aerial navigator was a good one for me, and when I later became a captain I met second lieutenant pilots who had been in training with me at Dos Palos.

Those of us assigned from Santa Ana to San Marcos were organised into a cadet contingent and sent to Texas by long, slow train. In World War II the Army never sent its flyboys to a new assignment by aeroplane – we were always on the train. Our train took us to San Antonio where we were off-loaded into Army trucks.

Those of us destined for San Marcos were placed on short and temporary do-nothing duty at Kelly Field. Along with nearby Randolph Field, Kelly was famous for being featured in flyboy movies of the time.

We had no regular duties at Kelly Field, but we were lined up in formation each day so that roll could be taken by a bored, disinterested sergeant abetted by a couple of high-ranking corporals. One day as the names were called out, one cadet proved to be missing. The sergeant called out the name again, as there was no answer on the first try:

'Wascsowskowicz!' the sergeant bellowed.

There was no answer.

'Wascsowskowicz!' the sergeant tried, yet again, louder this time.

'Which one?' screamed a cadet voice from the back row.

We were all rousted from the sack early one morning at Kelly Field. The Army weathermen had predicted a hurricane on the way, headed straight for San Antonio. We were all rushed to the flight line to tie down aeroplanes so they might not blow into New Mexico, but not being trained as sailors, we did this rather incompetently. Fortunately, however, there was no hurricane. The Army weathermen had demonstrated that same level of expertise that we were to see repeated many times. The following day an Army truck took our navigation student contingent to San Marcos.

The airfield at San Marcos was east of the small Texas town. Its barren landscape was punctuated with ugly tarpaper shacks, one of which was the barracks to which I was assigned. We began with every bed full, each occupied by some eager cadet and would-be aerial navigation officer.

San Marcos was a long and intense time of study and hard work. We were at it all day and half the night. We typically flew navigation missions two or three times a week, and I got to know the map of Texas like the back of my hand.

All our non-flying days were spent in the classroom. We learned about dead reckoning, winds, drift, and all the other techniques that enabled us to plot our course over the earth between solid, established geographic fixes. We learned the idiosyncrasies of the earth's magnetic field, and how the compass worked. We learned to do a careful job of calibrating navigation instruments.

The aeroplanes assigned to San Marcos as navigation trainers were mostly small, twin-engined Beechcraft. Each was fitted with three navigation desks, complete with driftmeter and all instruments. There were also one or two larger Lockheed aeroplanes, trainer versions of the 'Hudson' so-called bomber. There had been more, but this Lockheed design showed a remarkable propensity for crashing, and the aeroplanes were anathema to navigation cadets who heartily disliked being assigned to fly in one. The Beechcraft, on the other hand, was a most reliable little aeroplane, apparently indestructible in proper use.

In our barracks was cadet Dorger, who had been set back a few classes because of a lot of time spent in the hospital. Dorger had been a student navigator in one of the Lockheed trainers which crashed. The aeroplane had caromed off a fire truck while attempting to land, then had flown through the top of a hangar. Dorger, clothes and hair on fire, had jumped from the wreckage and run out of the hangar on two broken ankles. I admired Dorger as the bravest man I had ever met – had I his experience, I believed, I'd have demanded a different career immediately.

My first navigation mission was a memorable one. We flew a dead reckoning trip north out of San Marcos to Waco, and from there we headed south-east to Navasota. I had my head in the driftmeter most of the way, trying to make sure that my wind vectors were correct. Looking down at the ground through the optics of an aeroplane driftmeter is not recommended practice for those queasy of stomach – the earth below appears to rock and swing in most disturbing fashion.

As we came over College Station, Texas, the pilot noted that a football game was in progress in the stadium of Texas A & M, below us. He took time out from the navigation mission to circle the stadium a few times at low altitude. On about the third circle I tossed my cookies into the compass cover, and I was joined in this bout of airsickness by my fellow cadets. Fortunately, this was the one and only episode of airsickness I experienced in all my military flying days. The corkscrew flight over the Texas stadium apparently toughened me for all further such episodes.

Not all aeroplane trips out of the Navigation School at San Marcos were tough, nose-to-the-grindstone episodes with incipient airsickness. We had various pilots who flew our little Beechcraft for us. Most were understandably bored with the assignment – it was hardly as exciting as working in China with the Flying Tigers. Our pilots were, by and large, second lieutenants, but there were exceptions. The cadets' favourite pilot was Flight Officer Ball. Flight Officer was an Army warrant officer grade. Unlike standard Army warrant officers, with their brownish-red insignia, flight officers wore rounded-end blue bars on their shoulder straps. The flight officer grade was purportedly handed out to those graduates of a pilot school who could fly adequately, but who were deficient in one or more of the niceties of being an officer and a gentleman. Flight Officer Ball was a good-ole-boy from some-where down south, possibly a bit ragged around the edges, but he was a superb pilot.

A navigation training trip with Flight Officer Ball was a memorable and worthwhile experience. Ball always added a little extra flight time to cruise out over the Gulf of Mexico at balls-to-the-wall throttles and four feet of alti-tude. Such performances had an exciting effect on the sea birds, none of whom, fortunately, came through the windshield. If we were not out near the Gulf that particular day, Ball could usually find a chicken yard or a cattle pasture to buzz, causing remarkable psychological effects among the un-appreciative animals.

The physical training was tough at San Marcos. For this purpose cadets were assigned to the tender mercies of a corporal named Sullivan who took undisguised delight in ordering up one more brisk run around the long track or through the obstacle course. Cadets, with their natty uniforms and potential to become officers, were anathema to some G.I.s. Sullivan was apparently in the forefront of this cadet-hating category, but harrassed cadets did have one way to strike back. We marched everywhere we went on base. In informal formations, such as marching to the physical training area, we were allowed – encouraged, in fact – to sing. So the airfield at San Marcos rang daily with a gleeful cadet song whose lyrics proclaimed:

'S, U, double-L, I, – V, A, N spells CHICKENSHIT!'

As an essential part of keeping up the proper image, all of our activities were inspected regularly. Typically some high-ranking second lieutenant would come into the barracks, racking us all to stiff attention. He would proceed to disapprove foot lockers, bed sheets, and anything else in sight. Often the disaprovee would be sent off for a multi-hour stint on the kitchen deep sink.

One day we had a formal barracks inspection scheduled to be carried out by an actual captain. This scary super-officer was going to give us a thorough 'look-see'. Just prior to the appointed hour for his arrival we were all standing expectantly next to our respective bunks, but cadet Nemo had a severe problem. A diarrhoea attack was creeping rapidly up on him. At last he could stand the hydrostatic pressure no longer. He ran into the latrine at the end of the barracks to attend to his pressing need. As our cadet disappeared around the corner, the captain entered with his contingent of second lieu-tenants, each carrying a clip board. Each of us held his breath as the captain strode past our bunks and into the latrine. We figured cadet Nemo was a certain wash-out.

But then we heard the captain's voice say, 'It's not necessary to salute!'

Latrine cleaning duty was a regular cadet assignment. The Poet Laureate of our barracks, the one who had authored the Sullivan marching song, composed a latrine duty ballad to the tune of 'Sleepy Lagoon', a popular song of the time. His lyrics began:

> 'A filthy latrine,
> A urinal green.
> And two on a detail . . .'

As we proceeded through our training missions at San Marcos, the drop-out rate rose from disturbing to appalling: each week there were more empty beds in the barracks as those who flunked really did go off to gunnery school. We went on from dead reckoning, a navigation skill which I was able to master quite well, through radio, visual, and astral bearings up to and including celestial navigation itself. Celestial was tough. It required a lot of careful work with a bubble octant in a swaying aeroplane, and a half ton of mathematics calculation to build one reliable fix from star observations. In my previous life as a student I had never been particularly careful at arithmetic. Interestingly enough, I never made a mistake in mathematics while navigating an aeroplane. I was convinced that a navigation mistake in a military aeroplane could be a deadly one. Incentive is a powerful teacher.

This point was brought home to us by a visitor who came to our classes one day. One of our navigation instructor officers had a bombardier friend who had actually survived a full tour of missions over Europe in the Eighth Air Force. This bombardier, a high-ranking first lieutenant, spoke to us of his experiences in aerial combat.

His message was succinct and direct: 'It's your old ass up there, men!' he said.

I was actually interested in becoming as adept as possible in all skills and methods of navigation. Yet, as time passed at San Marcos, I decided that in the real world one made use of all possible information to confirm important decisions. Surely it should be the same in the real world of aerial navigation. I began to reconfirm my work in our interminable night celestial flights to El Paso and back. I learned the light patterns of places such as the city of Pecos, and I would augment the data of my star shots with a bit of unauthorised pilotage information gained by slyly peeking out the window as we went. After all, I figured, I would surely do the same under combat conditions. And I would never get to navigate an aeroplane on a combat mission unless I graduated from San Marcos.

Those cadets who washed out as navigation students were sad figures. Usually it took a week or so for the military administrative mills to crank out orders sending them elsewhere; meanwhile, they were around the air-base at San Marcos with nothing to do. However, not all of them moped. One of our barracks mates, a boy from Oklahoma, stood beside the road as we marched by to class, or elsewhere, and as we went by, our washed-out friend, with a broad grin, would mutter loudly, 'Thank God we got a navy!'

The survival rate at San Marcos was not very encouraging, but, somehow, I made it through to graduation. I got A in navigation and flunked cadet bedmaking. Of our original barracks full of cadets, less than twenty-five per cent were left to become navigators.

In early January 1944 I was handed my gold bars and my silver wings. I was also handed orders to show up at Blythe, California, two weeks later. As I left the San Marcos Navigation School for the last time, wearing my new uniform, I heard a formation of new cadets singing merrily on their way to the athletic field:

'If you don't know the man, it may spell Sullivan, but it's CHICKENSHIT to me!'

458th Bomb Group formation.

CHAPTER 4

CREW TRAINING

Many people on active duty in the army during World War II were granted no leave: instead, their orders were written to give them time to go home while changing stations. So it was at San Marcos. At the time this seemed to me to be a stupid procedure, but when I finally returned to civilian life after the war, and collected all my earned leave pay, it seemed like a brilliant procedure indeed. My orders upon graduation called for me to report for duty at the Army airfield at Blythe, California, two and a half weeks later. This impromptu vacation was very welcome. But, since it came unexpectedly, I had made no plans. I quickly decided to go to Blythe by way of Seattle.

Donning my brand new uniform with the second lieutenant's bars polished and in place, and my new crushed hat set at a jaunty angle, I took my heavy duffle and hitch-hiked north to Austin. There I bought a ticket on the night train to Fort Worth which was, at least, in the right direction.

The northbound milk train of the Katy Line was jammed full; it had no pullmans, only day coaches. It was on this train that I got my introduction to Jim Crow travel. There were no seats left on the train, allegedly, so I got to sit on my duffle bag in the car vestibule. Then I discovered that the car in front was mostly empty, only a handful of black people riding in it. I noticed that they looked embarrassed when I strode in and took a seat, before dozing off rapidly. I was awakened by the conductor who informed me that the car was reserved for 'coloured folks', and I had to leave. I resumed my seat in the vestibule for the rest of the night, cursing the separate but equal foibles of the South.

At Fort Worth all the trains were full and I could get no space headed north. But then as I wandered forlornly around the station I met a man from the Fort Worth and Denver City Railroad. He said he had an afternoon troop train headed north to Denver, and he was sure there was at least one bunk available on it. I bought a ticket and got on board. The whole train was full of sailors. I was the only flyboy on it. I felt like a porpoise among the whales but at least the train went to Denver. Denver luck was better. I got a berth on the Union Pacific *City of Portland*, which connected with the daily coast train northbound from Portland to Seattle.

The time at home was all too short. The news of progress of our aerial warfare was encouraging, but the casualty rates were alarmingly high. I had the gut feeling that I was at home for the last time, I told a bunch of lies to my girlfriend in the heroic hope that she would forget me when I didn't come back. That's the way they did it in the movies.

At the necessary and unwelcome time, I took the southbound through train to Los Angeles where I connected with the Phoenix-bound Greyhound bus across the desert to Blythe.

The air-base at Blythe was on a plateau west of the town. The city of Blythe is at a highway crossing of the Colorado River. While the river-bottom lands there are heavily farmed, the plateau where the air-base stood was barren desert – it looked even less attractive than the metropolis of Mojave. When I got to Blythe I was beset by a monumental homesickness. It might have been better had I gone straight from San Marcos to Blythe, and not stopped by Seattle. Probably every person on station in the wartime military has times of overwhelming desire to be back at home, safe with family, friends, and loved ones. It may be that my homesickness was amplified by the stark contrast between the park-like green world of Seattle and all of Western Washington, and the desolate world of the Southern California low desert at Blythe. With time, though, my homesickness abated as I got into the daily routine of crew training. I came to appreciate the beauties of the desert, especially the craggy and barren majesty of the Castle Dome Mountains which stood across the Colorado in Arizona.

At Blythe I was introduced to my crew, and to the B-24 bomber. Somehow the publicity department at the Boeing company had sold the public impression that the most glamorous big aeroplane in the world was the B-17 Flying Fortress. The B-24 Liberator was, by comparison, an ugly monster. The Liberator looked like an ugly monster. Especially when it was on the ground and taxying it appeared ungainly and awkward; however, it was the bomber we were assigned to fly. It had impressive range and load-carrying advantages over the B-17, and I was not about to tell the Government I'd rather navigate a prettier bomber.

The air-base at Blythe, which has since become the city airport, was a wonder to behold – nothing but arid desert was to be seen in all directions. Even in the winter-time the weather was often uncomfortably hot, so much so that just getting into a bomber that had been parked in the sun could be an exercise in will-power. Blythe Air-Base was shut down in hot weather because the place had asphalt taxiways, and the B-24s would sink in the sun-heated paving. The whole operation went to Mountain Home, Idaho, in the summer-time.

At Blythe I met the men of the bomber crew with whom I was to fly into combat. I was happy with them although it could have been otherwise. My crew First Pilot and Aircraft Commander was Bob Hayzlett. Bob was born in Loup City, Nebraska, a place where his maternal grandparents, immigrants from Sweden, had homesteaded. When Bob was nine years old, his parents moved to Corpus Christi, Texas.

With his youthful prowess at selling Liberty Magazines Bob Hayzlett had won a year's scholarship, at age thirteen, to attend Castle Heights Military Academy in Lebanon, Tennessee where he later became valedictorian of his graduating class. The Academy was owned by Liberty Publisher, Bernarr McFadden, and it was there that Hayzlett got the inspiration that caused him to volunteer to fly in World War II.

After graduating from high school, Hayzlett had taken a competitive exam for apprenticeship training at the Corpus Christi Naval Air Station. He was awarded a four-year civilian scholarship in master metalsmithing. At Corpus Christi at that time was Harold June, who had been one of Admiral Byrd's pilots on polar expeditions. June took the young Hayzlett along on test flights in Douglas dive bombers, Grumman Hellcat fighters, and various other Naval planes – anything with two seats. Secretly, June taught Hayzlett to fly, so when Army Air Corps recruiters came through Corpus Christi, Hayzlett took their tests, passed, and went off to be a cadet in pilot training.

After becoming a second lieutenant and an Army pilot, Bob Hayzlett was sent to Liberal, Kansas. There, at the air-base, he was introduced to the B-24 bomber. He had to learn to fly with four throttles in his hand instead of one. He learned, also, to depend on the essential help of a co-pilot.

Hayzlett was at Liberal in the Kansas winter. The weather blew across the plains all the way from the North Pole. Snow and ice were the norm for operations at the air-base.

The training planes at Liberal were not the cream of the B-24 production crop. They flew using fuel with less than the specified operational octane rating, and their maintenance left something to be desired. The uninspired

Lt Eddie Gniewkowski – as an aviation cadet.

mechanics on the Liberal flight line often worked with frozen hands. Flight accidents were frequent and fatal and the Liberal casualty rate threatened to exceed that experienced in combat flying. One day the Air Corps widows of Liberal staged a protest parade across the frozen base, shaking up the military training authorities considerably.

However, Bob Hayzlett survived, honing his careful approach to the risky job of bomber operations. This approach was to prove to our crew's benefit on more than one occasion.

Our crew co-pilot was Bob Stoesser from Elizabeth, New Jersey. Bob was a quiet and likeable young man, though he seemed always restive in his job, wishing, apparently, to be a first pilot and aircraft commander. I had some sympathy for his ambitions.

Our bombardier was Eddie Gniewkowski from Hamtramck, Michigan. Eddie was a very athletic person. He had been a golden glove boxer at age 19, and he was also a superb baseball player. He tried out with the Detroit Tigers, then got an offer from Kansas City, but didn't take the offer. Eddie's mother had died when he was fifteen, and he stayed home with his father to help raise his younger brothers.

Eddie Gniewkowski enlisted in the Army as a G.I. He became a bombsight technician, then applied for the admission to the Aviation Cadet programme. He was accepted and graduated from bombardier school. His considerable experience with bombsights made him a remarkably skilful bombardier.

Lt Eddie Gniewkowski (Left) and Lt Jackson Granholm at Blythe, California.

Our enlisted men were a great bunch, competent and devoted: there was Staff Sergeant Lynne M. Griefenstein, engineer and top gunner, Staff Sergeant Weldon J. Sheltraw was our radio operator, Sergeants Clair B. Stahl, Brownie G. Harvath, Dominic Giordano, and Carsie E. Foley were our expert gunners. Foley rode the belly turret, Stahl and Giordano manned the waist guns, and Harvath rode the tail turret. In its original configuration, like that of the aeroplanes we flew in training at Blythe, the B-24 had a greenhouse nose and a ball turret in the belly. So small was the aeroplane's ground clearance that the ball turret was retractable; it had to be pulled up for landing and taxying, and it was cranked down in the air for defence. Foley, being a little guy, fitted well in the retractable ball and had to depend on Stahl and Giordano to crank him up for landing.

All of us were young, single, and carefree, with the exception of Eddie Gniewkowski who was married. His wife, Dores, known fondly as 'Dee', followed him to Blythe. Dee was a tiny girl; even though she was pregnant, she weighed under a hundred pounds. There was no place for Dee to stay at the air-base, and Blythe had essentially no housing. Eddie had written to Dee, telling her to stay home in Detroit, but she came to Blythe anyway – she wanted to be near her husband, knowing that he was destined to go overseas soon to fly in combat.

On the way from Michigan to California, Dee got ptomaine poisoning. Having exhausted all her barf bags, she asked a Dallas druggist for help. He sold her Pepto Bismol, and to this day Dee credits it with saving her life, and that of her baby.

When Dee got to Blythe she went into the one and only hotel, but of course, there were no rooms. The hotel owner (apparently a self-appointed patriot) told Dee that, if she got a job at the air-base, he would find housing for her. Dee went out to the base and was promptly offered a job. She went back to the hotel to find out that the offered housing was a tent, out back in the sand.

But in the Blythe hotel Dee met a girl who was checking out the next day. The girl offered to let Dee share with her for the night, and take over the room. The room proved to be a converted chicken coop at the back of the hotel. It still had chicken wire on the windows which were boarded up on the outside. There were concrete floors (albeit cleaned of chicken droppings), one double bed, and a single light cord, hanging from the ceiling centre. Dee rented the chicken coop, and declined the job at the air-base.

Dee paid ten dollars a week for these opulent quarters, and had the additional privilege of the use of a half-bath in the back of the hotel. Eddie was busy all day, and often for half the night, with our training assignments at the air-base. He worried about Dee constantly and whenever he could get a night off from duty at the base, he went into town to stay with Dee in her palatial digs. The arrangement was hardly designed to promote a happy and tranquil married life.

Dee had lived in the chicken coop for about three weeks when she got sick again with a serious bladder infection. She kept the hotel owner awake all night by running in to use the bathroom, so, when next morning the owner asked Dee if she had a problem she told him she was pregnant. The hotel

From left to right –
Sergeants Carsie E. Foley,
Dominic Giordano, Weldon
Sheltraw, Clair Stahl in
London's Trafalgar Square.

owner, suffering from a sudden and rare attack of compassion, told Dee she could have the next vacancy.

The next vacancy proved to be a part of the lobby, surrounded by a partition. This magnificent area was rented for fourteen dollars a week – expensive by the standards of the time. The partition was only six and a half feet high, so the room was continually illuminated by the lights of the lobby, which were never extinguished. The regular rooms in the hotel were kept available for truck drivers, overnighting between Phoenix and Los Angeles. The hotel owner, looking to the future, intended to keep the good will of the truckers in order not to lose their patronage when the War was over. This partitioned section of the lobby, while more comfortable than the modified chicken coop, provided even less privacy for Dee and Eddie on those too-rare occasions when he could get away to be with her.

Since the lights were on all the time anyway, Dee began to play nickel and dime poker in the lobby with the truck drivers. Being a smart little girl, she often won enough to pay her weekly rent.

In her pregnant state, Dee had a craving for such foods as green onions and bananas. In one of the absurdities of wartime rationing, bananas were only for sale to people *with* small children. But the truckers, having high regard for pregnant Dee, the poker expert, brought her vast bunches of green onions and whole stacks of bananas.

The first of the Gniewkowski's children, Eddie Junior, was born back home in Michigan in August 1944, by which time our crew had been overseas for four months. Dee, like many wartime wives, faced her first labour and care of her first child without her husband there to help.

At Blythe, as we flew together, I learned to respect the men of my crew. As we tried hard to become a winning team, my admiration for each of them grew stronger. They were all excellent men, both officers and G.I.s. I was lucky to have drawn such a skilled crew.

We spent many days at Blythe flying formation with other B-24s. Lots of day and night navigation missions were a part of our busy schedule. We also attacked the bombing targets that were situated here and there about the desert.

To hit the bombing targets we carried bright-blue practice bombs. The practice bombs had the same aerodynamic characteristics as real bombs, but they were filled with white sand. Each had 'Inert' painted on it in big, white letters. When a practice bomb hit the ground it split open, making a large sand cloud which showed up well on our target strike photographs.

One bomber crew flying south out of Blythe had minor difficulty in flight. They jettisoned their practice bombs at low level, dumping a big salvo on a farm along the Colorado. The bombs were dropped from too low an altitude to split open properly and one went through the bottom of a rowboat. The commanding officer at Blythe got a terrified phone call:

'Somebody better get the hell out here right away!' the farmer said. 'There's bombs all over the bean field, and they're filled with Inert! . . . It says so right on them!'

There were tank tracks out in the desert. The American armoured troops, destined for duty in North Africa, trained at Desert Center to the west of us. Occasionally a tank would pull up to the air-base perimeter fence and the dried-out crew, dusty beyond belief, would get out, yelling to talk to someone. They had invariably become lost out in the Mojave, and needed directions on how to get back to Desert Center.

It was at Desert Center that General George S. Patton, 'Old Blood-and-Guts', had trained his men for their work in North Africa. One of the Patton stories, quite possibly apochryphal, concerned his talking to a man in G.I.-style coveralls. The man was working at the top of a telephone pole when Patton roared up in his jeep.

'What are you doing up there, soldier?' Patton demanded.

'What do you think? I'm fixing the wire, dammit!'

'That's no friggin' way to talk to an officer! You think you're in the goddam Russian army?'

'No!'

'What the hell's your company, soldier?'

'The Pacific Telephone Company!'

Patton was apparently not able to have the man thrown in the Army slammer.

We did a lot of flying with instructor pilots aboard. Some of them were highly skilled people from whom we learned a great deal; others were insane idiots who should have been sent off to the funny farm.

We flew with one of these crazy people one day to a bombing range in Arizona. We were over the Colorado River near the Mexican border when Mr Instructor decided that we were about to run out of fuel. My calculations showed enough gasoline in the tanks to go to Kansas City and back, but our instructor suddenly got his panic switch set. He called the Yuma tower, demanding landing clearance. Since Yuma was having a sandstorm at the time, he was informed that the field was closed, and was asked to go elsewhere, but this instructor pilot, a high-ranking first lieutenant and flak-happy returnee from a tour of duty, was not to be waved off. He informed the Yuma control tower that he was, by God, coming in whether they damn well liked it or not, and to get any crap off the runway to clear his path. He hauled the bomber into a tight turn, dived for the runway end, and levelled out at the last moment with an airspeed well above customary landing velocity for a B-24. There was a big cross-wind on the unauthorised runway our pilot had chosen. We floated a long distance, flaps down, flying at a severe crab angle to the runway. We had difficulty seeing the concrete because of the sand screaming horizontally across it.

At last the main gear crunched down, the nose wheel dropped to the concrete, and we rolled to the runway end. Just as our pilot began to turn off to the taxi-way, the nose wheel broke off the bomber, and we lurched to a screeching stop, aeroplane tail high in the air.

We left our bomber there, littering the field to the disgust of the Yuma ground-crew personnel, and rode back to Blythe in an Army truck. It was manifest that aerial combat was not the only situation in which flight hazards could be found.

On one simulated bombing mission our take-off was delayed by mechanical trouble. We had an instructor pilot on board, and we were to be part of a B-24 formation making a fake bomb run on Albuquerque. When we took off an hour or so late, the instructor pilot asked me to take us out on the assigned route, but then turn off to rendezvous with the returning formation over Phoenix. It was a classic intercept navigation problem of the sort we had studied at San Marcos. Somehow everything worked out, and we joined the formation square over downtown Phoenix. Much later I learned that this lucky mission had earned a recommendation from the training officers at Blythe that I be considered for appointment as a squadron or group navigator.

One of the pilots training at Blythe was Walter Williamson. He was a major, a high rank unprecedented among trainee air-crew officers. Williamson had been a paddlefoot, an officer without a flight rating, who had gone to flight school. When we went out to practise formation flying, Major Williamson was typically the formation commander.

One day we were out on a cross-country jaunt, all by ourselves over Arizona. We were relaxed, having a good time, flying our B-24 up the bottom of the Grand Canyon when we heard an irate voice on the radio. It was Williamson, leading a practice mission up at twenty-five thousand feet directly above us. He told us to get the hell out of the Canyon with our expensive government aeroplane.

Before Major Williamson could get really upset with us, another problem diverted his attention. The big fourteen-cylinder twin radial engines of the B-24 were designed to run on 100-octane gasoline, especially when supercharged at high altitude. But the high-octane gasoline all went overseas to combat units, and at Blythe, we worked with lower octane stuff. Hence our allowable operational parameters were cut well below optimum. Williamson's aeroplane, an old, tired one at best, was cruising with its intake manifold pressure a little high. A cylinder suddenly parted from its crankcase and blew out the top of the engine cowling. Williamson and his crew devoted their subsequent efforts to getting back to the air-base at Blythe safely.

At Blythe we adopted a useful operational practice which we were to continue throughout our days flying together as a crew. Bob Hayzlett, always a careful pilot, liked to fly with the bomb bay doors open about an inch. The B-24 had bomb doors that rolled up the aeroplane sides, like the cover of a roll-top desk. To fly with them cracked open, something not possible with a B-17, added minuscule drag, but also kept the bomb bay purged of gasoline fumes. Some models of B-24 had leaky gasoline transfer valves in the front of the bomb bay. These leaky valves could fill that compartment with an explosive mixture.

One evening at Blythe I was in the officers' club with Bob Stoesser. Various aeroplanes were taking off on a night practice mission, but we paid no attention. Suddenly the club shook with the impact of a nearby explosion, so we ran outside to look. There was a fire burning in the desert, south of the airfield.

Some unlucky crew had taken off southbound. The main east-west highway from Los Angeles to Phoenix went along the south boundary of the base and when the bomber was squarely over the highway, it exploded into small fragments. The debris, still burning, fell into the desert, well south of the field.

At the time the bomber exploded, the Greyhound bus from Los Angeles was rolling eastbound down the highway. So startled was the bus driver by the big bomber exploding directly over his bus that he lost control and rolled well out onto the desert floor, mowing down cactus before he came to a stop, which must have been a scary experience for the bus passengers. We never learned whether the deceased pilot had flown with the bomb bay doors fully shut.

Not all of the training work of our crew was routine. We were one of the crews sent out from Blythe on a night navigation mission to make a pretend bomb run on the city of El Paso. The planned attack was R.A.F.-style with each aeroplane flying alone, and with about five minutes' spacing between bombers along the assigned course.

We were about twenty minutes out, climbing east over Arizona, when Sergeant Sheltraw reported that all the ship's radios were out. However, being good soldiers, we elected to continue the mission, pressing on to victory. As we passed near Tucson the moon was up and we could see the huge, black bulk of Mount Lemmon looming up below us. Its eastern face was shrouded in black clouds and we could see lightning flashes below us down in the murk.

Soon we were riding thunderstorms, bouncing and churning through the turbulent clouds, and our path was punctuated by bright flashes of lightning. Sensible people would have turned back, but we were a brave new crew of the United States Army Air Forces, and we pressed on, holding to our briefed course, undeterred by a bit of rough weather.

Gniewkowski was over the Sperry bombsight, hoping to see El Paso through the churning clouds below. We were all tense. The horrifying weather outside gave this practice mission the semblance of actual combat. As we passed over the radio marker beacon west of El Paso I felt the bomber lurch suddenly. We took a severe nose-down attitude. The engines screamed, winding up to unprecedented high RPM. Clearly the pilots had given the ship full throttle – balls to the wall. We were in a near dive. I looked at the airspeed indicator – it read zero!

Thank God for Lynne Griefenstein's clear head! He spotted the trouble immediately, and ran forward, turning on the Pitot tube heat. Our airspeed Pitot tubes, protruding upward from behind the bomber's nose greenhouse, had filled with ice in the thunderstorms, but the electric heat soon melted them clear. When the ice had gone from the tubes the airspeed indicator wound up suddenly, settling out at about 270 miles per hour.

Hayzlett and Stoesser pulled our bomber out of its terrifying dive. We missed the high mountain west of El Paso but we'd had enough for one night. We turned around slowly so as not to bend our aeroplane any more, and headed back to Blythe without further incident.

When we arrived at Blythe, the G.I.s in the operations shack came out to greet us as though we were long-lost prodigal sons. The mission had been recalled for bad weather less than an hour after take-off, but with our radios out, we had not heard the recall. By the time we wandered home, the operations people had assumed we were dead, crashed in the mountains of New Mexico, and they could easily have been right.

Blythe was so far out in the boonies that there was no civilised place nearby. I did manage to hitch-hike into Los Angeles occasionally on rare weekends off from training operations, but the trip was so long that there was little time left to relax with my relatives.

At Quartzsite, Arizona, just across the Colorado River from Blythe, was an air-base full of women. These were girls training as wartime ferry pilots, who flew replacement combat planes to their operational areas, delivering them to the crews stationed there. Some of the big boys at Blythe had short-term paramours among the girls at Quartzsite. But our crew was more businesslike. We were at Blythe to learn to fly together as a team, professionally and with skill. The B-24 was our first love.

Our time at Blythe was short, but we were so busy it seemed long. We learned to live with our big bombers, and to operate them well. Most importantly, we learned to respect each other's skills, and to work together as a team.

When we finished our work at Blythe we were adjudged to be a well-trained and integrated crew. One afternoon we were put on the train for Hamilton

Field, near San Francisco. By now we were accustomed to the fact that whenever the Army sent us on travel orders it was always by slow train, never by aeroplane.

Being sent to Hamilton was a clear indication that we were destined to fly in the Pacific. During World War II more B-24 bombers were built than any other U.S. military aeroplane in all history, and most were used in the war in the Pacific. The B-24 was the longest-range American bomber in full production at the time, and it worked well for the Pacific theatre.

While our time at Hamilton was brief, it did give us the opportunity for an overnight pass to San Francisco. There was hardly a better place in the United States for military leave than San Francisco, so we made the most of our opportunity.

We sat around at Hamilton for a few more days, expecting to be given a new aeroplane and told to fly west. However, our expectations were thwarted by enigmatic military omniscience. We were put on a long, slow train full of troops and sent off to Camp Kilmer at New Brunswick, New Jersey.

As our train rolled across the Sierra Nevada and the Rocky Mountains, taking days to go a few miles, Bob Hayzlett developed a common traveller's problem. He became severely constipated. The wartime food on the troop train was probably no help. At any rate, Bob was doubled over with cramps, and running into the station at every jerkwater whistle stop on the way, looking for somewhere to buy laxatives.

In the middle of the night, out in Wyoming, Hayzlett finally felt relief coming. He went into the common john at the end of the ancient railroad car which served as our opulent travel accommodation. With a vast sense of comfort, Bob proceeded to make good use of the train's essential receptacle.

Train car crappers of those days dumped their contents onto the tracks whenever flushed with the gigantic brass lever provided for that purpose. These odd devices added a bit of water to the can's contents, to wash things down a bit, and, so the theory went, distributed the load along the tracks so that it was sparsely deposited in any one location. It was tacitly assumed that the material was biodegradable. Flushing the crapper in stations was manifestly frowned upon. Each train john had a large warning sign on the wall, alerting passengers to the fact that the can was not to be flushed unless the train was moving at full cruising speed.

Though the train had been rolling well when he began, by the time Hayzlett finished his welcome duty it had stopped dead on the tracks. Bob sat there dutifully for a long time. Finally, in desperation, he looked out of the window and saw nothing. The outside was totally black. Figuring that we were miles out in the Wyoming prairie, Bob flushed the Pullman crapper, dumping its ample contents out on the right-of-way. As he wandered back to his bunk he peered out of the car aisle window on the other side of the Pullman. The train was stopped with our car directly in front of the Cheyenne Passenger Station – the john window had been so dirty on the outside that Bob could see nothing through it.

We suspected that Cheyenne had good reason to remember Bob Hayzlett.

Camp Kilmer gave us our last chance for leave in the States. Stoesser went home to Elizabeth, New Jersey; Hayzlett, Gniewkowski and I took the train into New York City where we wandered around, looking at the sights, then spent most of the night in the ballroom of the Lincoln Hotel, listening to Count Basie's band.

For years I had collected the records of Count Basie. He fronted one of the greatest swing bands in the world, so witnessing a live performance was a dream fulfilled for me. The rock-solid work of the Basie rhythm section was everything one could expect; the heavy bass was punctuated by Basie's polite piano and the guitar of Freddie Green. Over it all drifted the whispering cymbal work of Joe Jones at the drums. My only disappointment was the absence of Lester Young who was, in my opinion, the greatest tenor sax man alive. Lester played psychedelic phrases with his sax laid casually and horizontally across his knees. But he had left Basie's band a few months previously to head his own small outfit in a Hollywood jazz joint.

This night at the Lincoln Hotel was to be our last taste of American culture in a long while. In the pre-dawn we took the Hudson tubes back to Jersey, there to meet Bob Stoesser who had borrowed a car to drive us all back to New Brunswick.

After three days at Camp Kilmer, we were trucked with all our baggage to the Brooklyn Navy Yard and marched aboard a troop transport ship staffed by a coastguard crew. In the middle of the night we sailed out into the Atlantic on our way to Europe.

When dawn came we found our ship was a small part of a vast convoy on the high seas. Those few of us who were aerial navigators kept track of where we were. We would sneak up on deck with a bubble octant and shoot sun lines.

There was another advantage to being air-crew – we did not get seasick. Our time spent riding bombers had made us immune to motion sickness so we were able to enjoy all the food that the paddlefeet were too ill to keep down. And having little else interesting to do, we stayed up half the night playing poker.

It took about a week of wandering all over the Atlantic before our convoy pulled into Clydebank in Scotland. We disembarked in late afternoon and got on a train, heading off into the British night and arriving about midnight at a place named Stone.

Stone was jammed with American aircrewmen with nothing to do. We sat around for a few days, then got on an aeroplane and flew to Northern Ireland, landing at Belfast. From there a truck took us to Cluntoe on the west shore of Lough Neagh. At Cluntoe we had a bit of schooling, but mostly did nothing for a month but sit around enjoying the green Irish scenery and taking invigorating walks in the daily rain.

Finally the orders came. We trucked to Belfast, got on a C-47, with a few other crews, and were delivered to various Liberator bases in England. Our outfit was the 458th Bomb Group stationed at Horsham St Faith in Norfolk, otherwise known as AAF Station 123, APO 558.

At last we were with a fighting outfit, ready to go to war.

CHAPTER 5

FIRST MISSION

In times of long ago the Saxon cathedral of Norfolk was at Elmham. William the Conqueror moved the See to Thetford. But the Conqueror's son, King William II Rufus, sent his Bishop, Herbert Losinga, to Norwich. There, beginning in 1095, Losinga built the vast Norman cathedral which still stands, a landmark for all of Norfolk.

The Norman kings set a huge castle on the round hill that is the epicentre of Norwich. Though it is a museum today, its vast bulk of white stone looks as though it was built last week. These two institutions, cathedral and castle, secured for Norwich its pre-eminence, held to this day, as the County Town of Norfolk and the biggest city in East Anglia.

Horsham St Faith, where the 458th Bomb Group was stationed, was at the end of the run of the northbound Norwich City bus line. The name, Horsham, found at various locations in England, refers to a place where

The hangars, administration and quarters at Horsham St Faith in World War II.

A photograph of Horsham St Faith taken in 1991. (*Courtesy Memorial Library, Second Air Division, USAAF – Norwich, England.*)

horses were kept. The name is written in the Domesday Book. The first known reference to a church of St Faith at Horsham in Norfolk is in a manuscript of 1163. St Faith was a virgin martyr of France who was immolated by fire at Agen in the Middle Ages.

To us however, Horsham St Faith was a big airfield. There we were assigned to the 752nd Bomb Squadron, 458th Bomb Group (Heavy), 96th Combat Wing, Second Air Division, Eighth U.S. Army Air Force. We were fortunate to be stationed there, as we learned in time. In all of the Second Air Division, the 458th had the only permanent station. We had brick buildings, excellent facilities, and entirely liveable quarters. Every other bomb group in Second Division was equipped with Quonset huts, freeze-to-death coke-burning stoves, and muddy surroundings.

When we arrived, the officers of our crew were given an upstairs apartment in one of the brick houses that served as combat crew housing at Horsham St Faith. The four of us could, and did, live quite comfortably in our second-story digs.

Our enlisted men, following the Army rules of apartheid and class discrimination, were given their own quarters elsewhere in buildings assigned to enlisted personnel.

We were unpacking our gear in our new digs when the air raid siren went

The officers' club at Horsham St Faith.

off, sounding loudly over the entire base. Since there seemed to be no strafing enemy aircraft in the vicinity, Hayzlett, Stoesser, Gniewkowski and I listened to the noise, then resumed our moving-in. Our crew enlisted men were more dutiful and well-disciplined. Sergeant Sheltraw ran from the barracks to the nearest bomb shelter. There he sat for a while, wondering why no one else was in the shelter. After a time the all clear sounded. Sheltraw went back to his new barracks to finish his unpacking. The rest of the airmen of Hayzlett's crew had run off in different directions, and they wandered slowly back to their barracks. After a time they were all present except for waist gunner Giordano. They wondered out loud what had become of him. At this comment a large pile of mattresses began to move in the corner of the room. From under the pile came Sergeant Dominic Giordano, flak helmet firmly in place, and ready for any emergency, however dire.

It was only later that our crew G.I.s found out it had all been a drill.

We soon discovered that we were prisoners on the base. All personnel were restricted to the base, and no one was allowed off – rumours were abundant as to why. The true reason was not long in coming. On 6 June 1944, the Allied Armies landed in Normandy and the invasion of Europe through France had begun.

The exact news came to us on the radio, as it came to the rest of the world. By this time each of us had bought a radio, and we kept it tuned to BBC, American Armed Forces Radio, or, sometimes, to German-operated radio on the continent. I could understand German relatively well, based on

Sergeant Dominic
Giordano.

my classes at the University of Washington, and I especially enjoyed
listening at night to the air raid warnings as the RAF went out to pound a
German City.

Four days after D-Day, on 10 June, 1944, we went out on our first mission.
The squeaky brakes of an operations jeep sounded outside our dwelling unit
long before the sun came up out of the North Sea (and it comes up very early
in Norfolk in June). We heard the footsteps of the duty sergeant on the stairs,
then a heavy knock on the door. The door opened and a voice said,
'Lieutenant Hayzlett's crew, Sirs, briefing in an hour!' It was a ceremony of
the dark hours that would be repeated many times before we went home
again.

On this occasion all of us were lying expectantly awake long before the jeep
and the sergeant arrived. We got up, took turns using the bathroom, put on
our flight coveralls, and walked over to the combat mess.

We had all heard horror stories from parents about the terrible quality of
Army food in World War I. The newspapers told us that only the best was
provided for combat troops of World War II. People back home were on
rationing so that our fighting men would be properly fed and nourished.

Army officers on duty in the Z.I. (the Zone of the Interior, meaning the North American United States) bought and paid for their own food. Now that we were on duty in a war zone, the food was provided free of charge.

The quality of food at the 458th Bomb Group combat officers' mess reflected the price we paid. Not that the food was non-nourishing or skimpy – it was in rather too ample supply. There was more of it than the quality of preparation warranted eating. This lack of tasteful quality may have been partly due to the form in which the food arrived to be subjected to the tender mercies of the men who prepared it.

There were no fresh eggs at breakfast time; the only eggs available were powdered. These were prepared by being whipped into a great sticky emulsion, then apparently fried in axle grease left over from the needs of the motor pool; the result was a well-vulcanised, plastic lump of lukewarm goo. Milk also was available only in powdered form. We were warned in lectures by the Flight Surgeon's staff never to drink local milk in England, but only to consume the G.I. powdered product. I found it unthinkable that a modern, civilised nation like Great Britain did not regulate the pasteurisation of milk, but such seemed to be the case. I never did have the nerve to find out if the medicos were wrong.

After enjoying breakfast at the combat officers' mess, we walked to the

Major Charles Booth,
Assistant Group Operations
Officer, 458th Bomb Group.

briefing hut. This establishment was one of the rare Quonset huts on our base. It was full of hard seats, and, at one end, was a platform. On the end wall of the hut, at the back of the platform, was a large, composite map of north-western Europe, England included. The map was covered with a green curtain until combat briefing actually began. Mission briefing was typically directed, conducted, and orchestrated by Major Charles Booth, Assistant Group Operations Officer. He was a good choice for the job. He was always smiling, happy, charming and erudite – even early on a God-awful foggy morning when everyone present was going out to look death in the face in the skies over Berlin. To listen to Booth you would think we had all assembled for a Sunday school picnic.

On his second combat mission in August of 1944, Booth, then a captain, flew as command pilot of the Group formation. The target was a ball-bearing plant in Berlin. Shortly after the formation crossed the coast inbound, a flak shell went off under the lead ship. Shell fragments ripped off the right side of the co-pilot's seat, injured both Booth's legs, and disabled the heating system of his electric flight suit. Booth, after ascertaining that he might possibly not bleed nor freeze to death, declined assistance until after his formation had bombed its primary target successfully.

For this gallant action he was awarded the Distinguished Service Cross. His colourful ribbon was admired by combat crewmen, as was his friendly personality. Chuck Booth showed that it was not necessary to spend all one's time worrying about death in combat. Rather one might perform successfully with a laid-back attitude, figuring that whatever came along would come.

At briefing Chuck Booth was assisted by various other people and the cast of characters varied with time, as we were to learn. Mostly it was made up of day people who seemed rather to enjoy getting up every morning before the crack of dawn. One seldom saw the office-holders themselves at briefing, but usually the assistants. Briefing was handled by the Assistant Group Bombardier, the Assistant Weather Officer, and the Assistant Group Navigator, for example. I was later to discover that the job-holders themselves were busy enough without having to attend every briefing session. But on this morning the Commanding Officer himself was present at briefing. It was our first opportunity to see him in person.

Colonel James H. Isbell was an impressive figure. He was the only full bird Colonel in the 458th. He stood out among all of us retreaded civilians as someone to be reckoned with, and someone not to screw around with.

Jim Isbell grew up in Union City, Tennessee. Both his maternal uncles were Army officers, West Point graduates. The younger uncle was in the Air Corps with a pilot's rating. At the age of fourteen, Jim Isbell set his mind on becoming a West Point Cadet, but the way to the Military Academy was not an easy one. When Isbell graduated from high school he asked his Congressional Representative for an appointment to West Point. The request was not granted. Jim Isbell went to a local college on an athletic scholarship. In his sophomore year, his Representative gave him a second alternate appointment to West Point. He quit college to study full time for the Academy entrance exam. The principal appointee failed. Isbell passed, but so did the first alternate, who accepted the appointment.

Flak bursts off the port wing.

Now, having been tagged out at third base, Jim Isbell decided to get to West Point any way he could. He enlisted in the Army and applied to attend West Point Prep School. He achieved his long-term goal on 2 July, 1934, when he was sworn in at West Point with a Presidential appointment won in competitive examination.

Cadet Isbell won four letters in football (he was team captain in 1937) and three letters on the heavyweight boxing team. He graduated in June 1938 and was commissioned as a second lieutenant. In September of that same year he began pilot training at Randolph Field, San Antonio, Texas. He earned his pilot's rating in August of 1939. By the time the United States became involved in World War II, James H. Isbell was clearly one of those too-rare people qualified to command an Air Force Group.

On the morning of our first combat mission, Colonel Isbell spoke about the kind of crappy formation flying that he didn't want to see. He was ever insistent on tight formations, and, as we would find out, he would frequently get his whole Bomb Group out to fly around England and tighten up their formation work on a day when others goofed off or slept in.

Isbell spoke plainly: 'If the German fighter pilots want to try flying through our tight formations, they're going to get their asses shot off. If we sock it in there tightly they'll leave us alone and go down the line looking for some sloppy-flying outfit to pick on.'

And he was right, as we found out in time.

When the briefing was ended, and the chaplain had said a reassuring prayer for those of us who might not return, we walked to the hut nearby where the flight equipment was kept. There each of us had a locker with flight gear in it. At Blythe we had flown in massive sheepskins to keep out the high-altitude cold, and we used old-style balloon-bladdered oxygen masks to breathe above fifteen thousand feet, but here in the E.T.O. (European Theatre of Operations) we had the latest in technology. Our flight suits were electrically-heated. When we got to our stations in the bomber we plugged into the nearest convenient outlet and rode toasty-warm all the way. The electric suits were thin and comfortable, like long underwear. They had heated bootees which plugged into the suit legs, and kept one's toes from frostbite.

In the States I had learned to like flying in a pair of old black engineering boots, civilian issue. I had brought these to England with me, and I wore them over the heated bootees. It was comfortable gear, and I had the strange belief that if I ever had to walk out of Germany, the boots would do the job for me.

The electric suits also came equipped with heated gloves. I learned in time not to use these. They made it hard for me to write. Writing was essential for a navigator, always at his logs and charts. If I kept my hands busy writing, they usually stayed warm. Also I could arrange to keep my log where the sun shone through the astrodome and the high altitude sunshine radiated plenty of warmth.

When we were fully garbed, we went out to get a jeep ride to the flight line. I carried my heavy navigation case in one hand and my parachute pack in the other. Navigators wore portable chute packs which snapped onto the front of the parachute harness. One needed always to put the chute pack in a handy place on board the bomber in case of need. Jumping out without it was inadvisable. The operations jeep delivered us to our bomber. The sight of the aeroplane was less than encouraging as we began our first mission.

The planes we had flown at training in Blythe had big greenhouse noses. There were mounts in the nose for 50-calibre machine guns, but we carried guns only for gunnery practice in training. The greenhouses gave widespread visibility to the navigator who rode the nose and were excellent for pilotage. One could see everywhere from them.

The B-24s equipped for aerial combat over Europe were quite differently modified. The front greenhouse was replaced with a big plexiglass turret mounting a pair of 50-calibres. Behind the turret in the nose compartment were two big ammunition cans, one on each side, to hold the belt loads for the nose turret guns. While the nose turret had its own doors, a second big pair of doors in the front of the fuselage allowed the turret occupant to get in and out of his chamber. These doors invariably leaked air, making the nose compartment of a combat B-24 the equivalent of a wind tunnel featuring freezing wind. The ammo cans made the nose compartment quite cramped for the navigator, and much more so for the bombardier who had to work wedged between them with his head under the turret. The aeroplanes were not built with crew comfort in mind.

In order to make up for some of the loss of visibility occasioned by the nose turret, a big plexiglass blister was installed on each side of the nose. These blisters were of a size and shape that allowed the navigator to put his head into each of them in turn and survey the surroundings. The turret and the side blisters gave the combat B-24 the external appearance of a gigantic grasshopper in flight.

The aboriginal belly turret of the B-24 had been discarded in the combat configuration. This disposed of considerable weight that could be made up in bomb tonnage, and it also avoided the necessity to crank the turret up and down.

The elimination of the belly turret was made possible by the wide fire arcs of the B-24's gun turrets. Both nose and tail turrets covered a much bigger angular range of sky than was possible with the turret guns of a B-17. The belly turret of a B-24 was actually superfluous from a defensive standpoint.

With this configuration of guns on our combat ships, Sergeant Carsie Foley was moved from his former defensive position in the belly ball turret to the nose turret and became our nose gunner. I don't know if his new job was any safer, but at least he had a broader view of the world – rightside-up, instead of upside-down.

The particular aeroplane of the 752nd Squadron assigned for our use on our first mission was an ugly mess. It was painted in foot-locker olive drab. The newer aeroplanes had abandoned camouflage paint in favour of honest, bare aluminium skin. They looked very shiny and technical alongside the older bombers. Our ship had its paint streaked with grease and oil indicative of leaking engines. It seemed to sag on its landing gear as it sat there, worn and tired. It was gross.

Not only had we been assigned an old, tired aeroplane, we had also been assigned an old, tired pilot. New crews were often capable of making fatal mistakes on their early missions. We had been given an instructor to help us make these mistakes in a professional manner. Every bomb group had a few folks around who, for one reason or another, had not completed their required tour of missions, but who no longer had a crew to which they were assigned. Our man was on his last, or next-to-last, mission, and damn glad of it, understandably. I've forgotten his name, but I didn't like his looks the first time I laid eyes on him.

He was a high-ranking first lieutenant, or some such, and very officious about it. He took over the first pilot's chair so that Hayzlett flew as co-pilot and Stoesser had to sit on the floor or stand between the seats. Mr Instructor then kept the intercom busy throughout the whole flight, mouthing us through the proper operational procedures to fly a combat mission.

We taxied out to get in the long line of bombers, then took off when our turn came. All of us were scared as hell – we were utter greenhorns, and we knew it.

We climbed out to the north to circle in wing assembly around Splasher Five, the radio beacon at Cromer on the coast. At the appointed time we swung out with our Group into the Wing attack line, holding our formation position somewhere down in the ass end of coffin corner. Our target was an airfield at a place in France named Châteaudun. It was alleged to be full of operational German aircraft and we were to crater it up a bit.

We went south over England and out over the Channel at Selsey Bill where a group of P-38 fighters wrapped comfortingly around the wing formation. We crossed over the coast of Normandy, where our troops had landed down below just four days earlier and then we were actually over occupied France. The enemy was below us. Down there was the big, tough German Army, ready to shoot our buns off.

I looked down a bit nervously from the side blister. It was green and quiet below, just like England. Everything seemed calm. Everything, that is, except our instructor pilot. His voice had become strangely high-pitched, and his comments singularly inappropriate. His demeanour, in fact, was alarming. He seemed suddenly to have adopted the view that he was a prisoner trying to escape and we were his captors.

About halfway through French territory towards our target the instructor pilot suddenly pulled out of formation.

'I don't like the way number three engine sounds!' he said. 'I think we better go home right away. The engine sounds funny!'

'I don't hear anything,' Hayzlett said.

'Look out there! There's oil on the wing, dammit! My God, we'll probably burn up! Oh, shit!'

'That was there before we took off,' Hayzlett offered.

I looked out of the blister at our Group formation disappearing in the distance, the fighter escort wrapped around them. We were all by ourselves over enemy territory. I remembered the Colonel's lecture about staying in tight formation no matter what. I looked out of the blister again and saw imaginary German fighters swooping in from all directions to make the final kill. I was torn between the desire to faint and to wet my pants.

By now the instructor was wracking our ship all over the sky. The compass at the navigator's station looked like a roulette wheel in action.

'What's happening?' I summoned the nerve to ask.

'The command pilot is assuming a new heading at his discretion,' said the idiot at the controls, 'We'll probably need to take some evasive action up here. It could be a dangerous situation. Oh, cripe!'

'You bet your ass!' I muttered into my oxygen mask, carefully switching off the interphone first.

'Bombardier!' the instructor pilot said.

'Yes, Sir,' Gniewkowski growled into his throat mike.

'See those woods down there. I think there's a target in there. It looks like just the place the Germans would hide something important. Bomb it!'

'What woods?' Gniewkowski said.

'Right up ahead there. Those big woods. It's clearly a target.'

'Bullshit!' Gniewkowski said.

'I said bomb that target, dammit! That's an order!'

'Yes, Sir!' Gniewkowski said.

I folded up my desk in the nose and got out of the way so Gniewkowski could get over the bombsight. He picked out the middle of the patch of woods, and we dumped our load of 500-pound TNT bombs into the sylvan scenery, destroying a few old trees.

Eddie Gniewkowski, with a disgusted look clearly visible over his oxygen mask, went back up onto the flight deck. Gniewkowski was always monumentally upset over a bad bomb-drop. He never made a bad one himself, in my experience, except for this dumping in the woods at the command of our crazy, *pro tem* aircraft commander. And Eddie could not stand flying in a formation where anyone else made a sloppy drop. As he departed the aircraft nose, sadly, he looked as though he might puke. I hoped that, if he did, he would do it in the lap of our instructor pilot.

By now my navigation log was an unholy mess, and my chart was worse. The insane instructor pilot was taking us all over Normandy, steering like a blind dog in a meat house. I was too scared and confused to follow him.

But, at last we got back to the Channel coast at a spot I recognised. We hadn't been shot flaming out of the sky, or even attacked. I gave the instructor a heading back to England and, surprisingly, he took it, holding course to within plus or minus ten degrees or so. I began to understand about the crew he didn't have. Probably they had devised some way to get away from him.

Halfway across the Channel I began to breathe easier. Maybe the Germans wouldn't find us after all. As we let down, got off oxygen, and neared Horsham St Faith we could see the tall spire of Norwich Cathedral in the distance.

'We better tool around till the formation gets back,' our self-styled command pilot said, 'we don't want it to look like we goofed off or something and got back early.'

'I thought we had engine trouble,' Gniewkowski said.

'Don't give me any smart ass! And remember to report that we hit a valid target.'

So we landed roughly in the middle of the homecoming crowd. We parked our ship and got out of it, happy to be alive and well.

Prior to our arrival with the 458th, there had been a change in the Commanding Officer's staff. Group Navigator Captain Ray Sandberg had left to join another bomb group and had been replaced by Elmer Mottern, previously the Navigation Officer of the 754th Bomb Squadron. I now got the memorable opportunity of meeting Elmer Mottern for the first time. We rode the jeep from the flight line back to the operations building. There the navigators were herded into line for debriefing. At a desk sat a glowering major, looking over the paper work of each navigator in turn. Major Elmer Mottern was the toughest-looking major I had ever seen.

He wasn't really of gigantic stature, but, somehow, he had all the demeanour of a grizzly bear. He was the Group Navigation Officer, and it had never occurred to me before that there could actually be a navigator in the whole world with the exalted rank of major. All my instructors in school had been lieutenants.

When my turn came I stood at attention before Mottern. I was filled with some pride – after all, I had been over France in a bomber, had survived, and had returned without injury or death. Elmer Mottern took my chart and log. He stared at them with considerable disbelief.

'You fly this mission?' he asked, in a notable South Carolina drawl.

'Yes, Sir!'

'Sure as hell cain't tell it by lookin' at this shit!'

And with this crushing remark I was summarily dismissed to rejoin my crew, return to quarters, and swap war stories about our first combat mission with the mighty Eighth Air Force.

That evening, up in our quarters, we held a conference of the crew officers. Our discussion centred around the question of whether we might go as a team to visit the Group Commanding Officer and ask, politely, that we would not be assigned again to fly with some crazy man as an instructor pilot.

We had been impressed with our introduction to Colonel Isbell at the briefing. He seemed like a no-nonsense kind of commander, highly capable and we felt sure that he did not intend his crews to pull out of the Group formation to bomb imaginary targets in French forests.

After due deliberation we decided not to ask to speak to the Colonel. That would make a big fuss, and get us noticed, something one ought to avoid in the military, we reasoned. So we cooked up an alternative plan. We decided that, if we got another instructor pilot like the one on our first mission, we would truss him up, hang him on the bomb racks, and drop him into a French forest.

753rd Bomb Squadron aircraft seen from the right waist window.

CHAPTER 6

THE LATRINE COEFFICIENT

The day after our first mission I got word that Captain Irving Burton wanted to talk to me. Burton was Squadron Navigation Officer of the 752nd Bomb Squadron. He had an office adjoining the Squadron's big hangar out on the flight line.

Burton had curly blond hair, twinkly blue eyes, and a warm personality. He was from Brooklyn, and his speech told me so instantly. Apparently Major Mottern had passed the word along that Burton ought to take a look at the log and chart I had brought back from our abortive mission to bomb the French forest. Burton had looked and he was just as appalled as Mottern was. He was, however, a bit kinder about it.

'What does this mean here where it says, "Pilot takes new heading?" That is what it says, isn't it?' Burton tapped his pencil slowly on his desk.

I explained the gruesome details of flying with our instructor pilot.

'I know that son-of-a-bitch,' Burton said, 'He's crazy!'

I agreed.

'Look,' Burton said in a fatherly tone, 'the navigator is, by God, in charge of directing the course of the ship. The next time you get some pilot who thinks he's going to tell you where the hell he ought to steer the thing, you straighten him out in a hurry.

'And if you have any more trouble like this, come and tell me. I'll get him straightened out.'

I began to like Captain Burton a great deal.

'And I'll try to see that you don't get any more insane people like this joker to fly with.'

'Thank you, Sir.'

'Come in and see me anytime. Maybe the next time we can have a more friendly chat.'

As far as I was concerned, my talk with Irving Burton was plenty friendly. He was about the only person in charge of anything who had smiled at me since I arrived at the 458th. I decided that Burton was a person I was happy to know.

Apparently I had managed to convince Burton that I was not a hopeless case. At any rate, we were scheduled up to fly a mission again the next day, and I was sent along as navigator.

We got a different instructor to help this time. We went off to bomb another French airfield at a place called Evreux. Everything went well, and we dumped the bombs on the target, making Gniewkowski and the rest of us happy.

Our instructor spent most of his time sitting on the floor next to Sheltraw's radio. He did offer some useful advice, but mostly he said, 'I'm just along to get credit to go home, fellows.'

This time I was ready for Major Mottern at debriefing. I had every damn time, position, and hiccup logged and charted. My papers had notations on the notations. I stood at attention and passed the log and chart to Mottern.

He glared at them with his grizzly bear stare.

'That's a little more like it,' he said, almost smiling.

Some of my confidence was restored by Mottern not biting off my head and handing it to me on a plate. Maybe aerial navigation in a combat zone would not be so bad after all.

Now that we apparently were to fly simple missions to French airfields, and only every other day or so, we relaxed a bit, and took some time to learn our way around the base. The airfield at Horsham St Faith was really an attractive place, well kept and well landscaped. The permanent buildings were attractive. We had lucked out on a place to be stationed.

Our air-base had big hangars clustered in a quarter-circle around the south taxiway of the field. In the back of the hangars were various buildings, built almost entirely of brick. Some of these, looking like private homes in a row, were set aside as officer quarters – one bomber crew living downstairs and one up. Hayzlett, Stoesser, Gniewkowski and I shared the upstairs of one such building. Our crew enlisted men lived in a big, long brick building

Horsham St Faith was blessed with large Type-C hangars. The aircraft shown is *The Pied Piper*, probably photographed late in the War. (*Courtesy Memorial Library, Second Air Division, USAAF – Norwich, England.*)

with numerous apartments or flats. On the base there was also a big building with two wings where a number of combat crew officers lived. This building housed the mess where we ate breakfast early in the morning before a mission.

Now that the invasion beachhead was more or less established on the coast of Normandy, we were no longer confined to base. We took the bus downtown to get acquainted with Norwich. These trips were for sightseeing, and to admire the mediaeval parts of the old city around the castle and the cathedral. Also, I used the time off to buy some things that I needed. The short nights of late Spring were occasionally chilly in East Anglia, and the only heat in our upstairs apartment was provided by a fireplace with a grate. We were provided with coke to burn in the grate, but trying to ignite coke by any ordinary means is like trying to set fire to a rock. So I bought a large bellows, hand operated, almost the size that a blacksmith would use. After considerable practice I learned to make a fire with coke, and the fire would burn for an unbelievably long time, once started properly.

We also spent our time getting acquainted with our fellow warriors of the 458th Bomb Group. We found that we were fortunate in being assigned to live in our little apartment in a detached unit. Those combat crew officers assigned to live in the huge brick dormitory building were about four to a room, and comfortable enough, but without the cosy privacy of home that we had in our little upstairs.

Off to the east of the combat officers' dormitory/mess was another big, brick residential building, usually known simply as the 'club'. It had somewhat more opulent living quarters. In this latter building lived all the wheels of the 458th – the Commanding Officer, the officers of Group staff, and other such exalted ones. Quite a few of the residents of this building were paddle-feet. 'Paddlefoot' was the Air Corps name for an officer without a flight rating as his military occupational speciality. Also patrons here, as we learned, were officers of the staff of 96th Combat Wing, Brigadier-General Walter Peck, commanding. The Wing was stationed at Horsham St Faith along with the 458th Bomb Group. General Peck lived in a nice private house in a quiet corner of the airfield. His command included the 466th Bomb Group at Attlebridge and the 467th Bomb Group at Rackheath as well as the 458th. Rackheath and Attlebridge were nearby bases.

We learned also that the club had a big and well-stocked bar, and a comfortable lobby for quiet conversation. I drank no booze at the time. I figured that I had enough going on to muddle my mind without adding alcohol to the muddling items, but I did enjoy dropping in at the club for conversation. The Eighth Air Force had people of all trades from all over the United States. To a small-town kid like me from the far-away Evergreen State of Washington these new friends were all fascinating, and I loved to talk to them.

Along with Stoesser and Hayzlett I dropped in at the club one evening and struck up a conversation with Lieutenant Irving Goldman. He was from New York State and was our Group Radar Officer. While Goldman was an engineer, he was also an attorney.

Near us was a lieutenant of about thirty, with dark hair, and a memorable voice, gravelly like that of Lionel Stander, the movie actor. Not only did this lieutenant have a memorable voice, but also he used it impressively. You got the impression that if he recited the ABC it would sound like the ten Commandments. The lieutenant of the stentorian tones was talking to an enlisted man who worked at the club. The topic was the G.I.'s English girl-friend who, allegedly, was becoming a bit cool towards her American paramour.

The lieutenant asked the G.I. if he gave his girlfriend presents. The G.I. replied that they had known each other too long, and were too well acquainted to mess around with anything sentimental like presents.

The lieutenant seized on this answer like a dog on a fresh bone. He gave a monumentally impressive lecture about the dangers of letting the sentiment go out of a romance. He told the G.I. that the whole problem with his girl-friend was his own fault for letting romance fade.

'Romance makes the world go around!' the lieutenant said, as though he were reading the preamble to the United States Constitution. 'Go get some flowers now, tonight! Take them to your loved one. Tell her she's wonderful, and kneel dutifully at her feet. Go and do it now!'

And the G.I., convinced, went off to do his romantic duty.

'Who the hell is that lieutenant?' I asked Goldman.

'Max Sokarl,' Goldman said. 'B.S. is his speciality.'

'What does he do?'

'He's an intelligence officer. But he's also an attorney, like I am. We don't get to practise too much law in the military, you know. Sokarl loves to put on enlisted men.'

'Is he a sadist or something?'

'No, he's not mean. He just seems to need continual intellectual stimu-lation, and he finds damn little of it in his job here. So, he keeps inventing it. You've heard about his invention of the latrine coefficient?'

'What in heck is the latrine coefficient?'

'Hey, Max.' Goldman beckoned to Lieutenant Sokarl, 'Come over here and meet Jack, and help me tell him about your latrine coefficient.'

Lieutenant Max Sokarl moved his chair closer, smiling. Goldman launched into the story of the development of the latrine coefficient. Sokarl added punch lines and colour throughout.

It seems that things were too quiet in Sokarl's squadron. Sokarl's good friend and patron, Major Pierce Manley, the Group Adjutant, had devised an extra job for Max. Sokarl was put in charge of a crew of enlisted men whose duty was to maintain latrines used by combat officers only. These enlisted men were 'basics', in Army parlance. That is, they had the lowest possible scores on Army entrance exams, and their I.Q.s were adjudged to be barely sufficient to let them serve in the military. It is possible, but not likely, that one of these men would, if he lived long enough to serve a hundred years or so, be promoted to private, first class. If so the promotion would be based on kindness, and not on ability.

Such was Sokarl's latrine crew.

Lieutenant Sokarl took a particular liking to a G.I. named George. He decided to test George's acumen. So one day he called him in for a chat.

Major Pierce Manley,
Group Adjutant, 458th
Bomb Group.

George stood, trembling, in a very raunchy imitation of attention, before the lieutenant's desk.

'Relax, George,' Sokarl said, 'Stand at ease. In fact, sit down right there. Here, have a cigar.'

'I don't smoke none, sir,' George said, 'You sure I can sit down?'

'Of course. Sit down. I just called you in for a friendly chat. We need to determine how things are going down there in your latrine.'

'Is somethin' wrong in my latrine? What's wrong? Ain't nothin' wrong I hope. I don't never need to get in no trouble.'

'Relax, George. There's nothing wrong. We just need to get a few facts together so we can keep the Commanding Officer informed. That's a vital part of our duties, you know – keep the Commanding Officer informed.'

'He's been usin' my latrine? I ain't never seen him in there no time. Oh, God, I'm in trouble, ain't I?'

'No, George, of course not. Relax. You're not in trouble. We just have to put a few facts together here for the Commanding Officer. You understand facts, right George?'

'What?'

'Never mind. Now let's see if we can compile a few simple statistics here. How many bowls are there down in your latrine?'

'How's that, Lieutenant?'

'I say, how many bowls are there in your latrine?'

'What?'

'Now think, George, you have a number of toilet bowls down there in your latrine, right?'

'Yes, Sir. I clean 'em every day.'

'I'm sure you do, George. Now how many are there?'

'What?'

'How many toilet bowls are there in your latrine, George?'

'I dunno.'

'Now think, George, you clean those toilet bowls every day, right?'

'Yes, Sir!'

'How many?'

'I dunno.'

'Concentrate, George! Imagine yourself walking by those toilet bowls. You have to clean them every day. Now how many are there?'

'About five, maybe, I guess.'

'Are you sure?'

'Yeah. Five.'

'Good! Five toilet bowls in George's latrine.' And Lieutenant Sokarl took from his desk a giant clipboard, stuffed with paper. On the top sheet he carefully wrote a large number five.

'Now, George,' Sokarl said, 'How many rolls of paper do you use each day in your latrine?'

'What?'

'I say, how many rolls of paper do you use each day down there?'

'I dunno.'

'George, you do put paper out there at the receptacle on each bowl so that the officers can use it, don't you?'

'Oh yes, Sir. I see they got paper. I put out rolls whenever they need it. They don't never run out of no paper, not in my latrine.'

'And how often is it that they need paper?'

'I dunno.'

'Now think, George. Each day you put out rolls of paper to replace those that are used up, right?'

'Yeah.'

'Now, on the average day, how many rolls is that?'

'About three, I guess.'

'Three rolls of paper?'

'Yeah.'

So Lieutenant Sokarl ostentatiously wrote a large three on the front paper of his clipboard. 'Now, George,' he said, 'we'll need to give the Commanding Officer and his staff some statistics here, O.K?'

'Some what?'

'Some facts about how your latrine is operating down there. Now you have five bowls, right?'

'Right!'

'And each day, on average, you use three rolls of paper, right?'

'Right!'

'Then how many rolls per bowl per day is that?'

'I dunno.'

'George, we're looking for a simple ratio called "the latrine coefficient". It's a measure of the use of your latrine. It will let the Commanding Officer see that you're doing your job efficiently.'

'He gonna ask me about it?'

'Actually, I doubt it, George. Not if we keep him informed, anyway.'

'O.K. I'll try, Lieutenant.'

'Of course you will. Now, George, if you have five bowls in your latrine, and every day you put out three rolls of paper, then how many rolls per bowl per day is that?'

George began to sweat visibly. He shuffled his feet. He wrinkled his forehead mightily and looked out of the window. He counted something on his fingers several times. At last he spoke:

'I dunno nothin' about them things, Lieutenant. All I know about is they're in the latrine there shittin' and pissin' an usin' up that-there paper . . . And I'm tryin' to keep it clean . . .'

And this was my introduction to Lieutenant Max Sokarl.

Next day, 14 June, we went on another mission to bomb a French airfield at Maison Ponthren. This time we flew in the high squadron bucket without an instructor pilot. We were on our own.

As we went across the French coast a few German flak guns opened up. I looked out and actually saw flak bursts in the sky. They were dirty puffs of black smoke well off to one side of the formation. They looked just like the pictures of flak bursts I'd seen in newsreels.

The flak was far enough away so that there was no sound, no impact, no nothing . . . 'Hell,' I thought, 'This flying combat missions is really no sweat. Anybody should be able to survive this easily.'

I was kidding myself and didn't know it.

Three days later, on 17 June, the story was different. The planners of Eighth Air Force high command seemed to have trouble making up their minds. We got up before dawn to brief for a mission, but before we could get to the flight line, word came that the mission had been scrubbed.

A short time later we were all called back into briefing again for another target. We were to attack a German installation at Tours, a city in France on the Loire river. This time we took off and got into assembly pattern over Cromer when the radio message came to abort the effort.

But the long days of the end of spring in England gave us daylight almost forever and after we landed we were called once again into the briefing hut. We were instructed this time to attack the airfield of Guyancourt in France. Our route was to take us out over the Channel at Beachy Head, then south over Normandy.

We went off again to the flight line and kicked the tyres of our weary B-24, its racks loaded full with 250-pound general-purpose TNT bombs. We took off and flew the mission this time, determined to crumb up the operations of the *Luftwaffe* on that French airfield.

On the French coast the Normandy beachhead was established, but pretty well stalled in place. The British troops of Field Marshal Montgomery were outside Caen, but could not punch into the city and drive the Germans out.

Our lead navigator of the day was a bit off course and took us directly over Caen. The city was full of *panzer* units and they opened fire. As I was to learn with time, the anti-aircraft fire of German tanks was highly accurate. They laid their first shells right to the middle of our formation, and for the first time I got the full impact of flak fire.

Gniewkowski was down in the nose with me. Though he was only to toggle on the drop of the lead ship this day, he always liked to practise at his bomb-sight, preparing for the day when he would lead the attack – performing the essential sighting himself – in the nose of the foremost bomber of the formation. When the intense sounds of the bursting flak shells hit our ears, I looked at Eddie Gniewkowski. His face was as white and bloodless as I'm sure mine must have been.

The sound of accurate flak aimed at your bomber is unforgettable. To this day I can remember it, and hear it, and have bad dreams about it. There is the loud crunch of the shell explosion, followed by the sharp rip of those fragments which penetrate the fuselage, and the rattle of those which bounce off. It sounds a bit like someone throwing big fistfuls of gravel down a huge tin pipe.

At about the tenth loud crunch a bomber of the 754th Squadron, flying formation to our right, suddenly pulled up and out of formation. This was the aeroplane of Lieutenant Moreley's crew, in bad trouble. The ship made a 180-degree turn, heading back for England, and feathering the right inboard engine. I watched this turning back with fascination from my side blister window. About the time our neighbour had finished his turn and was northbound, headed noticeably downhill, the bomber burst into flame. The whole ship lit up in a giant, blinding flash of fire.

There was a great fire in the sky where the bomber had been the instant before. The whole tail section fell off, and one parachute dropped out of the wreckage. The rest of the aeroplane, burning fiercely, fell spinning into the countryside of France below.

I fought off the urge to vomit in my oxygen mask. But the facts were made plain to me: one could die suddenly flying combat with the Eighth Air Force over Europe. I'd just watched some people do it. My knees were still shaking when we got back to Horsham St Faith four hours later.

But after supper, and a stroll around the flight line to calm down, I felt a little better. I was still too wound-up to go to sleep, though I'd been up well before dawn, and we were not scheduled for a mission the next day. So I strolled over to the big club where the atmosphere was relaxing. I listened to Lieutenant Al Albert play the piano for a while, then I joined a discussion-group centred, as usual, around First Lieutenant Max Sokarl. The Sokarl fables were some of the most diverting and relaxing fare to be found at Horsham St Faith, and, according to Irving Goldman, most of them were true.

CHAPTER 7

TO GERMANY, AT LAST

Our first six missions were all to locations in occupied France. That did not mean that they were simple missions, but we wanted to get over Germany itself – the big one. It would be bad news in later years to tell our grandchildren that we spent the war dropping bombs on French airfields. We looked forward (like idiots) to something more spectacular, like the famous raid on Schweinfurt which the B-17 groups had carried out. According to the legendary records of the Eighth Air Force, as we understood them, the Schweinfurt raid had resulted in more bomber crew casualties than any other attack on Europe. Surely that had been an event worth repeating.

Our wishes to fly over Germany were fulfilled on our seventh mission. We went to Saarbrücken on 16 July 1944.

Saarbrücken was in the midst of the Saar Basin, an area that had been detached from Germany after World War I and administered by the League of Nations. The Saar Basin, located in the south-west corner of the Rhineland, adjoined the French Department of Moselle, a part of the ancient province of Lorraine. Alsace and parts of Lorraine had long been disputed territory between France and Germany. Alsace and eastern Lorraine had been taken by Germany as a result of the Franco-Prussian War. At the end of World War I these areas were returned to France, and the Saar put into its state of international quasi-government.

In 1935, when I was in junior high school, a plebiscite was held and more than ninety per cent of the voting population of the Saarland voted to reunite with Germany. Saarbrücken was the largest city in the Saar Basin and heavily industrialised. The whole area was above a huge coal deposit, and the mines of the Saar provided much of the energy for the factories of the Ruhr to the north.

We were wakened early that mid-July morning, well before dawn. We dressed and walked together over to the combat officers' mess.

As Hayzlett, Stoesser, Gniewkowski, and I sat eating our breakfast, we saw an officer approaching us. He had no wings on his tunic. It was Lieutenant Max Sokarl, architect of the latrine coefficient.

'What the hell's he doing here?' Gniewkowski said, 'I didn't know he could get up so early.'

There were four organisational squadrons in 458th Bomb Group: the 752nd, 753rd, 754th, and 755th. Each had its own commanding officer, reporting to the group commanding officer. Each had its identifying letters painted large on the side of its aeroplane's fuselages, and each had its own squadron staff.

While Sokarl had a job in the 753rd Squadron as assistant adjutant, he also had one or more group jobs – jobs unwanted by anyone in his right mind. Sokarl was the private court jester of Major Pierce Manley, the Group Adjutant. Manley spent his spare time in thinking up odd jobs for Sokarl.

Group Adjutant Major Manley had, so the scuttle-butt went, a long and notable career with the U.S. Army. He had been a sergeant major – a multi-striper with long years of duty in China. In those rapid promotions and commissions which take place during a large-scale war, Manley had been moved up to the rank of major and when he served as our Group Adjutant, his vast army experience was invaluable.

Max Sokarl fascinated Major Manley. Here, in the available presence of a bright, highly-trained lawyer who could speak as impressively as Daniel Webster, Manley sensed an instrument to accomplish many things within the military – a place where accomplishing anything can be monumentally difficult sometimes.

Max Sokarl went his own way and did his own thing within the considerable latitude allowed by Major Manley, his self-appointed keeper. He approached us this morning with characteristic warmth and a bit of over-presumptuous friendship.

'My dear gentlemen,' Max Sokarl intoned. 'Pray you, be so kind as to permit a lowly paddlefoot to sit and partake of his repast here amongst your exalted presences. It is indeed an undeserved honour.'

Sokarl's smile was somewhere inbetween that of an innocent child and a crocodile about to devour its victim. While Sokarl's personality could be exceedingly grating on the nerves, there was an element of humour in it that made it impossible to dislike him. He was one of a kind. He sat down with us and began to eat his breakfast, ignoring the fact that the combat officers' mess breakfast was specifically for crewmen going on a mission that day.

'What the hell are you doing here, Max?' Gniewkowski asked, 'You don't have to get up this early. Besides, you should eat breakfast over there in the club with the bigwigs.'

'Ah, yes, you are correct. But I couldn't sleep, thinking of you brave men flying forth to do your duty. So I came to be with you. Is there a chance I could sneak aboard and go out to strike the evil enemy with you today?'

'You really are crazy,' Hayzlett said.

'Not at all,' Max said, 'You men are where the action's at. I'd love to go.'

'If we let you go, you'd change your feeble mind in a hurry,' Eddie Gniewkowski said.

'Your remarks cut to the quick, Sir, but they may be true,' Max said, 'Probably there's nothing I could contribute to the effort. But I would like to go along, just to feel fulfilled.'

'Come on, Sokarl,' Hayzlett said, 'I grew up on the farm. I know bull when I see it!'

And the four of us on Hayzlett's crew, having finished our early morning food, stood up as a body and walked out of the combat officers' mess toward the briefing hut. We left Max Sokarl smiling broadly and eating his toast.

After suiting up, truck-riding to the flight line, and warming up our bomber, we taxied out to the long line of B-24s awaiting the take-off signal. It came with the firing of a Very pistol from the control tower balcony. In our turn we rolled north on the long runway and lifted into the air without difficulty. At a thousand feet of altitude we levelled off, and made a left turn to avoid the traffic pattern of the Rackheath Air Base of the 467th Group. After a minute we turned right to resume our original heading, and resumed a steady climb. We cranked upward over Cromer and out to sea past the old city. Then we turned back, still climbing, and into our Group assembly pattern over radio Splasher Five, making a wide but steady left turn to form a big circle. At the time appointed we unwound from the circle and headed south-east. Our Wing formation left the coast at Lowestoft, still climbing out over the North Sea.

Our trip inbound to Germany was over Belgium and France nearly all the way. The lands below us were green and pastoral. The whole of western Europe looked peaceful, making it hard to believe there was a huge war in progress. No German fighter aircraft came up to attack us, and our formation made a big, right-angle turn to the left over Nancy.

We made our bomb run to the north-east across Saarbrücken, hitting a big factory that was our designated target. Our bombs blew huge holes in the roofs of the buildings below.

Flak was thick and relatively accurate. The crunch and rip sounds were very loud. It was a scary bomb run, and we were duly nervous all the way in to the target. We picked up a lot of new ventilation holes in our aeroplane's fuselage.

Shortly after bombs away, as the formation was in a gentle left turn and the flak was still crunching loudly, we heard a terrifying sound on the intercom. It was Brownie Harvath on the horn, speaking from the tail turret:

'Jesus!' he said, 'I been hit. I think it must be bad. There's blood all over back here!'

I was seized with a gripping fear for Brownie.

'Where are you hit?' Hayzlett asked.

'I don't know. But the blood's splattered all over on my window. I can't see out very well. It must be bad!'

'Can somebody help him?' Hayzlett asked.

'Sure, Boss!' Giordano said from his waist gun station.

I could picture Giordano grabbing a walk-around bottle and heading back for the tail turret. I had the silly hope that we wouldn't have a fighter attack on his side of the bomber while he was otherwise occupied.

'Oh, hell. Never mind. It's all right,' Harvath said.

'What's all right?' Stoesser asked.'

'It ain't blood after all. It's hydraulic fluid. Those bastards shot up my turret. I'm O.K.'

And that was indeed true. Harvath was unharmed. But he had a flak hole in a hydraulic hose. The tail turret was hydraulically-operated. The hydraulic fluid carried a bright red dye which made the thick fluid look like blood when it sprayed on something like the turret window.

I turned my attention back to my navigation work. I didn't need any more sessions of standing before Major Elmer Mottern at debriefing while he ripped my butt over the sad state of my mission records. But my hand shook and my knees rattled with unreasoning fear over the events of Brownie Harvath's episode in the tail turret. Visions of horror kept welling up in my mind, accompanying the memory of Moreley's bomber going down in flames over Caen as it had done on our fourth mission. I could picture us, all the men of Hayzlett's crew, following our friends into a flaming end in the German forests, so it was with difficulty that I kept reading my instruments and computing our course over this enemy land.

We were all happy that there was no hole in Brownie Harvath, but, as his turret lost pressure, he could no longer move it in azimuth or elevation. He could fire straight back if we were attacked, however, and twin 50-calibre machine guns barking away are pretty effective at scaring anybody.

As we flew north out of the Saar our formation lead navigator took us a bit off course and over the ancient city of Aachen, known as Aix-la-Chapelle to the French. This place was occupied long ago by the Romans. They called it *Aquae Grani* for the hot sulphur springs which are there. Aachen was Charlemagne's capital. The Holy Roman emperors, successors to Charlemagne, were crowned there until 1531. The 'la-Chapelle' in the French name refers to the oldest part of the cathedral which houses the tomb of Charlemagne.

The German gunners at Aachen opened up and put considerable heavy flak right in the middle of our formation. Off to the right a bomber pulled gently up and out of formation, taking a heading a bit east of north. One at a time, and rather deliberately, each crew member jumped out of the plane. I counted, and logged all ten of them in my log. They seemed to be in no hurry, and they must have spread out over quite a broad swath on the ground below. But the bomber kept flying, straight and level – it trailed no smoke, had no feathered engine, no manifest damage. For as long as we could watch and keep it in view, this B-24 flew straight and level at our altitude, headed apparently towards Denmark. At last it disappeared from sight, still flying well on its lone and unoccupied mission to God knows where.

Still off course as we headed for the North Sea and home, our lead navigator took us over downtown Rotterdam. There the German gunners opened up once more, putting more flak holes in our ships. But we got safely out to sea at last over The Hague, and back to Horsham St Faith without having any more crews bale out.

We were happy to be back in one piece from our first mission over Germany proper and we congratulated Brownie Harvath on having survived his ordeal in the tail turret.

The official mission records of the 458th for that day of 16 July in 1944 state that there was no battle damage, and all aircraft returned safely, so someone must have been asleep at the switch. How we could have a whole bomber missing, and not know it, seems a bit odd. We had clearly seen the aeroplane which left the formation over Aachen, and we had seen all its crew bale out.

After we landed at Horsham St Faith we walked carefully around the bomber we had flown. Our own unofficial count was one hundred and forty-eight flak holes in the fuselage. We were quite sure they had not been there when we took off. We had acquired them over Saarbrücken, Aachen, and Rotterdam. Our first trip into Germany had made us true veterans of the air war over Europe. We had sustained impressive battle damage, and come back alive.

We were not scheduled to fly a mission the following day. Though I was tired from our trip to Saarbrücken, I was also still nervous from the big flak barrages we had survived that day. I walked over to the club through the long British summer evening.

There, holding court as usual, was Lieutenant Max Sokarl. Sokarl told stories of fascinating content. He was, by his own modest admission, the greatest seducer of women of all shapes and sizes in the world and now that he was stationed in England he had a contest going with himself. He tried to set a record for getting into some friendly girl's knickers for the least expenditure of money. The Bell Hotel of Norwich was, according to Sokarl, the obvious spot to arrange a tryst, but it also required funding to schedule a room, and it required the application of some sneaky tactics to thwart the nosy interference of the proprietors, who were self-appointed guardians of British Victorian morals.

So Sokarl, taking advantage of the long, high-latitude, warm evenings of double British summer-time, would arrange to buy one portion of fish and chips to share with his paramour of the moment, then attempt to bed her down in a convenient countryside haystack.

He had, so he claimed, found a particularly eager local nymphomanic who took to haystacking like a duck to water. In fact, she often could not bother to wait for the fish and chips, but would run down the road to the nearest pile of hay in order to get with it faster and with considerable energy. Though this girl was hardly a beauty queen, what with a few missing teeth and all, her performance in the hay left little to be desired.

However there was a hitch in Sokarl's love action. Miss nympho had another boyfriend who took exception to her bedding down with Sokarl. This boyfriend was manifestly either a physical or mental cripple, or both, since it seemed every Englishman who could see lightning or hear thunder was in some phase of military service at the time. But nonetheless, he apparently resented sharing the favours of his darling with some dastardly American officer. So while Sokarl was in the hay, hard at work with his lady partner, and doubtless concentrating fully, the spurned boyfriend sneaked up on the opposite side of the great stack and set fire to the hay. By the time Sokarl noticed the towering flames, both he and his girlfriend were about to become burnt sacrifices.

Both were only slightly singed, but upon returning to the base, Max Sokarl drew some considerable wonder from the sentries on duty at the front gate.

Fortunately he was adept at fast and convincing talking and so was able to convince the night corporal of the guard that it was fully in compliance with the military regulations regarding uniforms for a lieutenant to come back to his duty station wearing shirt, tie, tunic, and no trousers.

Such was Sokarl's story. It was told so convincingly that we almost believed it.

B-24 over a German town.

CHAPTER 8

A BAD DAY IN GRÜNBERG

A sharp sound broke the stillness of the July night. I awoke instantly, tense and alert. Somewhere on a concrete circle out on the flight line a bomber engine started. Its vibration ground into my ears through my G.I. pillow, filling my mind with a vague uneasiness.

This breaching of the night's quiet was followed by the sounds of other engines. All across Norfolk twin-row Wasps of B-24 Liberators snarled into action, and far over the fields to the south and west their sounds were echoed by the wheezing coughs of Wright Cyclones as B-17 Flying Fortresses started their warm-ups. Engine joined engine, sound mounted on sound till all East Anglia echoed with a foreboding litany. The earth shook, warning the sky of impending action. The United States Eighth Army Air Force was readying for a mission.

The ground-crew people of the Eighth Air Force were a crusty lot, given to obscene descriptions and vile language concerning the great birds of

Ground-crews were highly important to us – a reliable bomber was the first essential for a good mission. (*Courtesy Memorial Library, Second Air Division, USAAF – Norwich, England.*)

destruction they tended. They never slept, working in the middle of the night to awaken their monstrous charges. Ground-crews were highly important to us – a reliable bomber was the first essential for a good mission. A common terror of every combat airman of the Eighth was to die, drowning under icy water, as his aeroplane, brought down with mechanical trouble, sank in the North Sea, taking with it more victims in the statistical list of those thousands of Americans who died in aerial combat. We were engaged in deadly business, and the results were often fatal.

Like many in England that 20th of July in 1944 I woke when the first engine started on the flight line. I knew that it would be a while before the knock came at our door, but sleep never came easily on the night before a mission. I had time to sleep longer before the duty sergeant would say, 'Lieutenant Hayzlett's crew, Sirs, mission today. Briefing in forty minutes!' but I could not.

I got out of bed reluctantly, bathed and began to shave. I looked around the corner of the bathroom door at Eddie Gniewkowski sleeping peacefully in his bed. He was apparently disturbed by nothing. You could start all the bombers in England, and Gniewkowski would sleep right through the noise.

I was halfway through shaving when the jeep pulled up outside and the sergeant pounded on our door. He gave the expected announcement, waking Gniewkowski, Hayzlett, and Stoesser, since we slept in the same room.

Our wake-up G.I. had been quiet and polite. Maybe he understood the tribulations of flying combat missions and had some sympathy for us. The fact that I could not sleep this night through engine warm-up did not lessen the impact of the actual announcement that told us that indeed we were to fly out on a mission.

If I live to be one hundred and fifty, I will never forget those rude awakenings in the British dark. It was bad enough to contemplate a day spent flying on oxygen through the freezing stratosphere, facing death from fire, explosion, or drowning, but to be rolled, unfulfilled with blissful sleep, from a warm sack in order to do it was too much. Ever since, and to this day, I resent being roused early.

Our wake-up sergeant was kind compared to some people assigned to that undesirable job. Private First Class Abdnour, a part of the clerical staff of the 753rd Squadron, had a particularly annoying method of waking crew officers. He seemed to take delight in shoving his flashlight square in the face of a sleeping pilot and bellowing, in a voice to wake the dead, 'Briefing in an hour – sign here!'

However, Abdnour went too far with first pilot Murray Loy, a good-ol-boy from Tennessee who bore considerable physical resemblance to a bull gorilla. Loy got fed up with P.F.C. Abdnour's dreadful wake-up tactics. He removed the slug from one of the shells of his G.I., 45-calibre automatic pistol, replacing the lead with a heavy wad of British newspaper crammed firmly in place. Loy placed this homemade blank cartridge in firing position, then put the gun under his pillow. When Abdnour next shoved the flashlight in his face, pilot Loy sat bolt upright in bed, yanked forth his John Roscoe, and aimed it directly at P.F.C. Abdnour.

'By God, Abdnour,' Loy bellowed, 'That's the last damn time you'll pull off this crap!'

Abdnour, wetting his pants on the way, ran for the door. Loy jumped from the sack, running right on Abdnour's heels. As Abdnour started down the stairs, stumbling three steps at a time, Loy fired over his head. The blast from the John Roscoe woke everyone for a half mile around. The sound of Loy's pistol was followed immediately by the screech of jeep tyres as Abdnour drove off for dear life. Someone else had to wake the rest of the crews assigned to Abdnour that morning. At his own request, the P.F.C. was subsequently given other duties.

When I look over the official lists of those targets hit by the 458th Bomb Group, I don't find the small German town of Grünberg. Yet my personal notes and recollections say that we bombed Grünberg. If not Grünberg, it was some little place out along the rail lines between Hersfeld and Giessen – someplace looking exactly like Grünberg.

We hit Grünberg as a target of opportunity. It was undesirable practice to bring the bombs home. Bombs were our deliverable commodity, and it was our job to rain explosive and burning destruction on Nazi Germany. If we could not find the assigned target, we picked another – a target of opportunity. The rules for selecting targets of opportunity were straightforward; with time we learned to make use of them whenever chance required.

The assigned target that day was the German city of Eisenach, which was

458th Bomb Group mission crew briefing. Col Frederick M. O'Neill is sitting front left and Major Charles Booth is front right. The Commanding Officer, Col James Isbell is standing in the foreground.

a target that made those of us on Bob Hayzlett's crew happy. Now we were actually going deep into Germany to attack a big, important target, not hitting a place right on the border, like Saarbrücken. We figured a long trip through flak and enemy fighters would be a way to demonstrate how tough we really were. With the typical fatuousness of youth, we had recovered rapidly from seeing the big collection of flak holes our ship acquired on the mission to Saarbrücken.

The four of us, officers of Hayzlett's crew, went to the combat mess for breakfast. When we had finished eating we walked over to the briefing hut and took seats well up front. Mission briefing was, as usual, directed, conducted, and orchestrated by Major Chuck Booth, Assistant Group Operations Officer, who was his usual happy, carefree, and smiling self this morning. Why not? He wasn't going off to Eisenach.

When the great, green curtain at the front of the room was pulled back, revealing the big map of Europe, there were loud moans from some of those present. The red mission route ribbon, defining our pending trip to Eisenach and back, extended a long way into Germany, above a lot of flak batteries. Eisenach was one of those German industrial cities out east in the foothills of the Thüringer Wald. Along with such neighbouring places as Gotha, Erfurt, Mühlhausen, and Weimar, it contributed to Germany's considerable industrial might. It was north and a bit east of Schweinfurt, that place where the Eighth Air Force had lost over six hundred men killed in combat in one day.

The operations jeep delivered to us to our bomber. (*Courtesy Memorial Library, Second Air Division, USAAF – Norwich, England.*)

Colonel Isbell was at our briefing this morning, as he usually was. He gave us a typical Isbell speech:

'You men are going in a long way today,' the Colonel said, 'and there's a good chance the German fighters will be up there after you. Don't make the mistake of depending on your fighter escort alone. They do a tremendous job, but you've got to hold your formations in there tight. Keep your gunners alert at their stations at all times. It's when you relax your vigilance that you're sure to get a fighter attack. They'll be looking for some sloppy-flying outfit. Make sure it's not us!'

When the briefing was over, and the chaplain had prayed for our safe return, we walked to the flight equipment hut, dressed for the mission and picked up our parachutes.

The operations jeep delivered us to our bomber. We started the engines, checked the controls, flaps, and magnetos, and taxied out into the waiting line when it was our turn. At the head of the bomber line was our garishly-painted Group assembly ship. At briefed departure time the tower operator fired a Very pistol. The crew of the assembly ship gunned all four balls to the wall and began to roll – we were off on our mission to Eisenach.

Assembly over the radio beacon of Splasher Five at Cromer was uneventful. The morning was bright and clear, the summer sun already well up in the sky.

The whole 96th Bomb Wing rolled out into Second Division attack line, unwinding from the radio Splasher like string from a spool. We headed south-east to Lowestoft and out over the North Sea, climbing relentlessly all the way, hauling our bomb loads up, up to attack altitude.

We crossed the European coast at Blankenberge in Belgium where our fighter escort joined us. This day our Wing had the chequer-board-nosed P-51s of 353rd Fighter Group protecting our tender buns.

Eddie Gniewkowski put on an oxygen bottle and went out on the bomb bay catwalk to arm our bombs. There was a propeller on the nose and tail fuse of each bomb. The propeller was held from turning with a pin and unless the propeller turned the correct number of turns, the bomb was not armed to explode. When Gniewkowski pulled the pins and put them in his pocket, he made our bomb load a live one.

This day we carried full loads of 500-pound, general purpose TNT bombs. These fat monsters in their heavy steel cases looked ominous hanging in our bomb racks, and they were.

We looked forward to a rough mission. We were going a long way into enemy territory and chances were the *Luftwaffe* would come up in force, to see how many bombers they could wipe out. It was a good day for shooting down big, lumbering aircraft, and if someone wanted to attack us over Germany, they would have a lot of hours in which to do it.

But our trip in was monumentally uneventful. Weather was superb all over Belgium, Northern France, and Rhineland Germany. The ground was totally clear, and we enjoyed the warmth of the high summer sun, shining through our plexiglass blisters and windows.

However, as we flew north of Frankfurt-am-Main the weather started to clobber up. Heavy clouds occluded large areas below us and by the time we went south of Kassel we were over complete cloud cover with no ground visible below.

It was about then that our Group command pilot began to hear the bad news on command radio channel: There was a big traffic jam ahead. The B-17 divisions were out to attack Gotha, Erfurt, Langensalz and Bad Frankenhausen. There were some scheduling difficulties, with one bomb group turning off to avoid another on the same bomb run, and command pilots bitching at each other about who-the-hell's target it was, anyway, and the German fighters had been seen over Bad Frankenhausen. There was a lot of specific radio yelling on the fighter channel, such as 'Look out for those bastards over there!'

Then we got the sad word on the horn from the lead ship that Eisenach was totally under cloud cover. We had no instructions to make anything other than a visual bomb run so the mission was a scrub as far as our briefed primary target was concerned.

We took a long look at that spot in the cloud cover which we believed to hide the city of Eisenach – there was no way the group could make a visual bombing attack on it. The 458th Bomb Group formation made a miles-wide sweeping turn, holding an Isbell-ordered tight formation all the way, and headed back for England. We were now free to pick a target of opportunity. Such a target, to make the choice simple, was anything inside Germany that looked good for bombing. It would be silly to carry the bombs home after we had freighted them over half a continent and now that we had to abandon the primary target, we looked for a good place to put our bombs.

We were flying south-westward somewhere up above the *autobahn* which went all the way from Koblenz to Dresden. The weather was bright and clear again, the visibility excellent, though we could still see the cloud mass to the east. Down below us, trending north-east by south-west, was a double-track railroad. Far ahead of us, beside the railroad, was the small town of Grünberg and there was a long freight train stopped in the middle of the town. We had no idea whether this place manufactured war materials, but it was definitely in Germany, and railroads were specifically recommended as targets of opportunity.

The word came over the horn from the lead ship. We would make a bomb run on the little town with the big train parked in it. We had a target of opportunity.

We swung well to the south when further word came from the command pilot in the lead ship. We were to bomb in Group formation, all at once. Since we didn't know what was in the town or in the train, we were to bomb at maximum intervalometer setting, blanketing the whole area with our five-hundred pounders.

I folded up my navigation desk and stood behind Eddie Gniewkowski, watching him crouched over the Norden. He always made sighting on every bomb run, leaving his bombsight disconnected from the bomb racks, hoping for the day when he might be a lead bombardier. Sweat dripped on his oxygen mask. He was an instrument of total concentration. It was as though Eddie and his bombsight were one. His head was pressed intently to the eyepiece and his big hands manoeuvred the dials with skill.

Our Group formation turned directly north towards the centre of Grünberg which put us exactly at right angles to the long, parked railroad train.

The attack formation of the 458th Bomb Group bore relentlessly down upon Grünberg. Five miles in the sky above this quiet place were thirty-six great machines of destruction, carrying five hundred and seventy-six heavy bombs. The bomb bay doors were open. The high, cold wind of the stratosphere whistled around the steel bomb casings.

At the appointed moment our bomb racks began to open. With the first bomb from the lead ship went two smoke pots, putting a trail through the sky to mark the target. Gniewkowski had pressed his manual release button. One at a time the racks opened, triggering the bombs out slowly with relentless precision. As I looked around us, long strings of bombs were trailing out of every bomber in the formation. And then, at last, they were all on their way downward, looking like great stacks of steel sausages, disappearing rapidly into the landscape below.

My view from the nose blisters was excellent. I watched the little German town below. All was quiet for quite a while, then the first bomb went off in a cabbage patch south of town. Another hit the potatoes in the next field to the east. Rows of explosive destruction began a relentless march towards the

A bomb drop on the smoke pot marker, seen here descending to the bottom right of the photograph.

centre of Grünberg. Chicken coops, barns, outhouses, greenhouses, farm buildings of every sort blew sky high, each propelled by a quarter-ton of exploding TNT and splitting steel. Then the houses began to go, bursting into the streets, and blowing across blocks. Neighbourhoods disappeared in an instant. The library, the city hall, the town meeting hall, churches, and business buildings all exploded and fell into the streets. The march of the terrible explosions continued through the railroad station, across the platforms, into the middle of the parked train, and beyond.

When the first bomb hit the train, there was an extra-large explosion; two or three more bombs hit the train's centre, causing big explosions in a few more cars.

Then, finally, the bombs quit hitting. I looked at the centre of the train where several cars were burning brightly. As I watched, cars fore and aft of our bomb hit began to blow up, and the pace of the explosions accelerated. One at a time, like rows of falling dominos, the railroad cars blew up east and west from the train's centre where we had hit it. The cataclysm continued along the rails till the whole train was destroyed, taking most of what was left of Grünberg with it. The engine exploded last, probably as its steam boiler was pierced by fragments. We had hit an ammunition train! In our blind luck, we had removed a lot of enemy war material. The load on that destroyed train would not be shot at our men on the ground, nor at us in the sky.

Our return to England was quiet and without incident. We picked up a bit of flak from the outlying batteries north of Frankfurt am Main, but no one hit anything. We let down across the North Sea taking off our oxygen masks at the Suffolk coast. The great stone needle of the Norman Cathedral of Norwich gave us a landmark from afar as we peeled off to land at Horsham St Faith.

We told our story at debriefing, but no one seemed to care much. Tough Major Mottern, apparently satisfied with my efforts, grunted at me and said, 'Next man!' Squadron clerks recorded the mission's target as 'Eisenach' in our flight records, misspelling it variously. Chances are the planners and G-2 people of Eighth Air Force were disappointed that we missed bombing our assigned target that day, but surely they were no more unhappy with that fact than were the citizens of Grünberg.

Word came to us after this mission that we had been selected to fly as a lead crew. On our next mission we would go out as Group deputy lead. Maybe there was a pay-off for destroying a train full of explosive war materials, even if it took a small town with it.

CHAPTER 9

MOVING UP IN THE WORLD

O n our next mission we flew as deputy group lead crew. That mission, of 25 July 1944, was an odd one that made the front pages of newspapers around the world.

For months the Allied troops had been stalled within the perimeters of the Normandy beachhead. Meanwhile, General George S. Patton, after much spoofing to fool the Germans as to our real military intent, had been given command of the U.S. Third Army and sent to France to stand by in Normandy.

The plan was for Patton to break out of the beachhead lines and carry out a great armoured sweep around the German armies containing the beachhead – a flanking movement on a grand scale, modelled after the classic attack of Stonewall Jackson at Chancellorsville. The third Army breakthrough was to be prefaced by a saturation bombing of the German troop positions at St Lô, a little French town in the department of Manche. Much of this massive tactical attack was to be carried out by the Eighth Air Force.

The briefing gave us clear directions as to where to drop bombs so as not to hit our own troops. These directions depended in large measure on landmarks to be seen on the ground. This was to be a drop based on visual sighting as radar was considered too inaccurate for such a touchy bombing.

The operations jeep delivered us to our bomber. Now that we were lead crew, we got to fly a brand-new aeroplane, shiny and with the latest equipment. When we flew as a wing crew we were typically assigned to some ancient, oil-soaked monster done up in olive drab with gruesome nose art scribbled on the front. When someone in high command had first decided to quit painting combat B-24s in Europe with ugly, foot-locker-brown paint, that decision sparked an interesting superstition: the first Group in 96th Combat Bomb Wing to go out with an unpainted bomber was the 466th, flying directly behind the 458th that day. The aluminium-skinned machine was shot down – the only ship loss of the mission. For a considerable time thereafter, a number of crews tried to avoid flying in unpainted bombers, but we didn't share the superstition; we liked our brand-new aeroplane.

Our aeroplane also had the latest in armour plating. The windows of the pilots' compartment were inch-thick and bullet-proof glass. Half-inch steel plates were fastened on the outside of the fuselage under the pilot's side windows. The pilots' seats were encased in welded steel 'coffins'. These latter left only some six-inch clearance between them, making it difficult for the pilots to get into their places (and, presumably, to get out, if necessary).

I wondered why the navigator's station had no such heavy protection, but reason clearly indicated that the aeroplane, if damaged, might get back home without a navigator, but it probably would not without a pilot.

These additional steel plates and seat-surrounding 'coffins' must have given reassurance to our friend, pilot Frank Hathaway. On one of the early missions which Frank's crew flew, a flak shell exploded under their bomber. A chunk of steel came up through the bottom of the aeroplane and through the pilot's seat, exiting out of the top of the bomber. It missed Hathaway's family jewels by a scant few millimetres. Thereafter, Frank Hathaway became famous in the 458th for flying combat missions sitting on his flak vest instead of wearing it.

We took off and assembled as usual over Splasher Five at Cromer. As the Division line formed and we moved south across England, it was obvious that we were part of a gigantic parade of heavy bombers, all headed for Normandy. We crossed the French coast and could see a high column of smoke ahead, reaching almost to our flight altitude. Gniewkowski got over his bombsight as though he were in charge of the drop, synchronising and adjusting. He never misidentified a target in all my experience flying with him. We forged ahead over this huge smoke column, dropping our bombs on the lead ship's trigger as we were supposed to do, but seeing check points on the ground was very difficult in the target area.

We turned off target to the right in a sweeping turn. Eddie Gniewkowski came up from his bombsight with a disgusted look on his face. It looked to him as though some formations were dropping short, hitting the area occupied by our own troops. He was happy, though, that the 458th had apparently hit the right spot.

As we learned later, Gniewkowski's fears were correct. Some of the bombs had fallen on our own troops, and American soldiers were killed by the bombs of American aeroplanes. Among the one hundred and eleven of our own people killed by American heavy bombers was Lieutenant-General Leslie McNair, an infantry commander. He became the highest-ranking American soldier to die in the campaign kicked off at the Normandy beachhead.

However, the Germans got theirs in fuller measure. Over five thousand tons of general purpose TNT bombs, plus many tanks of flaming napalm were dropped on the German defensive positions south of St Lô. General Bayerlein, commanding the Lehr *Panzer* Division, reported over seventy per cent of his people out of action, many of them dead.

Early in August, just after the saturation bombing of St Lô, Major-General James A. Hodges was relieved of command of our Second Division. He was replaced by Major-General William E. Kepner who, until that time, had commanded all the fighter operations of the Eighth Air Force. Hodges was to say later, speaking to groups of air war veterans, that he had been removed from command because Second Division B-24s dropped short at St Lô.

Our work on combat operations now consisted entirely of lead crew efforts. Some of the missions again were short ones into France where we hit targets ahead of Patton's rapidly-advancing American troops. On 7 August we were deputy group lead once again on a mission to bomb a factory in Ghent, Belgium. The factory was used by the Germans to manufacture some war-important materials. The target factory proved to be totally under clouds, so we went instead to attack a target of opportunity, a huge and ominous-looking building north up the Schelde River at Sas van Gent in the occupied Netherlands. We did a great job of blowing huge holes in this building and setting it on fire. When we returned home, proud of our strike photos, the intelligence people informed us that the place processed sugar beet.

It was about this time in August that Captain Burton sent word that he wanted to see me. I was pretty nervous; I wondered what vast navigational screw-up had now been attributed to me.

Burton asked me to sit down across from him at his desk.

'Guess what?' he said.

'I don't know, Sir.'

'I'm going home. I've finished my missions. Not only that, I'm still alive. I'm going home. Isn't that great!'

'Yes Sir,' I said, agreeing that it surely was great, but wondering why he had singled me out as someone with whom to share the good news.

'And you can have this desk,' he said.

'That's nice, but where would I put it? I mean, I don't think there's room in our quarters, you know, and . . .'

'No, you don't get the picture. The story is that you are now the Squadron Navigator. I've recommended you to take over my job, and everyone in command concurs.'

'No crap?'

'No crap!'

'What do I do?' I asked. 'When do I start? I mean, I think that's very nice, and I thank you. But I don't know what to do. I'll need a lot of coaching, or something.'

'I'll be here for a week or so yet,' Burton said, 'I'll run you through all the procedures and the paperwork. There's not really all that much to it. But you'll have to watch your boys. We do get sent a few dummies along with the navigators.'

'And I'm not one of them?'

'Hell no.'

'I hope I can trust your judgement.'

'Cut the crap!'

Captain Irving Burton was as good as his word. He ran me through all the procedures and paperwork to the point where I felt comfortable being Squadron Navigator of the 752nd Bomb Squadron. Then after a week or so he went home to the U.S. and I never saw or heard from Burton again. But I did develop a good new friend in Major Paul Betzold, the Squadron Operations Officer; he was most helpful and a great coach.

I must have done at least a passable job as Squadron Navigator, for in a short while I was promoted from second lieutenant to first lieutenant. It was a rank I had hoped to attain if I lived through my mission tour, but I didn't expect it so early in the game.

The most discomforting thing about my job as Squadron Navigator was the fact that I had to deal with Major Elmer Mottern, the Group Navigator. He was a terrifying, no-nonsense sort of a person, and I still smarted from his expert chewing at the time of my first mission.

When Mottern phoned me with his down-south rebel drawl I always had the impression that I was about to be sent immediately to Libby Prison without stopping to pass go. The calls were usually about some confused kid on an early mission. Mottern had dissected the navigator's log and chart at debriefing, and he would call me to demand better performance.

'You see the log this shit-head turned in?'

'Well, I . . .'

'Take a good look at that mothah. I dunno what the crap he thinks he's doin' up there, but he sure as hell ain't navigatin' his damn airplane.'

'Yes Sir!'

And I would look at the crappy mission records of the latest navigator on Mottern's bad boy list. Mottern was always right, the navigation effort he had complained of was pathetic. Thus, in the exalted chair of the Squadron Navigator, I got in some valuable practice at military chewing. I tried to look and sound as fierce as Mottern did, but I'm sure I never brought it off convincingly enough. Besides, a first lieutenant chewing on a second lieu-tenant is nowhere near as fearsome as a bull major with all the pleasant personality historically credited to Confederate Major-General Nathan Bedford Forrest.

One day my office phone rang. It was Mottern on the horn:

'Granholm, git your ass up here to my office on the double!'

I shook in my boots. 'Sweet Jesus,' I thought, 'What's crapped out now?'

Mottern shared his office with Major Fred Vacek, the Group Bombardier. Vacek was out when I arrived. I stood stiffly at attention before Mottern's desk and looked at him carefully, seeking some clue to my fate.

'Sit down there, goddammit,' he said, 'Don't stand there like some goddam aviation cadet.'

'Yes Sir.'

'I'm goin' home. I've finished my tour. Ain't that a goddam pistol! Son of a bitch!'

'You mean?'

'That's right, goddam it. You're the new Group Navigator, you poor bastard!'

'But all the other squadron navigators have a lot more experience than I do. I don't know up from sideways yet, really.'

'Hell, Granholm, they're a bunch of old farts like me. They'll be goin' home too. We need some new blood around here. You're it!'

'I don't know what to say.'

'You don't have anything to say. Isbell's already signed the orders. You're deep in the dog shit whether you like it or not. You got to shape up now or the Colonel will have your ass run up the flag pole.'

So I packed my brief-case and moved into the exalted territory of upstairs in the headquarters building. I also moved out of the quarters occupied by my crew and moved into the club. This was a requirement because I was now

Commanding Officer's staff, and scared to death of my new and bigger responsibility.

Elmer Mottern stayed around for a couple of weeks to show me the ropes. He was magnificent. I discovered that he was a real and very admirable human being, and a wonderful good friend. His tough-as-hell image at debriefing was only a part of his ball game, and he really knew how to be Group Navigator. My short briefing from him was one of the most intensive I ever had, and one of the best organised.

Mottern had built his legend during his time with the 458th. He had come over with the group as Navigation Officer of the 754th Squadron. After Ray Sandberg transferred to another Bomb Group, Mottern moved up to the Group Navigator's desk.

On 25 April 1944 the 458th Bomb Group had led the entire Eighth Air Force over Germany. As First Group, of First Wing of First Division in the bomber attack stream, the 458th headed for the railroad marshalling yards at Mannheim. Colonel James Isbell flew as command pilot that day, and

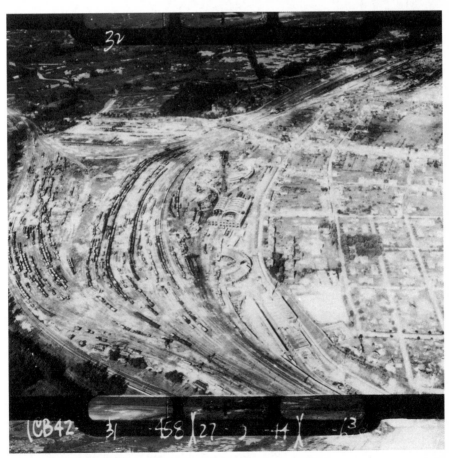

A bombed railroad marshalling yard in the Ruhr Valley.

Major-General William E. Kepner on the left and Colonel James 'Big Jim' H. Isbell on the right.

Major Elmer Mottern manned the lead ship navigation desk in the bomber's nose.

The fighter groups were still short of long-range escort aircraft. P-51s with drop tanks were still in short supply in England at that time, and fighter escort for the bombers of the Eighth was supposed to swap groups over France. But near Vitry, the escorting fighter group left the bomber stream about fifteen minutes before their replacements showed up. The 458th was out front with no friendly fighters around.

Big Jim Isbell, looking out of his right side window, saw a bunch of Messerschmitt Me-109s climbing off to the side of the formation. This batch of tough mothers, in a sweeping left turn, swung around in front of the bomber stream and came in head-on at the lead ship, 20-millimetre cannons barking fire.

The deputy lead bomber took two hits and pulled out of formation, spinning rapidly into the fields of France below. A shell shattered the top turret of the lead ship, blowing the plexiglass dome all over the sky. Isbell had looked back to see the feet of the engineer/top gunner hanging out of the turret, blood running down his flight suit into his boots. A German shell went through the waist section and into the tail turret, exploding when it hit the plexiglass window. Miraculously, the tail gunner survived with a scratch on one finger. Another shell hit in the bomber waist section, taking out all the oxygen system. The waist gunners switched to walk-around bottles, later to cross the bomb bay catwalk gingerly and ride home in the nose section where there was still enough oxygen for all.

Yet another 20-millimetre shell hit the bomb bay, creaming the hydraulic pump. Miraculously, this shell did not set off the load of incendiaries in the bomb rack. A shell ripped through the nose compartment, messing up Mottern's maps, and setting fire to the fuel tank of the auxiliary power unit. This small engine-generator, used for electric power on the ground before the main engines were running, was known fondly as the 'putt-putt' from the deafening noise it made in operation. A roaring fire broke out in the tunnel between the nose and the flight deck. Mottern ripped off his oxygen mask and intercom cords, grabbed up a casualty blanket, crawled down the tunnel and smothered the fire. Then he burst up through the flight deck floor doors, looked around at his startled fellow crew members and said, 'Somebody gimme an oxygen bottle, dammit!'

That performance was pure Mottern.

Now that we were flying lead ship all the time, Hayzlett's crew had been augmented with a pilotage navigator. This was a rated navigator who rode the nose turret in place of the enlisted gunner. With his pile of maps jammed into the turret with him, the nose turret navigator could presumably aid with the pilotage and make up for some of the poor forward visibility of a B-24 lead ship. Carsie Foley, our nose gunner, moved back to the waist compartment where he spelled Stahl and Giordano at their 50-calibres and became chief operator of the chaff box.

By this time in the hostilities we had begun to carry copious quantities of aluminium foil strips. This stuff, looking like decoration for a Christmas tree, was dumped out into the stratospheric air where its falling clouds of metal served to confuse the images of the German radar. All lead ships were modified with little chutes in the waist through which to push chaff bundles. Foley kept busy throwing out this material. By the end of the War, nearly all of Germany was to be decorated with it.

The first pilotage navigator we were assigned was afraid to get the nose turret out of index. He worried that, if he did so, he would not be able to get the turret doors open to get out in an emergency, so he rode up front all the way like a frozen statue, afraid to move the turret or to charge his guns. I wondered what would happen if we had a head-on fighter attack. I mentioned the surprising performance of this man to Mottern one day.

Mottern snorted. 'Ain't that a bunch of crap!' he said. 'If I wanted to get out of that goddam turret, I sure as hell wouldn't let a little thing like doors stop me'. And, looking at Mottern, sitting there like a grizzly bear, I knew the statement was true.

A few days later we had a new man on the crew – Mottern had arranged for us to get a different front turret navigator. I felt a little sorry for the man who had been replaced because of my brief comments to Major Mottern, but I didn't feel all that sorry. We now got a nose turret pilotage navigator who did know how to operate his turret, and made use of the knowledge.

In retrospect it seems to me that something was missing in the organisation of our training programmes. Back in the early days when all B-24 bombers had greenhouse noses and the navigator lived there, standing at his fold-down desk, many navigators were sent on to gunnery school – they were expected to man the nose 50-calibres when the need arose. But now that only the lead ships had a navigator in the nose turret, the people had no gunnery experience. Quite possibly our man who had been afraid to get his turret out of index also did not know how to charge his guns. I had never been to gunnery school, but I thought that I would sure as hell learn how to use the nose turret and its guns if I were required to use it. Many German fighter attacks were head-on.

After his time spent indoctrinating me, Elmer Mottern went back to the States. I bought his portable typewriter, which I still have as a treasured keepsake, but I've never seen nor heard from him again. One day a short time after Mottern's departure my phone rang. It was Colonel Isbell. 'Granholm, can you please come into my office for a few minutes?' he said.

Major Manley, the Group Adjutant, was standing at Colonel Isbell's side when I entered. Manley had a wicked smile on his face.

I stood at attention before the Colonel's desk, admiring his giant office.

'I've arrived at an important decision, Lieutenant Granholm,' the Colonel said.

'This is it,' I figured, 'the bad news!'

'I've decided to make you a captain!'

And the Colonel personally removed the single silver bars from my uniform tunic, replacing them with impressive-looking double bars.

He shook my hand.

'Congratulations!' he said. 'You've earned it.'

Manley handed me a bunch of official looking papers.

'Thank you, Sir,' I said, 'I hope to live up to your expectations.'

I had been a first lieutenant for exactly one month.

CHAPTER 10

AN AZON MISSION

On 16 August 1944 word came to everyone at Horsham St Faith that the 458th had a stand-down day scheduled for the 17th. The combat crews were all told that there was no mission for the day following – a rare event. We all went over to the club and stayed up till midnight.

At the club I fell into conversation with Captain John J. Van de Rovaart, our Group Armament Officer. Captain Van had been a salesman of ladies' lingerie in civilian life. For this previous career, he had been dubbed with his paddlefoot military nickname of 'Sanitary Sam, the Panty Man'.

Van de Rovaart was a meticulous person, always perfectly groomed. He had the shiniest shoes in the Bomb Group and his uniform looked like it belonged on a clothes store mannikin.

Van himself was equally precise. As we sipped our soda water in the club lounge, he gave me a learned lecture about aircraft bomb bay doors. The bomb doors of a B-24, built of an assemblage of connected pieces, were cable-actuated to move up the sides of the fuselage when opened. They worked like the cover of a roll-top desk. The cables on each door corner were hard to align, and the doors would often bind and stick in their slots when someone tried to slam them open.

So great was the casualty rate of bent and broken bomb bay doors, that Captain Van de Rovaart had built a bomb bay door mock-up in the corner of one of the hangars. There he conducted classes, trying to run all the bombardiers, lead and wing ship, through his tutelage. This school for bombardiers was set up to show them how to actuate the bomb bay door control handle gently and with repeated short bursts of energy in order to ease the doors open safely.

But, in the heat of battle, with flak bursting all around, and *Luftwaffe* fighters boring in for the kill, the last concern of a bombardier was the integrity of the aircraft bomb doors. The bombardier, wracked with terror for his life, would slam the door control handle wide open. When the doors stuck in their slots, the bombardier dropped his bombs through them, ripping them fully or partly from the slots. The sight of B-24 bombers coming home from a mission with bomb doors flapping in the breeze was a common one.

Invariably the bombardier of such a plane would report his trouble as 'equipment malfunction'. The multitude of such reports drove Van de Rovaart mad.

'Isn't that a lot of bull?' he said to me, 'They always say that the bombs just sort of fell through the doors when they weren't looking. What a total pain in the butt!'

I agreed with Van. 'Bombardiers are no damn good,' I said, 'the paddle-feet run Eighth Air Force. Without them we'd be lost!'

'I didn't mean that,' Van said, 'I just wish I could teach them to do it right.'

But he never did. Van really cared; his sense of precision made him long to see everyone do everything right the first time. This, of course, was a hopeless wish in the middle of a big War, or any other time, for that matter.

After a time Van and I became saturated with soda water. He went off to get some sack time, having an early morning scheduled for the following day when he intended to lecture newly-arrived bombardiers on the proper use of bomb doors.

I went around the corner to attend the current Sokarl lecture. Lieutenant Max was in rare form, as usual. His topic for the evening was how the presence of the American forces in England had saved the country. The saving was not in a military sense, according to Sokarl, but because the Americans were changing the stodgy mental state of the British. Actually I had heard parts of this lecture before, so I went home to bed, having nothing much better to do.

Having been assured of a stood-down day on the 17th, those of us on Hayzlett's crew were astounded to be wakened by the night duty sergeant at some ungodly hour in the British dark.

'Briefing this morning, gentlemen,' the sergeant said.

'Bullshit!' Gniewkowski snorted from his sack. 'We're stood down, dammit! We get the whole day off.'

'I just follow my orders, Sir. I don't make the rules,' the sergeant said, 'Sign here please, Sir.' And Bob Hayzlett signed the sheet while we all grumbled.

The sergeant was right. We were scheduled out as group lead on an AZON mission. Someone had determined that, as a visual lead crew of an ordinary bomber, we were to lead the mission, sight and drop, and the AZON bombers would all drop with us. Each of the AZON bombardiers could then steer his personal bomb to the target.

During all of the United States involvement in World War II there were many projects to invent new weaponry and to improve existing items. Various people had paid attention to the hit accuracy of the bombs we dropped and while the Norden and Sperry bombsights were excellent instruments, their performance was dependent on the information that the bombardier had cranked into them. The aerodynamic characteristics of a falling bomb were pretty well known, but the precise knowledge of aircraft drift at altitude was sometimes sketchy, and knowledge of wind currents in the five miles of air between the bomber and the ground was non-existent. It would be nice, presumably, if the bombardier could steer the bomb as it fell on its way to the target.

The AZON bomb was the brainchild of Jim Rand, that Rand who provided half the name of the Remington–Rand Corporation. With government help, he had built a system including radio and servo links which permitted the bombardier to steer his bomb in azimuth (side to side) after it fell from the bomb bay.

The AZON bomb itself was a standard 1,000-pound TNT job, fitted with a one-million-candlepower, red flare in the tail assembly, and a radio receiver. In each AZON bomber was a transmitter which output the bombardier's signals. The receiver passed along steering commands to the bomb tail fins, enabling the bombardier to steer the bomb as it dropped. Thus, it was hoped, super-accuracy might be achieved, letting the bomber hit not only the barrel, but also the pickle.

Ten B-24s of the 753rd, Squadron, 458th Bomb Group, were equipped to drop AZON bombs. They had bombsight modifications and radio transmitters installed. These aircraft were easy to identify, since they had three antenna masts protruding downward under their tail sections.

The use of AZON, of course, was dependent on good visual conditions, a requirement that the European weather offered somewhat seldom, especially in the winter-time. Results achieved by the 753rd Squadron's AZON bombers were spotty at best. The AZON ships operated in the 458th Bomb Group for several months, then the operation was suspended, and the bombers were converted back to conventional bombing use.

In other aircraft, such as medium bombers which flew at lower altitudes, and in other theatres with better weather, AZON bombs later proved their worth.

It may have been a good idea to have us lead out the AZON bombers and make the primary target identification, sighting, and bomb drop. It was surely a compliment to Gniewkowski's skill, but it seemed to me that it might have been a good idea to tell us first. That way I might not have stayed up half the night tossing the bull with Van de Rovaart in the club. A bit of previous practice might also have been useful.

When we had finished showering, Sergeant Brownie Harvath, our tail gunner, came bounding up the stairs to our opulent officer quarters; he was red in the face, and clearly pissed off.

Apparently our awakening to go lead the AZON mission had come up as an afterthought on the night duty sergeant's list of things to interrupt his solitaire game. Our enlisted men had been awakened in their quarters, had gone to the combat mess to get breakfast, and had been told by the mess sergeant that they were out of luck. The place was closed, it was alleged, and that was just too damn bad.

Sergeant Brownie Harvath, who had come up to the job of being our tail gunner out of previous duty in the field artillery, was not about to take such military chickenshit lying down.

'You go fly the mission for me, you son of a bitch,' he told the mess sergeant, 'and I'll stand here in the goddam mess-hall and tell combat aircrews they can't have breakfast!' Naturally, this got our crewmen no breakfast.

Bob Hayzlett was a quiet man, but he could get excited at times. As he listened to Brownie's tale of woe, his face turned stern. He left with Brownie Harvath in tow. Where Hayzlett found the combat mess officer to wake him up I don't know, but that Bob Hayzlett's speech should have gone down in the annals of great military lectures is not to be doubted. He painted a vivid picture of those lazy folks who stood over the breakfast griddle, but did not have to go forth at dawn in a freezing bomber to get their ass shot off.

Lt Robert Hayzlett in 1944.

Breakfast was promptly forthcoming, and very well prepared for our crew enlisted men.

The briefing session was small and cosy as there was only a short squadron of AZON crews. We learned that our target was a bridge in northern France and from the way we were to approach the target, and the clear pictures we had of it, I figured Gniewkowski could wipe it out all by himself and forget the AZON bombers with their 'Mickey Mouse' equipment. But I may have had too much confidence in Eddie Gniewkowski.

We took, off, still grumbling, into the morning mist. There was not much to assembly; a couple of turns around Horsham St Faith did the job. The sky was ours. All the rest of Eighth Air Force had the day off.

We climbed to operational altitude as we went south across England. The clouds got thicker and thicker below us as we went, the weather looked more and more crappy.

We flew a bit to the west of London, the red-nosed P-47s of 56th Fighter Group joined us north of Guildford. These big jugs looked fearsome as they wrapped around our formation. Joining them at Chichester were some 150

P-51s of several groups. I began to hope the *Luftwaffe* would come up trying to shoot down our little AZON squadron. We had over two hundred tough fighters as escort.

Below us, through gaps in the broken clouds, we could see the old Norman Cathedral of Chichester. It was readily identifiable as the only church of that size in England with a tall bell tower standing alone, away from the main body of the building. It made a good steering beacon for aeroplanes crossing the south coast at Selsey Bill, which we often did.

As we set out across the English Channel, the clouds got ever thicker below us and by the time we got to the French coast there was complete cover below us. No landmarks were visible on the ground; we had no radar on our ship, and I had to depend on the British gee navigation system for position fixes. The system was working well that day.

We turned east at the assigned initial point to begin our bomb run and still we could see nothing below us. Gniewkowski was over his bombsight, coupled to the autopilot. He flew the aeroplane automatically. I set the gee co-ordinates of the bridge on my navigation cathode ray tube display, and gave minor steering corrections to Eddie, trying to head us towards the bridge. About four minutes out from target, Eddie Gniewkowski gave up.

'Forget it!' he said, in considerable disgust, 'I can't see a damn thing down there!' Eddie hated to be unable to hit his target.

Eddie reported the problem to Major Charles Breeding in the command seat. Breeding called me on the horn.

'What do you think about trying to go under the clouds and hit it?' he asked.

'Well, Sir, it seems to me that we'd never be able to hold formation going through that cloud deck, and our fighter escort would be very likely to lose us and not find us again.'

'I guess you're right,' Breeding said, 'but let's take another run at it.'

'Yes Sir,' I replied. I gave Hayzlett a heading to go back to the initial point and try the bomb run again. Now the fighter group commanders were on the horn, bitching at Major Breeding.

No one had told the escort about two bomb runs.

Our second run was as abortive as the first – we could see nothing below us. We peeled off the bomb run and headed for home.

The rest of the trip was without incident. We got back to Horsham and landed through a thin fog. The AZON bombs would have to wait for another day to be dropped on a target. Though we got mission credit for flying over enemy-occupied territory, the whole day had been a big pain. I wondered who had planned this impromptu mess.

That night at the club I resumed conversation with Captain Van de Rovaart.

'You're right,' I said, 'Bombardiers are no good. You should have seen how we wasted the day today.'

'I never said that!' Van replied, 'I love bombardiers!'

CHAPTER 11

MISSIONS TO MAGDEBURG

By late summer-time of 1944 a good deal of the glamour had gone out of flying combat bombing missions over Europe. We had been into Germany, had been shot at repeatedly, and had developed a jaded attitude about the whole thing.

Part of our common attitude may have originated in the monumental exhaustion brought on by flying a combat mission. The tired feeling which came with such a concentrated effort went to our very bones. We often came home to Horsham St Faith too worn out to sleep.

Another aspect of our job was the deep and all-pervading fear that lived with us always. Death surrounded us on every mission day. Our friends showed up as virile young men, and left in coffins, when their bodies could be found.

As a youth I had grown up as a ward of my grandmother. When she was a girl she had worshipped in the ancient Cathedral of Rochester, a massive pile of stone built by the Normans beside the Medway near London. As a legacy of that dear lady I had been brought up in all the mediaeval and episcopal tradition of the Church of England. So it was that, occasionally, finding need for a respite from our daily routine of destruction and death, I went into some corner of Norwich cathedral, there to kneel and say my prayers. The huge old church, with its thick walls and delicate overhead lierne vaults, gave me a personal navigation checkpoint as important as its stone tower was in our flight pattern.

There, in Losinga's time-honoured church, I prayed shamelessly to be spared a death from fire, drowning or explosion.

A disenchantment with our work was especially typical of Bob Hayzlett. Always Mr Careful, he became convinced that certain command pilots of the 458th were asinine incompetents. We were briefed always to fly at some integral altitude above sea level, such as 24,000 feet. Bob decided that the gunners of the German flak batteries were aware of this practice, and set their shell fuses accordingly, partly out of laziness. He always liked to lead his formations at some non-integral height, 500 feet above or below briefed attack altitude, for instance. Some command pilots objected to this practice, saying it would screw up the bombing accuracy. But the Norden bombsight was easily set to bomb from any altitude, and Gniewkowski didn't care what our flight height was, as long as he knew it.

Hayzlett's crew had been transferred from the 752nd Squadron to the 755th Squadron under a plan in which all the lead crews of the 458th Bomb Group were assigned to the 755th. That squadron became the one made up of lead crews only. The hard-working and long-suffering people who flew the wing positions of the attack formations were distributed among the other three operational Squadrons. 755th Squadron, at the time, was commanded by Major Don Jamison, a Californian and science graduate of U. Cal., Berkeley.

We sometimes went out on combat missions in our B-24s under conditions that seem impossible in retrospect. If a commercial airline flew passengers in such circumstances, the Federal Government would put it out of business. I recall pre-dawn take-offs in the English fog in which it was not possible to see the wing lights from the cockpit. The pilots set the directional gyro to the runway heading, shoved the throttles to the bulkhead in balls-to-the-wall position, let the brakes off, and rolled it.

In our take-off pattern from runway 04 at Horsham we had a turn to make at about a thousand feet of altitude. This let us avoid interference with the take-off pattern of our neighbours at Rackheath.

One new crew went off in the fog one morning, out the proper distance, made the turn, and dug a wing into a potato patch, killing themselves. They had apparently forgotten to read the altimeter or note the rate-of-climb indicator. Such was the attention span of a new crew and the climb-out performance of a bomb-loaded B-24.

My observation of this, and similar screw-ups, was that, if a crew survived its first five missions, it became essentially indestructible. Flying combat in the 8th was an experience enhanced by possession of a steep learning curve. We had two kinds of aircrews: the quick and the dead.

Though I had moved my digs into the exalted precincts of the club, I still flew with my crew. We were inseparable buddies.

When we became lead crew we had moved nose gunner, Sergeant Foley, to the waist and replaced him in the front turret with rated navigator, Lieutenant Frank Shepard, to do pilotage. Later, as the 458th got its own aircraft equipped with H2X radars, we added yet another navigator. This man, Lieutenant Bert Kemp, properly trained on the equipment, operated the radar set. As lead navigator of the bomber and the formation, I was nominally the boss of these two.

In the B-24 radar lead ship configuration I got to move upstairs where I sat at a more-or-less comfortable desk just to port of the top turret. There I was emplaced back to back with the pilot. Apparently some design genius had decided that B-24 navigators were all fated to ride facing the rear. But at least, in this new office, I didn't have to stand all through a nine-hour mission.

Frank Shepard rode in the goldfish-bowl seat, out front in our nose turret. Bert Kemp operated the H2X when we flew a radar ship. He was our secret weapon, letting us see in the dark or through clouds.

On those lead ships of the 458th which were equipped with H2X navigational radar (commonly known as 'Mickey' sets, possibly from their Mickey Mouse performance), the radome which housed the dish or scanner was installed in the hole previously vacated by the ball turret. It was necessary to crank this radome down after take-off and up before landing, just as

A lead B-24 dropping bombs through heavy cloud. Note the lowered radar dome used to aid navigation in these conditions.

had once been done with the ball turret. Otherwise it would be dragged on the concrete or tarmac and badly damaged.

The Mickey set operating console, not a small contraption, was installed just to starboard of the top turret, making the aircraft flight deck rather crowded. In its initial configuration the radar set faced the rear of the plane. This configuration was later changed because some radar operators got confused as to the direction the aircraft was going. But the lead navigator was still left with his seat facing the rear, an orientation he shared with the tail gunner.

I inadvertently got into trouble over this turning-around of the radar sets. The order to reinstall radar consoles had come down from Division, signed by General Kepner's adjutant. One of the equipment officers in 458th had decided that the consoles would not fit turned around the other way and he voiced his gripe to Colonel James Hogg, our Air Executive. Hogg asked my opinion. Being busy at the time, and not having seen or paid attention to the order from Division, I said 'If it won't fit, it won't fit,' or something equally brilliant. The next day my phone rang.

Lieutenant-Colonel Carl Barthel, the Second Division Navigation Officer was on the horn.

Seen here when a major, James Hogg later became a Colonel and Air Executive Officer of the 458th Bomb Group.

Barthel was no Elmer Mottern. His chewing was much more civilised and polite, but just as effective. The punch line was 'Do you just ignore the commanding General's orders?'

'No Sir!' I said, sensing immediate court martial in the offing. I spoke pleadingly to Colonel Hogg. He got the problem resolved immediately, and the radar consoles were all turned to face forward in the aeroplane.

Compared to the Boeing B-17 bomber the B-24 was the ugly duckling of World War II. It could not achieve the swan-like look in flight that the B-17 had. The publicity people (if any) who promoted the image of the Liberator were no match for the professionals of Boeing who successfully pushed to the reverent members of the press the mistaken belief that the Flying Fortress was *the* American heavy bomber of World War II.

Fred Vacek, our Group Bombardier, had a different view of why the B-17 fliers of Eighth U.S.A.A.F. got all the publicity. All the B-17 bases, Vacek noted, were close to London. Our B-24's, on the other hand, were stationed up in the corner of East Anglia, around Norwich. It was too far from the London pubs, Vacek proclaimed, for the ignorant and lazy American journalists to bother visiting and writing about B-24 bases. They wrote about B-17s instead.

There were always gripes from operational theatres about B-24 performance. But, in Europe at least, combat-modified ships were invariably operated in conditions that exceeded design specifications. When a new model came out with performance upped, more crap was loaded onto the aeroplane. Our lead ships carried radar, guns, gee equipment, personnel armour, eight thousand pounds of bombs, and a crew of thirteen. They flew like boat anchors. Hayzlett grew so unenamoured of heavier and heavier aeroplanes and worse and worse handling that he would sometimes order the ordnance men to unload a bomb or two from our lead ship so he could get it airborne before the end of the long runway. He had paid attention to his pilot schooling on the subject of aircraft weight and balance.

I always wondered why the 458th flew so many missions to Magdeburg. It seemed to me that every other time we led the Group it was on a mission to Magdeburg. I recalled having hoped in our early mission days that we would actually go on the attack deep into Germany, but now I got tired of hauling bombs to Magdeburg and I wished I could go back to France for a change.

Magdeburg was a German city about halfway between Braunschweig (Brunswick) and Berlin. We bombed it repeatedly. On sunny days I could look down, especially with the binoculars, and see the old city clearly. It looked to me like nothing was left of Magdeburg except a huge collection of muddy craters and the sad remnants of a destroyed mediaeval cathedral.

Trips to Magdeburg were a pain in the butt. There was the long haul in both directions across the North Sea, then there was the interminable ride back and forth across Germany. Our route took us in and out so that we essentially got no flak. It was pretty dull.

One day, however, we were on our way east to Magdeburg, leading the Group in. We crossed the Dutch coast at Bergen aan Zee and the four-gun German flak battery there opened up as usual, hitting nothing. Their bursts went off up above our formation, and off to the side.

Suddenly there was an ungodly loud noise – an ear-splitting blast that shook the whole aeroplane and woke up everybody.

'What in hell was that?' Hayzlett asked.

'Sorry!' Griefenstein said from the top turret. He had inadvertently discharged his twin fifties. The bark of our own weapons, though comforting, was also startling.

The P-51s of our fighter escort had met us ten miles off the coast; their formation commander was on the horn instantly.

'Hey, it's us, dammit!' he said, 'Hold your fire, please!'

The fighters flew in little boxes of four – two leaders and two wingmen. They flew ovals to the side of us – forward up the line of the bomber stream, then back – always alert – always protecting their big friends. Another bunch of fighters wove a cross-stitch above us, back and forth, meeting over the top of our formation with the completion of each node.

The Fourth Fighter Group, stationed at Debden, often escorted 96th Bomb Wing; the red noses of their aircraft nicely matched the red tails of our bombers.

My hometown friend, Wilbur Eaton, flew in Fourth Fighter Group. I always looked out of the window to see if I could spot him. Though I never identified him for sure, I felt better knowing he was up there with us.

The loud blast of Griefenstein's exploding guns was only an addition to the continual deafening racket in which we flew. Part of the overwhelming internal noise of an operating B-24 was made easier to bear by the fact that we all wore leather flying helmets, modelled somewhat on those originated by the ancient aces of World War I. Ours had huge pads which contained the earphone pieces of the aircraft intercom or 'horn' (any communication system on which humans spoke was 'the horn' in World War II terminology). The pressure of these huge ear pieces became totally unbearable after some six hours of constant wearing. My ears hurt for hours after I returned from a mission.

Over these leather flight helmets we wore a steel flak helmet when the exterior flying-steel weather conditions warranted. We had no G.I. flak helmets, so we had ours made in the shop by kind paddlefeet. They welded semi-cylindrical extensions on each side of standard trench helmets so that the modified flak version would fit over our monstrous earpieces. These welded extensions were ugly, with a combination of black and rust colours around the weld seams. I considered mine to be so raunchy that I took it to the paint shop and had it customised. The paint shop people, happy to have an artistic challenge, polished it smooth, then painted it overall sparkling blue with a great golden figure eight, surrounded by silver wings on the front. It became known as my 'Flash Gordon' helmet after the Sunday comic's space hero of the day. I should have donated it to the Smithsonian when the War ended.

Flak helmets could be dangerous in other ways than those related to German anti-aircraft shells. Some unknown design genius of B-24 equipment had supplied with each aeroplane a contraption called the 'relief tube'. At the ungodly hour at which we woke to fly a mission, typically having had too little sleep, it was essential to drink numerous cups of coffee to wake up. The effects of such excess consumption of mildly diuretic liquid often overtook us about over Bergen aan Zee. It was for hydrostatic emergencies like this that the relief tube was designed. However, at high altitude it never functioned as intended.

The relief tube was located downstairs under the flight deck in the tunnel that led to the nose compartment. It was installed next to the front bulkhead of the forward bomb bay on the starboard side of the ship and consisted of a plastic funnel attached to the end of a flexible plastic tube. The tube connected to a short metal pipe which extruded an inch or so through the outer skin of the aircraft fuselage at the bottom. A hook was provided on the bulkhead for hanging the funnel when it was not in use.

The theory of relief tube use was simple enough. You unzipped several layers of flight clothing at the fly aperture. Then, carefully placing your genito-urinary member into the funnel, you tried to accomplish the desperately-needed urination.

Manifestly the relief tube was a sexist design. A female crew member, of which we had none, would have had a tough time.

The design thought behind the relief tube may have been excellent, but the actual practice was exceedingly difficult. At the intense cold of bomber operational altitude, one's essential organ was usually so shrivelled as to be almost impossible to find under three layers of clothing, let alone place in the funnel. If you were, however, so adept as to be able to get in the funnel and let go, the first charge of warm liquid, upon hitting the metal pipe to the outside, froze instantly, forming a solid plug. The subsequent liquid filled the tube, then the funnel, and then the undergarments, electric suit and coverall trousers of the urinator, making the rest of the mission most uncomfortable travelling indeed.

For such reasons we abandoned all thought of use of the relief tube. Our alternative method required more skill, but was less likely to result in a dampening accident. The flexible bomb bay doors of the B-24, when retracted, fitted upward snugly around the fuselage. This design created less drag than that generated by the bomb doors of the B-17, which hung out in the airstream when opened. We always flew with the bomb bay doors opened about an inch. The gasoline transfer valves were located on the front bomb bay bulkhead, and they sometimes leaked. B-24s occasionally exploded suddenly in the sky from an ignited build-up of gasoline fumes in the bomb bay, occasioned by leaking transfer valves. Bob Stoesser and I had witnessed such an event during our crew training days at Blythe. The inch-wide crack of partially-opened B-24 bomb doors caused enough airstream burble in the bomb bay to purge gasoline fumes continually. But it induced only minuscule additional drag. It also made the task of urination possible without using the relief tube.

To urinate with style, you took a walk-around oxygen bottle, and went down into the tunnel below the flight deck. There you opened the front access doors through the bomb bay bulkhead and stepped carefully out onto the catwalk. It was not a bad idea to wear a parachute pack, for if you fell off the catwalk the bomb doors were typically not strong enough to hold up a falling human body, and the next step was five miles down into Germany.

Standing on the catwalk you unzipped and took very careful aim. The name of the game was to aim well enough to urinate directly through the inch-wide crack of the bomb bay doors. When you stood, the urine stream had enough velocity to carry outside the aeroplane and disperse in the airstream. It was a bad no-no to miss your aim and piss on the bombs. The frozen urine could immobilise the bomb's fuse propellers. The bombs would then fail to arm when dropped, and would hit as unexploded duds. At the successful culmination of this elaborate hydrodynamic procedure you would be standing on the catwalk, feeling much better, and letting it all stream out smoothly through the inch-wide door crack. That was the point at which the irate voice of Brownie Harvath, the tail gunner, came screaming over the horn in indignation:

'Who's pissin' up there? Cut that out, dammit! It's splashin' all over my window back here. I can't see anything but frozen piss! What if there's a fighter attack?'

Staff Sergeant Weldon Sheltraw, our radio operator, was a busy man during a mission, especially after we became a lead crew. He was always sending messages from the command pilot, or taking messages to give to the command pilot. Frequently he was too busy to carry out the elaborate procedure for catwalk urination. One day as we droned east toward Magdeburg Sheltraw was overcome by the consumption of excess morning coffee. He made hurried use of a convenient nearby receptacle – his flak helmet. He put the helmet under his radio desk, thinking to empty it later and wash it on his return to Horsham St Faith.

Midway down our bomb run we flew into super-heavy flak. Sheltraw grabbed his flak helmet to put it on. But by now a film of ice had frozen across his forgotten urine. The flak helmet would not fit properly. Sheltraw reached up and pulled it snugly into place. He was rewarded with an unexpected shower bath.

Sheltraw had added yet another reason for us to look with displeasure on trips to Magdeburg.

Second Air Division bomber attack stream.

CHAPTER 12

THE MYSTERY OF THE MISSING BUS

While the flying of combat missions was a career aimed at keeping one from growing old, we did have compensations. Surely our lot was better than that of the foot soldiers who froze at night in some rotten foxhole. One of our compensations was found in the happy evenings we spent at the club. There we had a bit of home, a little corner of America, our own hideaway in the midst of wartime England.

So attractive was the club at Horsham St Faith that officers of neighbouring bomb groups often visited us in order to get away for a while from their ugly digs of Quonset huts and coke stoves. One could find them happy in the bar, or just sitting around enjoying the atmosphere. A frequent visitor while he was commanding officer of the 466th Group at Attlebridge was Colonel William Cleveland. Typically he would drop into the Club to organise a gigantic crap game.

Among the navigation officers of our Group, those for whose performance Jim Isbell now held me responsible, were some lead crew men who had been with the 458th since its organisation in the States. Some of them had personally taken part in a memorable event purportedly organised by the remarkable Max Sokarl.

Speaking to these navigators, and to others of that group which formed the Sokarl fan club during his nightly fable sessions at the club, I learned what was apparently the whole story of the Wendover bus.

Bomb Groups did not just happen, people were not just stuffed together into a fighting outfit and sent forth overseas. There was considerable prior staging, organisation, and practice. The 458th Bomb Group trained and organised at several bases in the United States prior to joining the Eighth Air Force in England. When Lieutenant Max Sokarl was sent to help, our Group was in training at the air-base at Wendover, Utah.

Sokarl had passed the bar in 1931 and set up practice as a criminal defence attorney in his home town of New London, Connecticut, when World War II came along. Since he had no sympathy with the draft, Max volunteered and went to boot camp at Fort Devens, Massachusetts. In December of 1942 he was admitted to Officer Candidate School with the U.S. Army at Miami, Florida and in March of 1943 he graduated as a shavetail with no particular speciality except his law degree and his hyperactive mind. Though he had high academic grades in O.C.S., he collected an impressive series of upper-level reprimands. But Sokarl was immune to reprimands, and, in fact, was immune to much of military life and discipline.

Max was next sent to the School of Military Intelligence at Harrisburg, Virginia and upon graduation, he was assigned to the 458th Bomb Group.

There was no particular intelligence work for Sokarl when he arrived at Wendover. German and Japanese spies were not much in evidence on the Utah desert nor the Bonneville salt flats. The 458th, at that time, flew only practice missions, so there was not much enemy damage to be evaluated. But Sokarl, with his stentorian voice, ex-cathedra mode of speaking, and nimble mind, came early to the careful attention of Major Pierce Manley, the Bomb Group Adjutant.

Manley convinced the then commanding officer of the 458th, Light Colonel Robert Hardy, to appoint Sokarl as Group and Post Provost-Marshal, reporting, of course, to the Group Adjutant. What better job for an attorney, Manley reasoned, than law enforcement? Thus began a relationship that endured as long as Sokarl was with our Bomb Group. Whenever there was an opportunity for Machiavellian intrigue, or a need for something out of the ordinary, Manley would see that Sokarl was given the job. In his days with the 458th Sokarl served as assistant squadron supply officer, assistant recreation officer, assistant liaison officer for public education, and group fatality and graves registration officer.

Way back in 1943, which seemed an age ago to us in 1944, military clerks all over the United States were busy cutting travel and assignment orders for military personnel. At stations, airfields, and bases from Maine to California officers and enlisted men newly assigned to the 458th Heavy Bomb Group packed their bags and boarded trains to travel to western Utah. Among such were those trained and skilled in the vital profession of aerial navigation.

'Where in hell is Wendover?' was a question asked over and over again by those who hoped not to be stationed out somewhere in East Poophead surrounded by cactus. Duty near a big city, or at least near some semblance of civilisation, preferably with an ample supply of wild women, was much to be preferred. Married men, of course, hoped that their wives would be able to live somewhere other than in a tarpaper shack or a cockroach-infested chicken coop, if, in fact, wives could follow along at all.

To Wendover they came – persons of all specialities – ground-crew and flight crew. Pilots, navigators, bombardiers, engineers, gunners, armourers, mechanics, carpenters, clerks, flight surgeons – they all came. Every kind of skill needed to complete the capability of a bombardment group was sent to the wilds of western Utah. Also sent were people like Sokarl, whose skills were hard to match with the needs of a bomb group. Sokarl was to find his own niches and create his own jobs, or else succumb to boredom.

And Max Sokarl was about the last person on earth to succumb to boredom.

One hot night at Wendover, Sokarl and Manley were busy at professional drinking in the officers' club when they were joined by Captain Ray Sandberg, the Group Navigation Officer. Sandberg was in a vile mood. Sokarl and Manley, in their happy mood, sought the reason for Sandberg's dissatisfaction with the state of the world.

Sandberg told how he had sought the blessing of Colonel Hardy upon a trip which he wanted his more-expert navigators to make to Hamilton Field, north of San Francisco. There was to be at Hamilton a demonstration of a new, electronic device which promised to revolutionise the whole art of aerial navigation. It was important that Sandberg's men be able to see this new technological wonder at first hand. Sandberg himself intended to go, quite naturally, and if his men were to find spare time for drinking and wenching in the city by the Golden Gate, so much the better.

To this proposition Colonel Hardy responded with a stern lecture about the waste of government funds on unnecessary travel, and about the imminent departure of the 458th Bomb Group to combat assignment so that they might all play their essential part in saving the world from Axis terror.

In brief, the Colonel's answer was, 'Hell No!'

Sandberg was still smarting from the Colonel's expert mouthing, and was feeling rather self-righteous. Sokarl and Manley, in their feel-no-pain state, sympathised mightily with Sandberg. They gave learned lectures on what a professional, chicken son-of-a-bitch the Colonel was. But Max Sokarl, possibly inspired by officers' club booze, went one better. He offered to solve the problem.

'This is a simple matter,' he said, 'Be out in front of the PX with your guys at three tomorrow afternoon.'

'Are you kidding?' Sandberg asked.

Lt-Colonel Robert Hardy, the first Commanding Officer of the 458th Bomb Group.

'Hell no. When you have a problem that requires the application of pure thought, just hand it to Sokarl.'

'Has this kid flipped out?' Sandberg asked Manley.

'What the hell? Give him a chance.'

'You better not fuck up on this, kid,' Sandberg warned, 'I'll have your ass!'

Second Lieutenant Max Sokarl, totally unawed by being seated between two semi-inebriated higher-ranking officers, put on his best cool.

'Just be there, Sir,' he said, 'Leave the arrangements to me.'

The following morning, rather late, Max Sokarl wandered into Major Manley's office.

'I guess I better figure out what to do to get Captain Sandberg and his people to San Francisco,' he said.

'Sounds wise.'

'You got any good ideas?'

'Not me. All I got is a hell of a hangover.'

'I think I know how to swing it.'

'Watch your ass.'

'Yeah, I'll try. If somebody were to steal your coat temporarily, the one hanging there with the gold major's leaves on it, would you notice?'

'Not if I was looking out the window at the time.'

'Are you expecting to look out the window today?'

'I was thinking of looking out the window right now.'

'Good. When were you thinking of looking back at your coat rack?'

'In about an hour and a half. I got to get out of here early today. I don't feel all that well, and I'm going to need to disappear later in the afternoon.'

'I see. Well, I hope you continue to enjoy that view out the window. It sure as hell is a beautiful desert.'

Captain Sandberg was standing in front of the PX, along the sidewalk where the civilian bus stopped, at exactly three o'clock in the afternoon. With him were all his expert navigators. They were joined by a major not familiar to them, one who looked remarkably like the older brother of Lieutenant Max Sokarl, presuming Sokarl had an older brother.

The bus from Wendover pulled in on time, and a few people got off. The bus driver got out to stand on the sidewalk, picking his teeth. The unidentified major strode up to him, carrying a particularly officious-looking clipboard loaded with papers. As the bus driver stood there, the major began to read to him in stentorian tones, apparently quoting from the text of the clipboard.

'By the authority vested in me by the President and the Congress of the free and sovereign United States of America, I hereby impress and confiscate this vehicle and its operational personnel into the temporary official service of the said Government of the United States . . .'

'What's all that mean?' the bus driver asked.

'It means that you, and your bus, have a most important mission to perform. Furthermore, this is a top secret mission, and you are hereby warned not to speak to anyone about it, nor to divulge the contents of this conversation, nor your destination, to anyone, at any time, ever!'

'Yeah, but I . . .'

'Are you willing to do your duty as a citizen of the United States of America?'

'Well, yeah, but . . .'

'Then listen carefully. I do not repeat! You are to take these men here, as I shall designate, aboard your bus. You are to go where this officer here, this high-ranking captain in the Army of the United States, tells you. If you need funds for fuel, or for any other legitimate purpose, he will supply you. You are not to communicate with any person about this secret mission. You are not, under any circumstances, to tell anyone, ever, where you have gone or what you have done there. Now prepare to load your bus!'

'Yeah, but what about my run back to Wendover?'

'Leave that problem to us as the cognisant military authorities.'

'I gotta go home and get my shaving gear and tell my wife that I'm going.'

'Didn't you understand me? You are not to speak to anyone about this mission. This is a secret mission. Please prepare to load your bus.'

'Yeah, but my boss . . .'

'Don't worry about your boss or your wife. The cognisant and duly consti-tuted military authorities will take care of all that. Now please load your bus. We are wasting time!'

'Well, all right.'

Captain Sandberg and his navigators climbed on board the Wendover bus, each being officiously checked off on the clipboard by the unidentified officer. The bus door shut, and they drove off towards the main gate.

News of the mystery of the missing bus soon spread far and wide. The county sheriff had his men combing every back road and by-way, but there was no clue whatever. The wife of the missing bus driver was admitted to the hospital by her doctor for treatment of her hysterical condition.

Four days later the Wendover bus pulled in front of the PX once again and Sandberg and his men got off. He thanked the bus driver and gave him five dollars. There was no sign of the mysterious major.

The owner of the bus company was both happy and astounded when his lost vehicle pulled into the garage. He spoke excitedly to the driver:

'Christ, Fred! Where the hell you been?'

'I can't tell you.'

'What the hell you mean you can't tell me? You been gone four fuckin' days with my goddam bus. I been worried sick. The whole town's been lookin' for you. We figured you was killed or some shit, and you stand there and tell me you can't tell me where the hell you been.'

'I'm sorry, but I can't tell you. I just can't.'

'Why the hell not?'

'I can't tell you why not.'

'Goddammit, Fred, you tell me where the hell you been or I'm gonna wipe the garage floor with your ass! What the hell you mean you can't tell me?'

'It's a secret.'

'What's secret?'

'I can't tell.'

'Fred, you gimme any morra that crap I'm gonna bust you one. Secret my ass! Where the hell you been with my bus?'

And after many extended and dire threats, and much cajoling, the bus owner finally extracted the story of the secret mission to San Francisco from the very reluctant Fred:

'What goddam major told you to go? What's his name?'

'I dunno.'

'You dunno! What the shit did he look like?'

'I dunno. He looked like Army. You see one major you seen 'em all.'

'Dammit, Fred, you musta hadda study hard to get so goddam dumb. Geez, I never heard such a dumb buncha crap. But I'm gonna find out who the hell done this. I'm goin' out to the goddam air base and find out who the fuck stole my bus. And you can bet your dumb ass I ain't gonna take no military bullshit for no answer.'

So it was that the irate owner of the Wendover bus line appeared in his Cadillac at the front gate of the air-base demanding to see the Commanding Officer. The corporal on duty was polite, but firm:

'I'm very sorry sir, but the Commanding Officer does not see civilians. He suggests you write your question to the War Department.'

'So he ain't gonna talk to me, huh? That's a lotta stupid-ass crap to hand to a tax-payin' citizen. I s'pose he's too goddam busy to care if he's gotta buncha damn thieves in this outfit!'

'The Colonel's office suggests you see the Adjutant, sir.'

'See the what?'

'Major Manley, sir, the Group Adjutant. He takes care of many problems for the Commanding Officer.'

'I'll bet he does. Well, hell, I got to talk to somebody. Let's give it a try.'

'Yes sir.'

It was a most solicitous and polite Major Manley who gave gracious reception to the owner of the Wendover bus line. As the story unfolded Manley looked more and more concerned.

'Why, this is a very bad thing that has happened to you, sir. I just can't understand it. I don't know who can have convinced your bus driver to do such a thing, and right in front of the PX too. But you can rest assured that we'll give this a very serious and thorough investigation. We'll get to the bottom of it. And we'll assign it to the best man we've got. A job like this is exactly in his line.'

'Who's that?'

'Our Provost-Marshal, Lieutenant Sokarl. He heads up our criminal investigations. Also he's a fully-qualified attorney and lawyer. Investigations of this kind are exactly what he's good at.'

'Sounds good.'

'Yes, I think we'll get the kind of action you need from Lieutenant Sokarl. Just let me call him here and see if he can see you now.'

And Major Manley dialled his desk phone with great deliberation. He gazed out the window while awaiting an answer.

'Major Manley here. Yes, Lieutenant Sokarl. The Commanding Officer has asked that I bring this case personally to your attention. This is clearly of top level importance. Yes, indeed . . .'

Thus was the owner of the Wendover bus line led expectantly to sit across

the desk from the businesslike, impressive, and manifestly competent Second
Lieutenant Max Sokarl. On Sokarl's desk was the omnipresent clipboard,
filled with blank paper. Sokarl proceeded to take about a half ream of notes
as the interview went on and on through the afternoon:

'Now, let's see, sir, we'll need the serial number of the bus.'

'Well, I don't know that offhand.'

'Do you remember the engine number?'

'No.'

'Yes, well we'd better have you come back and bring the registration slip
with you. Now about the tyres . . .'

'What about the tyres?'

'Do you know the make, serial number, and date of purchase of each of
the bus tyres?'

'Geez, no. Why is that important?'

'Well, you see, there may be distinguishing marks about the tyres – the
tread pattern and all – so that we could trace the tyre tracks in case the bus
ran out across the desert.'

'But my driver was driving it all the time. He went down the pavement to
San Francisco, the damn idiot. There wouldn't be no tyre tracks out in the
desert.'

'So your driver says. But has it ever occurred to you that he might suffer
from hallucination?'

'You know, you got a hell of a good point there. He's dumb enough to
think he done most anything.'

'You see, sir, in cases of this nature, absolutely everyone is suspect. The
whole thing could be a fabrication.'

'A what?'

'Made up.'

'Oh yeah. You really think so?'

'Well, of course we can't make preliminary judgements without having all
the facts at hand. That's why I want you to help me carry out this investigation for you by bringing me all the pertinent information I've asked for
here. Have you ever been fingerprinted?'

'No. Why should I be fingerprinted? I'm the one who had his bus stole. I
ain't the guy that stole the bus.'

'Yes, I understand. But, you see, in sending my report to Washington I'll
have to reassure the officials of the Federal Government that, in fact, you are
who you actually claim to be. It's one of those formalities we have to observe.'

'You gotta send this stuff to Washington?'

'In a case of this serious magnitude, we have got to keep higher authorities fully informed.'

'Well, I'll be.'

'Of course, we'll keep you fully informed.'

And, after three trips to the air-base to bring superfluous documents,
including his wife's birth certificate, to Lieutenant Sokarl, the owner of the
Wendover bus line began to get regular and voluminous written progress
reports on the investigation into the case of the missing bus. These were very
difficult to read, and they quoted heavily from military regulations and the

United States Constitution, but, at least, they indicated that Lieutenant Sokarl was, if nothing else, exasperatingly thorough.

Occasionally the bus owner would be summoned out to the air-base for a two to three hour interview spiced with highly baffling questions.

And the voluminous reports came to the bus owner. They came until word went around that the 458th Heavy Bomb Group had left the base at Wendover, possibly to go to Europe.

CHAPTER 13

HAULING GAS

Following the saturation bombing we had done on the area of St Lô, General George S. Patton's army had broken through the German lines. Patton's people advanced rapidly in a great arc across Northern France. 'Old Blood-and-Guts' drove his armoured troops mercilessly. He was the equal of Stonewall Jackson in rapid manoeuvre.

Patton's people captured a large number of German soldiers in this fast trek into enemy-held territory. And Patton, true to style, earned the annoyance of his superiors by publically complaining that British General Bernard Montgomery was too slow in breaking through the strong German position at Caen. Had Montgomery got 'the lead out of his ass', in Patton's terms, he would have completed the other half of a pincer movement resulting in the capture of vastly more German troops.

Whatever might have been, both Patton and Montgomery ran past their supply lines. East of the French City of Lille, the Allied armies ran out of fuel and their tanks came to a halt. Thus it was that the pundits of high command determined that the 458th Bomb Group, among various heavy bomb groups, should contrive, in the latter half of September, 1944, to haul gasoline to the Allied armoured troops in France and Belgium.

We went into five days of stand-down from combat missions while our ground-crews refitted bombers, converting them to gasoline tankers. Bomb bay tanks were installed and filled with tank-octane fuel. Fighter-plane-type wing tanks were loaded into the waist sections of some bombers. Also filled with ground-vehicle fuel were the Tokyo tanks, as our ships' outer wing tanks were called. The trip to Lille from Horsham St Faith was a short one for a B-24, and the Tokyo tank capacity was not needed for the aeroplane to fly such a distance.

The 458th hauled gas during the last two weeks of September. While Hayzlett's crew made trips to Lille, I did not go along. I contrived to get some other navigator assigned for those trips. I had plenty of Bomb Group paperwork, plus reports to Wing and Division to catch up on. Besides, I figured that I had come to England to fly combat missions. Had I wanted to be in the transport business, I would have volunteered for that kind of half-assed, no-mission-credit job. This was doubtless a raunchy attitude, but it was my view of the world of bomber operations at the time.

Nor was gasoline-hauling the totally safe operation one might imagine. One bomber loaded with gas took off from Horsham St Faith and crashed a short distance out from the runway end. With the vastly flammable load the aeroplane carried, there was no chance for anyone on board to survive.

Colonel Isbell sent a number of headquarters staff officers to France to take care of the gas-hauling operations. In command at Lille was Lieutenant-Colonel James A. Hogg, Assistant Group Commander and Air Executive, also known as 'Old Iron Ass'. With Hogg was Major Charles Booth, Assistant Group Operations Officer, and a number of other field- and company-grade officers. The gas we hauled to Lille was destined to fuel Montgomery's tanks. When our bombers got to Lille, they were unloaded by the British who lived in little tents across the field from the digs of our American flyboys. The British people used a hand-operated pump called an 'octopus'. The pump had a single input hose which was dunked into the aircraft tanks. It had eight output hoses, each of which was put into a five-gallon jerry can. There was a British soldier, either in the bomb bay or up on the wing, to crank the octopus pump by hand. There was an additional soldier on each output hose to change jerry cans when each got full.

The British shut down this operation twice each day for tea.

The octopus pump method might, all going well, result in a gas-loaded B-24 being emptied of its fuel cargo in two or three days. Back at Horsham St Faith, Big Jim Isbell had begun to wonder what in hell had happened to all his bombers. He went over to Lille on the next trip out to see for himself.

Captain Sam Lakin.

Struck by the gross inefficiency of the British unloading operation, Colonel Isbell remembered that each Liberator came delivered with a 50-gallon-per-minute, gasoline-powered pump.

Radioing ahead for Captain Sam Lakin, our Group Supply Officer, to meet him at the ramp, he took the next bomber back to Horsham. When Isbell landed, Lakin was standing there.

'Sam, where are all those portable, gasoline-driven pumps we used to have?' Isbell asked.

'I have them all stored,' Lakin said, 'They're over here in a little building I found, just for that purpose.' Sam Lakin was, as usual, our ever-competent, ever-resourceful supply officer. He was a gem among all of us rough-cut rocks.

Isbell sent ten pumps to Lille on the next ship out, along with a sergeant-technician who knew how to operate them. The fuel unloading operation at Lille went into high gear.

Meanwhile, the rest of the Eighth Air Force continued to attack targets in Germany.

Of the memorable heroes of my youthful days, Wilbur Eaton ranks high. He was a few years older than I was. He lived in my home town of Puyallup, Washington. Eaton was particularly remarkable, in those depression years, for having a steady job, which gave him the economic clout to own and drive an automobile.

Eaton was tall and handsome. He had dark, wavy hair and twinkling blue eyes. He was always witty and happy. Bill Eaton had an irresistible natural charm. He also was afraid of nothing.

Eaton used to defend me from those older boys, the home town bullies, who liked to try to trap me up an alley and pound the crap out of me just to keep in practice. When they found out that Eaton was my friend, they left me alone.

When the war came along, Bill Eaton volunteered. He went off for flight training as a sergeant in the Army, under a programme that was then in operation. Eaton went to primary school at Santa Maria, California, then on to basic flight training at Merced. He graduated as an Army pilot from Williams Field at Chandler, Arizona.

After his graduation, Eaton was sent to Peterson Field, near Colorado Springs, there to train for photo reconnaissance work in P-38 aircraft. He was moved up from Sergeant to Flight Officer, a warrant grade. Having held this rank for a short time, he was commissioned as a Second Lieutenant. From Colorado he went on to join the Seventh Photographic Group of Eighth Air Force at Mount Farm, near Oxford, England.

On his twelfth photo trip over Germany, Bill Eaton had the oxygen system shot out of his P-38. Descending rapidly, to avoid passing out, he injured his ears with the rapid compression effects of diving, and spent some time in the hospital, recovering.

Out of the hospital, but not yet back on flying duty, Eaton and two friends borrowed a jeep and were sightseeing through the English countryside. They drove by the airfield at Debden and were fascinated by the P-51s of Fourth Fighter Group. They motored onto the base and asked to speak to the

Commanding Officer. Colonel Don Blakeslee, commanding Fourth Fighter Group at the time, told these errant airmen that he could use them. He arranged for their transfer, sent them off for training in P-51 combat operations, and added them to his cadre of hot-rock fighter pilots.

Fourth Fighter Group was originally formed out of the American 'Eagle Squadrons'. When the United States entered World War II, RAF Squadrons 71, 121, and 133, whose people were American volunteers serving with the British, were transferred into the U.S. Army. Thus Fourth Fighter Group, originally equipped with Spitfires, had operated out of England prior to the existence of the Eighth Air Force. The Commanding Officer of the Fourth, Colonel Blakeslee, an ace in his own right, had been one of the original American volunteers. But, by the time Eaton joined up, Fourth Fighter Group was a part of Second Air Division, Eighth United States Army Air Force. The red-nosed P-51s of Fourth Group were often assigned to escort the bombing missions of 96th Combat Wing. They gave us a great sense of security as they surrounded our bomber formations.

Bill Eaton flew fifty-six combat missions with Fourth Fighter Group before he was sent back to the States for quieter duty. Around the time of his tenth mission as a fighter pilot, he was promoted to First Lieutenant.

Eaton was out on a strafing mission over Germany that September of 1944 when the radio word came that England was fogged in, and the fighter planes should seek a place to land on the continent till the weather cleared over the British Isles. With four of his friends, Bill Eaton elected to go into Lille. When his wheels hit the runway, Eaton's ship skidded off into the grass. He cut the switch, killing the engine, and rolled into a small ditch, upending his P-51, nose first into the dirt. Thinking that his aeroplane's propeller might be damaged, Bill Eaton rode home two days later on an RAF Lancaster Bomber that had also stopped over at Lille.

The gas-unloading operation at Lille was pretty dull for our people. When Major Chuck Booth saw Eaton's red-nosed P-51 parked among our bombers at Lille, he was intrigued. He had never flown nor been checked out in a P-51. But Booth was, after all, a rated and qualified Army Pilot, he figured he could fly anything.

Eaton's aeroplane had some gas in it. Booth opened the canopy and got in. There was no check sheet in the plane. However, Booth managed to fire up the engine, and taxied out onto the field. Colonel Hogg stood watching from a safe distance.

Booth's initial taxying of Eaton's P-51 was a bit erratic, since, at first, he could not figure out how to unlock the tail wheel. So he gave the engine enough quick throttle to lift the tail, then kicked the aeroplane around with the rudder in order to turn it. After a few such oddball turnings, he noticed a small placard on the instrument panel which read, 'To unlock tail wheel, push stick full forward.' After he complied with these instructions, the P-51 was considerably easier to taxi.

Having figured out how successfully to taxi the P-51, Booth decided to take it up for a ride around the traffic pattern. He taxied back to the ramp, shut the engine down, and got out to look for a parachute. He couldn't find a seat pack of the kind fighter pilots customarily wore. So he borrowed a bomber pilot's back pack. He told Colonel Hogg he had decided to take the fighter up for a trial flight.

'You'll bust your ass!' Hogg said.

Filled with the desire to prove that the solemn-visaged Hogg was full of it, Booth, wearing his back-pack chute and mud-caked galoshes, got back in the P-51 and fired it up again. He taxied out onto the field. By now quite a crowd of bomber pilots and crewmen had gathered to snicker a bit and watch the show.

Lining up with the runway, Chuck Booth set all the trim tabs to zero. The check-list would have told him to crank in some thirty degrees of rudder trim, but he didn't have a check-list.

The British flight controller gave the P-51 a green light. Major Booth shoved the throttle to the firewall. The gigantic Rolls engine wound up as the fighter accelerated rapidly forward.

Booth could not see forward over the aeroplane's nose. A B-24, which Booth was used to flying, with its tricycle gear and big office windows up high in front, had excellent forward visibility. But the P-51 had an old-fashioned tail wheel, its huge prop and engine blotted out the scene ahead until the tail became airborne and lifted off the runway.

Booth, used to a four-engined bomber, had not fed in ample rudder to correct for the torque of the big, single engine and the massive prop. By the time the tail came up and he could see ahead, he was aimed some forty-five degrees off the runway, charging through the grass straight at the British flight line on the other side of the field. He stamped hard on the rudder pedal, but it would hardly budge. Booth held the P-51 on the ground as long as possible to build his airspeed, then hauled back on the stick, mushing, in a half-stall, over the British aircraft and the power lines alongside the field. Fortunately there was a valley on the far side. Booth nosed down into it to let his speed build.

The down-run gave the fighter ample airspeed to zoom out of the far side of the valley, screaming upward into the French sky.

Booth levelled it off. But now he was faced with another problem. His leg, flak-injured from his early mission over Berlin, had begun to shudder un-controllably. He had tensed up from stamping on the rudder pedal. Booth pounded on his leg, trying to relieve his muscle spasms.

When his leg trembling abated, Chuck Booth looked up and around. He climbed up to about five thousand feet. He decided that, having had so much trouble in take-off, and since there was not much gas in the P-51, he'd better take it back in. Besides, he was heading for the German battle lines at a rapid pace, if he had not already passed them. He turned and headed back for the Lille field. Booth spotted the airfield below. By now he was feeling a bit more comfortable flying the P-51. He made a low-level fighter approach down the runway, turned, but went out about five miles to come back in a straight-in approach.

Booth got the wheels down – three green lights showed on the instrument panel. He gave the fighter twenty degrees of flap, and, to his surprise, made an excellent landing. He taxied over to his audience, gunning the engine a few times to show his prowess.

Booth unstrapped and stepped out of the P-51. He was happy still to be alive.

Colonel Hogg had a rare smile on his austere face. 'You idiot hot-dog show-off!' he said.

'Jim, that's the closest I've come to being killed in this whole damn war,' Booth retorted, a bit annoyed at the Colonel's jibe.

Two British soldiers were standing nearby. They wanted to know who might help them put up their tents up again, and repair the damage to their tipped-over tea table. These items had been blown down by the buzzing P-51. Booth made them happier with the present of a couple of bottles of French booze.

A day or so later the gas-hauling operation was completed. Our bombers all came back home to resume combat operations.

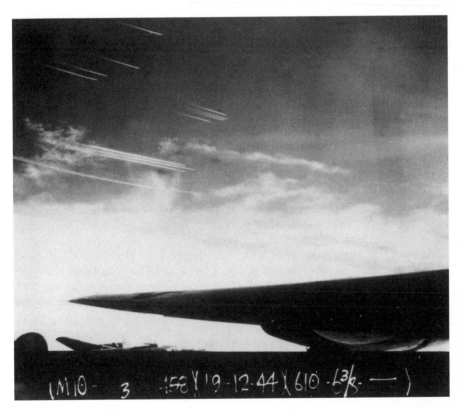

B-17 Formation overhead.

CHAPTER 14

OIL REFINERIES AND CANAL TRAFFIC

Otto von Bismarck, the Prussian Chancellor responsible for building a united Germany from the post-Napoleonic remnants of the Holy Roman Empire, was also the person who visualised the Kiel Canal. Construction began on the Canal in the reign of Wilhelm I, first of the Hohenzollern kings of Brandenburg-Prussia also to be Emperor of all Germany. The canal is officially named 'The Kaiser Wilhelm Canal'.

The Kiel Canal cuts across the isthmus of Jutland to the south of Denmark. It connects the North Sea at the Elbe estuary to the Baltic at the Bay of Kiel.

This Canal, some sixty-one miles long, was widened in 1905 to take bigger ships. It gave the Germans an inland passage between the naval bases at Kiel and at Wilhelmshaven, saving a dangerous voyage around the northern tip of Jutland through the straits of Kattegat and Skagerrak. The Canal was of considerable use to Germany in both World Wars.

During World War II Germany had continual need for petroleum supply. Nazi occupation of the Balkan oil fields helped fill this need, but there were still shortages. To keep their war machine well fuelled and oiled, the Germans built numerous synthetic oil refineries. These made oil and liquid fuels from the ample German supply of coal.

Among the German synthetic oil plants was the one built near Brünsbuttelkoog at the west end of the Kiel canal. The 96th Wing was sent out one late summer day in 1944 to take this oil plant out of production. Bob Hayzlett's crew was chosen to lead the 458th Bomb Group that day and the 458th was first out in the Wing combat line.

We took off early in the morning and assembled over Splasher Five at Cromer, as usual. As the Wing peeled off to join the Second Division penetration line, our assembly ship, First Sergeant, went back to Horsham St Faith.

We went out of Cromer north-east across the North Sea. This trip was about as long an overwater haul as we were to make on our various routes out of England to attack Germany

Our flight across the sea was uneventful. There were scattered clouds below, but as we flew north of the Frisian Islands, the air below cleared and we were in bright sunshine with excellent visibility all the way to the water surface below.

We crossed the coast of Denmark at Esbjerg, just north of the island of Fano. Jutland looked as flat as a billiard table, and as green. Below us were the farms and fields of this small, peaceful country. It was the place where my paternal ancestors had lived before moving into the Holy Roman Empire to become public administrators. I knew from my visits to the Castle Museum in Norwich that Denmark had not always been peaceful. There were on display numerous historic relics of the many raids and invasions of the fierce pagan Danes into East Anglia. The part of England where we were stationed had been part of the Danelaw for many, many years. A Danish king of Viking days, Sven Forkbeard, had captured most of England. His son, Knut the Mighty, had completed the job to become the first of the long-ago Danish kings of England.

But things were different now. Denmark, no longer a great military power and unable to raise any effective defence, had been overrun in a few days by Hitler's troops. However, the Danes had not given up. When Hitler decreed that all Jews in Denmark must wear yellow armbands, King Christian X appeared on the streets of Copenhagen, proudly wearing a yellow armband. His action was exemplary of the determined non-co-operation of the Danes with their German captors. Below us were proud and defiant people. The Danish underground was as active as any in Europe, and many Danish patriots were put to death by the Nazis for their part in it.

From Jutland we flew east across the Danish islands of the Baltic. Over Odense we began a sweeping turn to head south-west over the island of Langeland and the Bay of Kiel. We crossed the German coast at Eckernforde, north of the city of Kiel. Out of the right nose blister window I could see below, stretching across the isthmus of Jutland, the outline of the Danewerke, that great earthen fortification that the Danes had built in olden times to keep out the Saxons and the Wends who were apt to invade Jutland from the south.

Our bomb run took us parallel to the Kiel canal. Eddie Gniewkowski was over the Norden bombsight, concentrating, correcting, steering the Group formation as he made minor adjustments in his sighting. Flak bursts broke out, flashing amidst the bombers of our formation, as the German defence batteries below us opened fire, trying to shoot us out of their national airspace. Our escort fighters moved up a little higher, avoiding the flak, but still protecting us adequately.

At the bombsight-computed time the racks opened and our bombs went down. They were dropped at a close intervalometer setting so that the concentration on target would be tight. All the ships in the Group dropped sharply on Gniewkowski's smoke flares. The falling bombs made a compact clump, dropping down below us.

I watched the target closely, looking out of the nose blister windows. The bombs seemed to burst all at once; the great explosions below were all in the refinery area. Gniewkowski had made a flawless drop. In the synthetic petroleum plant below, great fires erupted. Huge billows of black smoke belched upward from the stricken refinery.

The 466th Group, behind us, dropped into the smoke cloud originated by our attack. By the time the 467th Group, third in the Wing attack line, was over the target, the smoke had risen to our flight altitude. A monstrous fire was blazing at the bottom of the vast smoke column. We had put the German oil refinery out of business.

Flak fire along our canal route had been continuous and heavy, though relatively inaccurate. I didn't see much of the flak from the tiny window at my backward-facing desk, though I did hear it when the shell explosions were close enough. By now the waist section of every B-24 was fitted with dump chutes into which the gunners could stuff chaff at will to be dropped overboard. The falling clouds of metal foil served to confuse the German radar by generating false images, making it hard for the flak gunners below to locate the bomber formations. Of course, if the weather were clear, chaff was of no use, since optical sighting was far more accurate than radar.

This day the visibility over the target was unlimited. We could see a hundred miles in every direction. So too, of course, could the German flak gunners on the ground.

Nonetheless, when we were well out over the North Sea, off the Frisian Islands and on our way home, I heard our waist gunners talking to each other on the intercom:

'Are youse trunnin' out chaff?' Dom Giordano asked.

'Yeah,' Stahl replied, 'Are you?'

At least the action of decorating the North sea with shiny foil gave the waist gunners something to do on a long, boring trip back to Horsham St Faith.

My office as Group Navigation Officer was upstairs in the operations building at our air-base at Horsham St Faith. It was a room I shared with Major Fred Vacek, the Group Bombing Officer. Living in the same office with Vacek was interesting.

Fred Vacek was out of Chicago. He was an American of Polish ancestry, a fact for which Eddie Gniewkowski admired him. Vacek could not be described as handsome – he was not exactly ugly, but Chuck Booth, our ever-smiling Assistant Operations Officer, invariably referred to Fred as 'Boot-Nose Vacek'.

But, good looks aside, Vacek was a superb bombardier and an excellent administrator. He had the respect and confidence of Colonel Isbell, which he surely had earned. Vacek had a quiet and often subtle wit. Hardly anyone – at least anyone that Vacek outranked – ever came into our little office without Vacek remarking politely, 'Kindly shut the fucking door.'

Fred Vacek roomed at the big club for a time with an officer whose name I have forgotten. This officer was, according to Vacek, a self-appointed great lover who would, on occasions when Fred was not expected back at his quarters, bring his girlfriend in for a roll in the sack. Willing to go along with a good gag, I made a phone call to the officer, at Vacek's urging. The call went something like this:

'Major, Sir, this is Sergeant Dorkmann at base facilities.'

'Yes, Sergeant, what can I do for you?'

'I'm afraid it's somewhat bad news, Sir.'

'What the hell is it?'

'Your facilities request has been disapproved, Sir.'

'What the hell request is that? I don't remember any damn request.'

Taken on the day that Major Frederick Vacek completed his tour of missions, this photo shows from left to right, Major William Routon, the Author, Major Vacek, Major Charles Booth and Major John Davis.

'It's your request to have a douche bowl installed in your living facilities, Sir.'

'Goddam it! Who the hell is this anyway? That son-of-a-bitch, Vacek, put you up to this, didn't he! I'll have his ass . . .!'

At this point I hung up the phone. Vacek was doubled up with hysteria listening at the other extension.

By October 1944 the 458th had acquired a relatively large number of radar-equipped lead ships. No longer did we have to borrow these aeroplanes from the 466th Group. Bert Kemp flew every mission as our radar operator and Frank Shepard had earned a permanent seat in the nose turret.

We soon got a mission on which to see if navigation radar worked. There was widespread distrust of our airborne radar navigation sets among air-crews and our formations typically flew with a visual lead ship as group deputy, just in case. Actually, none of the navigation equipment of Eighth Air Force was worth a public celebration. But radar and gee navigation, both British inventions, were a hell of a lot better than nothing.

On 26 October 1944, our crew was picked as group lead. We were to attack the aqueduct at Minden, Germany. There, in a concrete bridge-like structure, the waters of the Ems–Weser Canal met those of the Elbe Canal above the Weser River, whose waters flowed beneath the aqueduct. At this time in the war, the rail transport of Germany was in bad shape, having been royally pounded by the U.S. Eighth, Ninth, and Fifteenth Army Air Forces, so the canals which met at the aqueduct were of essential military importance to the Nazis. Through them, via the junction with the Dortmunder Canal, traffic flowed in and out of the Ruhr Valley, centre of Germany's industrial might.

We took off and assembled as usual over Cromer. We climbed east over the North Sea towards the Dutch coast. When we made landfall above Noordwijk aan Zee, Bert Kemp was the only one who could see the land below. The cloud cover was ten-tenths with the top of the murk almost up to our cruising altitude, but we pressed on, carrying out our assigned mission. We turned over our initial point above the airfield at Quackenbrück, and I gave Hayzlett the heading for Minden. He turned on the bomb run, and put the ship on autopilot. Kemp kept calling out the ranges to Gniewkowski who was over his Norden in the nose, cranking in corrections, cursing and muttering because he could see nothing but clouds below him.

We must have made fifteen or twenty rechecks of all our navigation data on that bomb run. Shepard kept reporting that he could see only clouds from the nose turret, he could give us no input to verify my dead reckoning, or Kemp's radar fixes.

At the computed time the bomb sight ran its course and triggered out our flares and bombs. The rest of the ships in the 458th formation dropped on our flares. We made a slow and sweeping right turn and headed home.

Gniewkowski came up on the flight deck as we let down over the North Sea. He took off his oxygen mask.

'Hell!' he said, 'We probably hit some bean patch.'

Later that afternoon a P-38 photo ship, piloted by one of those brave loners who worked in recon, went down on the deck and took pictures of Minden. We got the word later – the aqueduct at Minden had been destroyed – broken in two by our bombs. We were both ecstatic and astounded. Next day the overseas edition of the *New York Times* carried big headlines:

'FLYING FORTS BREAK KEY GERMAN AQUEDUCT.'

Once again the publicity experts of the Boeing Company had snowed the gentlemen of the press. The performance of our ugly B-24s was ignored.

Fred Vacek shared our happiness with the results of the mission to Minden. The following day he commented to me as we sat in our joint office:

'Maybe the damn Mickey radar sets are worth something after all,' he said. 'But the fuckin' newspaper idiots are no damn good. They sit on their ass in the London bars. They think every bomber is a B-17'.

CHAPTER 15

A CASE OF MURDER

The club of the 458th Bomb Group at Horsham St Faith maintained a well stocked bar. The bar was well stocked due to the efforts of Captain Samuel M. Lakin, the Group Supply Officer.

Sam could find anything that existed in the world, and trade anybody for anything; he'd have been the best horse trader in the cavalry if the Army still used horses.

With a war proceeding in Great Britain, the export sales of Scotch Whisky were not very brisk. Sam Lakin would make trips to Scotland, put in an acceptable offer for a quantity of top-drawer Highland booze, and consummate the deal with funds from the officers' club. He did a superb job.

One of Sam Lakin's good friends was Lieutenant-Colonel Frederick O'Neill. Shortly after the AZON effort was shut down, O'Neill had been relieved as Commanding Officer of the 753rd Bomb Squadron and moved up to a new job as Group Operations Officer. At Group he replaced Light Colonel Bruno Feiling who, having flown a lot of missions as Group Command Pilot, completed his tour of duty and went home. In his new Operations job, O'Neill became my immediate boss.

Captain Irving Goldman and I, apparently not having enough else to do, thought up the idea of a training facility for navigation: our motivation for this was the short supply of new navigators. I had the idea that if a G.I. gunner, engineer, or radio operator could be taught the rudiments of dead reckoning and use of the British gee system, he would be able to get his crew home if they got lost from formation. The scheme was no more grandiose than that.

I got an enthusiastic approval from Colonel O'Neill, so Goldman and I appropriated a room, built up the equipment, and went to work. I set aside the services of a highly-competent wing navigator as full-time instructor (when he wasn't on a mission).

Shortly afterwards Sam Lakin came home with a receipt for a half-warehouse full of booze up in Scotland. Colonel O'Neill assigned himself to fly the booze run, a job which he greatly enjoyed. He ordered cargo racks to be installed in a B-24, grabbed a co-pilot from somewhere, and started looking for a navigator who could find a whisky distillery in Scotland.

All the navigators were out on a mission, or downtown, or someplace. I was over at the air-base at Hethel, looking at some new and experimental navigation equipment, so Colonel O'Neill descended upon the new navigation 'training' facility, and appropriated some poor G.I. who was standing around. He ordered this luckless individual to go with him to Scotland and

Captain Irving Goldman.

what is a sergeant to do when ordered by a Lieutenant-Colonel? The man went.

They got to Scotland and loaded the booze without mishap, but on the way home the weather turned bad, and darkness was falling. O'Neill, the load of Scotch, and the poor G.I. 'navigator' were lost somewhere out over the North Sea. There were mixed feelings at Horsham St Faith, with some praying that the booze would be saved and O'Neill lost. But after considerable frantic yelling on the horn, O'Neill had the control tower talk him safely home with the whisky, and all was well.

All was well, that is, except for O'Neill's professional chewing on me for having tried to send him to his death with an incompetent 'navigator'. I did not respond to this tirade, but offered no excuse. I felt the attack unprovoked, however. I didn't send him off to Scotland with some novice, and I didn't drink the club's booze.

There were other attractions at the club besides the booze which Sam Lakin procured. There was typically a crowd around First Lieutenant Max Sokarl, listening to the mad and wonderful tales he told. There being no particular regular work for Max, he performed a number of simultaneous and inconsequential jobs. These were such simple jobs for him, that he arranged to have a cot in his office, and his sergeant had orders that, when

Lt-Colonel Frederick
O'Neill, Operations Officer,
458th Bomb Group
(Photographed when a
Major).

Max was sacked out on his cot, he was not in. From this grew the practice of referring people sequentially from the supply office to the grave registration office to the recreation office, etc., ad infinitum.

Major Pierce Manley, the Group Adjutant, had developed the practice of giving Sokarl the administrative responsibility for every weird and strange problem that came along. An example of such was the claim for the dead horse:

A Norwich farmer came to Horsham St Faith, insisting that he had been leading his horse across a bridge over the river when he and his animal were buzzed by an exceedingly low flying bomber. The horse, badly frightened, leaped the bridge parapet into the river, and was drowned. The farmer believed that the buzzing bomber was probably American, since the British flew at night; the aircraft looked like it had a red tail with some kind of stripe; and, besides, the air-base at Horsham St Faith was nearby. He wished to be rewarded with sixty pounds sterling for the loss of his animal.

This was manifestly a case for Max Sokarl. He wrote down the answers to endless queries on his clipboard, wishing to find out such things as the name and age of the horse, the colour of its tail, the height of the bridge parapets in millimetres, and the names of the farmer's wife and children, for example.

In return, Sokarl gave the farmer interminable and content-free investigative reports, but no money.

Among the people who had occasion for making frequent calls to, and requests of, Max Sokarl was Lieutenant Al Albert, Assistant Group Adjutant. He would call repeatedly on some assignment Manley had cooked up. With each call, Sokarl being sacked out on his cot, Albert would get the reply that Max was 'out' and he should call the graves registration office.

One day Albert called and said, 'This is Colonel Frebus! You tell that son-of-a-bitch to get his ass up here to Headquarters right away!' Sokarl appeared in Manley's office about ten seconds later, standing at attention. He and Albert negotiated an agreement about being in for future calls concerning the Group Adjutant's business.

One such call resulted from the visit of two British ladies to the air-base. Manley referred their complaint to Sokarl. They were mother and daughter and both were obviously pregnant. The other parent in each case was, they alleged, a sergeant named 'Billy' – no last name specified. But they were not unhappy about Billy's expertise in the bed – their complaint was that he had stolen their bicycles, and they had not seen him since.

Sokarl offered the opinion that such despicable action was bad for international relations, and proceeded to issue voluminous reports about the unsuccessful search for the stolen bicycles.

Al Albert had talents other than those of Assistant Group Adjutant and Sokarl-motivator, he was also a great pianist. His keyboard recitals at the club were popular, as allegedly were the ones off-base at various pubs. He had gifts too as a lyricist. To the tune of 'After the Ball is Over' he wrote and frequently performed at the club the unofficial Flight Song of the 458th Bomb Group:

> *'After the mission's over,*
> *After we all get back,*
> *We get interrogated:*
> *Where did you see that flak?*
> *How were the German fighters?*
> *What time were bombs away?*
> *Do you have any bitches?*
> *That's all for today!'*

An event that was to make life much more exciting for Max Sokarl occurred on 3 December 1944. At the south-eastern corner of the perimeter of the air-base at Attlebridge was an impressive British manor-house known as Honingham Hall. This place was the residence of Sir Eric Teichman who was a former Counsellor at the British Embassy in Chunking, China, and an expert in Chinese culture and language. Upon his retirement from diplomatic service he had purchased Honingham Hall and during the London blitz he and Lady Teichman took as their temporary wards all the children of a London orphanage.

Sir Eric had invited officers of the 466th Bomb Group at Attlebridge to join him from time to time in the pheasant shoots he held on his estate. He was a gracious host, and welcomed his friends most warmly.

On 3 December 1944, Privates Leonard S. Wojtacha and George E. Smith of the 466th took their G.I. carbines and went on an impromptu hunting trip into the woods of the Honingham Hall estate. This they did in spite of the fact that it was against regulations to go into the wood, or hunt, or even to carry firearms off the base.

Sir Eric Teichman heard the noise of their guns in the woods and went to see what was happening. When he accosted them, Private Smith, shooting from the hip, felled Sir Eric with a single shot, killing him instantly.

It was the next day before a sorrowful Lady Teichman found Sir Eric's body in the woods where the two G.I.s had left it.

The incident was investigated by a joint team of U.S. Army C.I.D (Criminal Investigation Division) men and officers from Scotland Yard and by 6 December they had pretty well identified Wojtacha and Smith. They confronted Wojtacha who spilled his guts, fingering Smith as the actual murderer. When Smith was confronted, he confessed immediately.

Smith was locked in the military slammer and a general court martial was scheduled for him on the charge of murder.

It was, of course, necessary to find a competent defence counsel for Private George E. Smith. Apparently the Adjutant of the 466th Bomb Group spoke of his need to Major Pierce Manley, old regular Army expert of the 458th. Manley recommended that great criminal attorney, First Lieutenant Max M. Sokarl.

Sokarl got the job of defending Smith. While he found that the task had certain distasteful aspects, he came back to the club at Horsham St Faith each evening to recount the case's progress to us, members of his fan club, in the most glowing terms.

While he may have wished not to admit it too openly, Sokarl always sought the input of Irving Goldman when he was on one of these cases. He respected Goldman as a deep thinker and an accomplished attorney. Sokarl had once been called upon to defend an American G.I. in a court martial in which the enlisted man was accused of rape for having impregnated an English girl of minor years. The liaison was apparently friendly, but statutory.

Goldman expressed his philosophy about winning in one of our bull sessions at the club: 'If the law is against you, argue the facts. If the facts are against you, argue the law.' It was Goldman's view that, in this rape case, Sokarl had both the facts and the law against him. So Goldman thought up for Sokarl the unique defence that there would have been no crime under British law, and we were guests in England. Therefore, if the girl wished to shack up with whomever, there was actually no cause for trial. Sokarl went into court with this defence and won an acquittal, prompting all kinds of outraged letters from higher command of the Judge Advocate General's Department about whose law was being enforced, anyway.

Alleged murderer Private Smith proved to be a rather unusual person. His buddies of the 466th described how he kept pets in his quarters in order to have animals available for torture and abuse. His Army personnel record was a continual litany of desertion, AWOL, and drunkenness. Smith was one of a family of ten children, and he liked to brag that he gave his parents more trouble than had his five brothers and four sisters combined.

While he was in custody, Smith wrote various essays under titles such as

'My life in the U.S. Army,' 'What I Think of the Man I Shot,' and 'What I think About my Lawyer.'

Sokarl took Smith into court where he pleaded 'not guilty.' Sokarl argued insanity on behalf of Smith, showing that he had served eighteen months in a Pennsylvania reformatory for grand theft auto, and had been accused in eight previous courts martial in his two and a half years in the Army. According to the testimony at Smith's trial, he had been sent to overseas duty as punishment for continual bad conduct – rather an insult to those people who had become Air Corps through an inflated sense of patriotic glory. Sokarl had Private Smith disrobe for the court to show that his body was covered with strange, obscene, and odd tattoos.

The decision of the court martial was unanimous: 'Guilty!' The penalty: 'Death.'

Major-General William Kepner reviewed the case for Second Air Division, seeking the counsel of his officers of the Judge Advocate General's Department. They concurred that the trial had been fair and the defence expert. The sentence of the court stood.

Lady Teichman, in an illustration of charity worthy of St Paul's description, wrote to General Eisenhower, begging him to spare the life of Private George E. Smith, but General Eisenhower declined to act. She then wrote to United States Ambassador Winant, pleading with him. She indicated that things were bad enough as they were, and her husband would not have wanted Smith's blood on his hands when so many were dying already in a great and terrible war.

But there was no action from the United States Government and on 8 May 1944, a Tuesday, Private George E. Smith was hanged by the neck until dead at the U.S. Army Disciplinary Training Center. With him when he died, at his personal request, and possibly his only 'friend' on earth, was First Lieutenant Max M. Sokarl.

On the death, some years later, of Lady Teichman from natural causes, Honingham Hall was willed to the permanent use of the London orphans who had lived with the Teichmans during the war.

Around the bar at Horsham St Faith, Sokarl had his stories to tell.

'I figure it was a victory,' he said, 'that I got the son-of-a-bitch hung instead of shot.'

CHAPTER 16

CHRISTMAS EVE 1944

In November of 1944 freezing weather came to East Anglia. Our countryside, which was typically green and with ample fog and rain, now enjoyed clear days and crystal nights in which the earth's heat radiated rapidly off into outer space. Each morning found our airbase and the surrounding countryside white with frost. When washboard clouds blew over, we got showers of snow instead of the usual gentle rain from heaven.

For several weeks I had a cold with continual sniffles and a sore throat that got steadily worse. I worked late one night in my navigation office, feeling terrible. As I was about to quit and go to bed, I realised that I was weak, shaking, and burning up with fever. I walked, shivering all the way, to the base hospital and checked myself in. The flight surgeons diagnosed my problem as strep throat – bad news.

I lay in the hospital for over a week while the flight surgeons pumped me full of penicillin and eventually I began to feel better.

In the adjoining hospital bed was Charlie Giesen, a pilot of the 752nd squadron. Charlie was from Ida, Louisiana, a little town way up north of Shreveport near the Arkansas border.

Charlie Giesen might have been the type specimen of all those American young men who volunteered to be aviation cadets and to take pilot training for the glamour of it and the shine of the silver wings on the left front uniform pocket.

Giesen suffered with nervous stomach, and the reason for the state of his stomach was not hard to discover. He kept telling me of his need to get off combat operations.

'They're gonna shoot me down.' Giesen said, 'They're gonna get me.'

'Forget it,' I said, tired of his depressing complaints, 'Anybody who can survive five missions is indestructible.'

Giesen was in about the middle of his tour of missions. He should have been looking forward to finishing and going home.

'They're gonna get me,' Giesen said, 'it's bad out there!'

'I know how bad it is, dammit. I work for the same outfit you do, remember? But look at our losses. The Germans have had it. They can't put up a good fighter attack any more. And their flak never hits anyone except by accident.'

'They're gonna get me. . . They're gonna shoot me down.'

'If you keep up that attitude they will get you. I hope they shoot you down if it'll make you shut up for five minutes. How about some peace and quiet in here?'

'They're gonna get me. They got a flak shell out there with my number on it.'

Nothing I said could make Giesen shut up, or feel better about his antici-pated fate. So it went, hour after boring hour, listening to Giesen's worries, trying to kid him into a better attitude. Finally Charlie Giesen was released from the hospital, sent back to active duty, and I got time for quiet naps and magazine reading. A few days later I was released, feeling much better. My crew had flown several missions while I was on the sick list.

It seemed to me, as a non-qualified observer whose opinion was of no consequence, that the Allied High Command was stuck on dead centre. Nothing much had happened on the ground for months.

'Blood-and-Guts' Patton was not sent forth on another of his spectacular poundings through German-held territory. Except for our continual bombing in bad weather, it looked like the Allies sat around fat, dumb, and happy.

In mid-December the Germans ended the lethargy. Field Marshal Gerd von Rundstedt commanded the massive German counter-attack that drove rapidly through the Ardennes Forest into Belgium, blasting a great bulge in the battle lines and threatening to split the Allied forces and reach the sea.

The German weathermen did their work well. Probably we should have tried to hire some of them. The start of the Battle of the Bulge marked the beginning of seven days of fog and foul weather that kept us on our bases in England.

For each of the seven days I was rousted from the sack around three a.m. to go to target briefing, then to breakfast, then to general briefing, then to suit up, ride to the flight line, and wait. We waited each day till about eleven a.m., then scrubbed the mission for weather. The pressure was awful. It was bad enough to go forth and fly a mission, but to be alerted every day and then scrubbed and stood down was a terrible mental strain. I began to have bad dreams each night.

Finally, on the eighth day, 24 December, 1944, the sun came up bright and clear out of the North Sea. Some fifty or more Liberators, five combat squadron boxes of the 458th lined up behind the Group assembly ship. This would be the biggest mission we had ever flown. Any B-24 that could haul potatoes was out on the flight line that morning.

We were in group lead position with a mickey ship. Bob Hayzlett rode first pilot's chair, and Major Don Jamison, commanding 755th Squadron, flying as Group leader, had the co-pilot's seat. We took off, climbing out on our assigned dog-leg, hauling loads of general purpose bombs up into the morning sky. We flew out to Cromer, there to circle Splasher Five radio beacon. The rest of the group came up behind us to the wing assembly area.

The whole sky above the north coast of East Anglia was filled with Liberators. They fell gradually into place behind their respective assembly ships. The 96th Bomb Wing wound into its wide circle around Splasher Five, the three assembly ships of the 458th, the 466th and the 467th flashing their scintillating identity lights and punctuating the morning sky with Very-pistol flares. Our red-tailed neighbours from Attlebridge and Rackheath formed with us in the great aerial ballet that went round and round the Splasher. The thunderous noise of the wing assembly woke the whole town of Cromer, and shook the bells in the tower of the old Church of St Peter and St Paul, far below.

At the appointed time the 96th Wing swung out into place in the Bomber Attack Stream of Second Air Division. The Third Air Division of B-17s went first over Europe that day. They were followed by the First Division, also equipped with Fortresses and we came last with our slab-sided boxcars.

Visibility was monumental after a week of murky weather; we could see many miles in every direction. As we climbed out over the North Sea I vacated my seat behind Hayzlett, and my little window with the clear view of the left inboard engine. I went down the hatch, forward through the tunnel, and stood up in the nose astrodome, from where I could see fore and aft, through the whole sky. The Third Division was crossing the Belgian coast, the First Division was over the Channel, while the tail end of the Second Division followed far behind us, still cranking upward out of the English countryside.

From East to West, horizon to horizon, the sky was filled with the bomber attack stream of Eighth Air Force. This was the biggest aerial mission ever launched in World War II, or in any war . . . two thousand and thirty-four heavy bombers.

I looked long at this monumental parade of destructive power, knowing somehow that earth would not see its like again. Then I went back to my navigation desk on the flight deck. There I could tend to my books and avoid looking out of the window in case there was any mayhem.

As we crossed the Belgian coast we were joined by the red nosed P-51s of The Fourth Fighter Group. They wrapped around our Bomb Wing like a sock around a foot, parading their defensive patterns above us and to the sides, stitching the high sky with their cross-weaving. I strained to see if I could identify the ship of Bill Eaton, my hometown friend, but my window was too small, and I could not be sure of the number on any P-51.

Bob Hayzlett had consumed one too many cups of coffee at breakfast. He unstrapped himself from his steel coffin seat and went by my desk with his mask plugged into an oxygen bottle. He climbed down to the bomb bay catwalk, to follow the standard procedure for non-use of the relief tube. Our briefed route called for us to make a turn at the Belgian coast, but Hayzlett was not in his seat. I called to Major Jamison on intercom – no answer; he was plugged into the command channel. I wrote out a note with the new heading on it, got up and handed the note to Jamison – no response.

By the time Bob Hayzlett came up from the bomb bay we were headed south-east while the rest of the Eighth Air Force headed east. There wasn't much I could do about it, believing that I was not empowered to give orders to a command pilot major about how to do his job. But Hayzlett came back to his seat very unhappy. He turned our formation back into the attack stream of bombers, and muttered a few unseemly remarks into his oxygen mask.

Our target was a small road junction and railroad siding in the forest, a place in western Germany called Schönecken ('Beautiful Corner' in German), near where the borders of Belgium, Germany and Luxembourg meet. Schönecken was reported to be full of German tanks and supplies. It was an unexciting target, and a difficult one to identify. But Bert Kemp at the H2X radar, our precious mickey set, took ranges and bearings from Dutch and Belgian cities, fixing our position, even over open or wooded country. Frank Shepard, riding nose turret, provided visual fixes from the ground below. This day he was confused by the nondescript pattern of the Ardennes below, buried in a heavy fall of fresh snow.

But the radar kept us on course, and I had no misgivings about target identification. Eddie Gniewkowski could spot a mosquito on a rose-bush below us. He never had a problem with target identification. My seat, with its clear view of the left inboard engine, was not an exciting place to ride for enjoyment of the scenery, but I didn't care. Keeping my head in the books was often less disturbing than watching the flak and the mayhem.

When we crossed the initial point and opened the bomb bay doors the story was different. I had the hatch doors open. From my seat at my navigation desk I had a vast, panoramic view, through the bomb bay, of the ground below us, spread out like a great map. It was the best spectator seat on the bomber for the duration of the bomb run.

The Ardennes Forest was filled with snow. Here and there were roads and intersections and an occasional small village, but mostly there were trees and snow. It was from this forest that the Belgae came to launch their massive attacks against the Roman army of Julius Caesar. Now in this same forest von Rundstedt hurled mighty forces against the retreating Allied armies.

My job on the bomb run was primarily that of recording position and logging the time of bomb drop, Gniewkowski flew the ship automatically via his electronic link to the autopilot. Hayzlett and Jamison sat, hands off controls, and watched the show.

While I looked down through the bomb bay, I saw blunt-nosed fighters below us. Thinking they might be Focke-Wulfs, I took out my binoculars and looked down carefully. They were Republic P-47s, 'Fat Friends', on a strafing attack far below.

As I put the binoculars back in their case, the whole visible space below the bomb bay was filled with a huge explosion. A flak shell had burst some fifty feet under the bomb bay catwalk, so I dived into my flak vest and helmet. Our Radio Operator, Sergeant Weldon Sheltraw, told me later that I set an all-time speed record for this manoeuvre.

The woods below us were filled with German *panzer* units. The German tanks were built so their guns could elevate to ninety degrees, making them usable for anti-aircraft fire, and those tank crewmen could shoot. They put up some of the most accurate flak rounds I have ever flown through. They aimed for the lead ship, knowing that to bring us down would do maximum damage to the attacking formation.

Their first shell went off square under our catwalk – if there had been a slight change in fusing, we'd all have been blown to bits. That shell was followed by more, almost as accurate.

Information set forth at our briefing that morning had told us that we would fly on our bomb run over a battery of four flak guns. With the *panzers* below us, it looked more like we were over four thousand flak guns.

Major Maurice Speer in front of Catton Hall on Church Street in Horsham St Faith.

A flak shot hit the gee-H ship flying deputy lead off to our right. This was Jack Roberts' ship with Major Maurice Speer riding command chair. The number one engine and the VHF transmitter were both creamed by the flak burst. The engine ran away, madly overspeeding, then froze up with the propeller refusing to feather. The big bomber rolled far left and began a sweeping turn through the front of the group formation.

Hayzlett, looking out of our right cockpit window, saw Roberts's ship, vast wings vertical in the sky, hauling buns straight towards us. He yelled at Jamison, 'Cut the autopilot!'

Major Jamison, staring at Hayzlett in disbelief, had not seen the deputy lead bomber roaring towards us on a certain collision course.

'We're on the bomb run!' Jamison said, knowing that to turn off autopilot would disconnect bombsight control and ruin Gniewkowski's sighting.

Bob Hayzlett grabbed the control wheel with both hands and with his back hard against the pilot's seat he shoved forward with all his might. Our bomber nosed down suddenly as Hayzlett overcame the autopilot.

The left wingtip of Jack Roberts's ship cleared us by some ten feet.

Hayzlett had saved our collective ass.

'What the hell happened?' Gniewkowski asked, growling on the horn.

Major Donald C. Jamison,
Commanding Officer, 755th
Bomb Squadron.

As Roberts's bomber swung down to the left and away from the formation, he ordered the bombs dropped, his smoke pots went out with the bombs. About half the people in the 458th Bomb Group formation toggled off with him, dropping bombs all over the woods below.

Roberts cranked in full rudder trim, but still the bomber would not fly straight with the unfeathered prop dragging at it. Roberts and Speer both got on the foot controls, shoving at the rudder, and cranking full right on the control wheel to pick up the sinking left wing.

Roberts made a complete 180 and headed for home. About half the 458th Bomb Group turned off the bomb run and went home, trying to follow Roberts. This was a terrible operational no-no, but these people were possibly to be forgiven in the midst of a gunnery demonstration like this one. Maybe they honestly thought Roberts was flying the Group lead ship. The smoke from the flak bursts was thick enough to obscure visibility. It looked like the whole German Army was shooting at us.

Speer and Roberts could not hold altitude with their ship dragging so badly, but they made it across the Channel and back to Horsham St Faith, finding a bit better lift at lower altitudes.

Another flak shell went off right under our bomb bay catwalk. Instantly thereafter I saw a sharp spray of liquid hit the nose fuse propeller of the one-ton bomb in the right forward bomb bay, about six feet from my foot. Our gasoline transfer valves were in the bomb bay, directly ahead of the bomb noses. This liquid shower on the bomb was a gruesome sight and I considered leaving quickly by the nearest exit, but that would have been too selfish. So then I considered yelling for everyone to jump, but intercom silence on the bomb run was a crew rule we tried to follow. Besides, what the hell was there to say that was encouraging? Quite possibly we were to be blown into atoms as our gasoline supply went up in a single momentary great explosion. I watched in fearful fascination, seeing the liquid build up on the bomb casing in syrupy thickness. Then I saw its colour . . . bright red. It was hydraulic fluid.

Hydraulic fluid is relatively non-flammable. Maybe we were not doomed to disappear instantly in a blinding flash in the Belgian sky, but it was too soon to be sure. The highly accurate flak fire from the tanks below continued all through the bomb run.

As the bombs went away, our ship lightened suddenly. The other ships of lead squadron dropped with us. A moment later a flak shell went off directly under the lead ship of First Squadron, low element. This was the bomber directly behind and below us, heading the low-hanging triangle of the squadron formation box – it was Charlie Giesen's ship.

I saw Giesen nose down, and out of formation. There was no external sign of damage to his aeroplane . . . no fire, no feathering engines. And then,

The following bomber of the lower formation element as seen from the bomb bay. This is the view I had of Lt Giesen's bomber on 24 December 1944 prior to its demise.

suddenly, the whole tail section of Giesen's aeroplane fell off, taking the tail gunner in his turret straight down into the trees below.

The fatally-stricken big Liberator eased lazily into a right turn. We could see the squadron letters, 7V, painted boldly on the left side of the fuselage. As Giesen's ship swung more and more to the right, the turn tightened until it was a downward spiral, a tight spin and with the tail section gone, Giesen had no control whatever. I could picture him in the cockpit, terrified, pulling with all his might to move elevators that were no longer there, stamping wildly on rudder pedals that did nothing.

I looked anxiously for hatches to open, for crewmen to leap out, for the bomb bay to spill forth escaping people. There was nothing – no sign of anyone baling out.

Ten, fifteen, twenty turns Giesen's ship went, down and down into the snow and the trees of the Ardennes Forest. I watched until it hit the ground, five miles down, and exploded in a vast ball of fire. Charlie Giesen had been shot down in a gruesome fulfilment of his own prediction.

As Giesen's aeroplane exploded, setting the forest on fire far below us, there was a quiet comment from the waist section.

'Oh, Jesus!' said Dominic Giordano, peering over his 50-calibre at the disaster below us. In my mind's eye I could see him crossing himself.

We held course and speed until the bomb explosions went off on the ground, hitting the road junction directly below us. It was always a great

The unlucky crew who were lost with Lt Charles Giesen, seen here third from left in the back row.

temptation to change course at bombs away, taking evasive action and getting the hell out of there. This was especially so after we had witnessed a frightful sight like Giesen's spectacular departure, but to change course would have been unprofessional. We needed our strike photos showing that we had creamed our target. Besides, when the scream of falling bombs became audible on the ground, anti-aircraft fire often became much less accurate.

We made a sweeping right turn to go back across Belgium towards England, and at that point I reported the hydraulic leak. The pilots checked the pressure. It was zero!

There was plenty of time on the way home to figure out how to try to land safely: we could crank the landing gear and flaps down without hydraulic pressure: we could retract the radar dome the same way. A hydraulic accumulator, equipped with check valves, was intended as a back-up system. It was supposed to give us enough pressure for one thorough brake application. Probably we could stop on our own runway at Horsham.

If we wanted to avoid the risk that the hydraulic accumulator might not work, we could go to Woodbridge, the British emergency field on the coast. Woodbridge had a runway five miles long – you could roll most anything to a stop on it.

But we knew that roast Christmas turkey awaited us at Horsham St Faith, and we really didn't want to spend the evening in a cold truck, riding home from Woodbridge.

At the English coast we turned the group lead over to the number three ship, and pulled out of formation to cruise alone and vote. Major Don Jamison, riding the command seat, refused to pull rank. He announced that his vote would count the same as the tail gunner's. We voted to go home.

The tricycle landing gear of the B-24 gave it minimal ground clearance. There was also a big metal skid on the tail so that if someone stupid removed all four engines at once, the bomber would, hopefully, get no structural damage as it tipped over backward. The pilots decided to come in short and tight on the runway, haul back on the controls, and drag the skid as long as possible before hitting the brakes.

Then we got another bright idea. We would leave the radar housing cranked down and drag it too. It would ruin the radar dish, but it would make a lot of extra drag.

The other ships of the 458th had all landed by the time we got into the traffic pattern over Horsham. We told the control tower about our problem. As we lined up with the runway, we could see rows of fire engines and ambulances parked on each side of it. This was not the comforting sight it was probably intended to be.

We hit the concrete about two feet from the near runway end, both pilots hauled back on their control wheels, and radar dome and dish ground away in a spectacular shower of sparks. When the radar was gone, the tail skid hit the runway with a screech that could be heard in Scotland. As we lost speed, and the nose wheel dropped to the runway surface and rolled, both pilots hit the brakes. They worked. I was nearly catapulted through the flight deck bulkhead. Our ship left skid marks of about two hundred feet, and it stopped safely in a monumental cloud of rubber smoke.

We got out and walked to the waiting crew jeeps and left our bomber on the runway. It was someone else's problem now.

As we ate our Christmas turkey late that evening, Lieutenant Spinner Barnes, the mickey set maintenance officer, came by to complain about the loss of his valuable radar equipment but he left gracefully when Major Jamison politely suggested that he shut up.

Our Christmas was not the merriest in memory. Charlie Giesen and his crew were gone. They joined the long list of over six thousand men killed in combat operations of Second Air Division. Giesen's crew was made up of ordinary airmen. They were not famous. Their spectacular deaths were not reported to the world, except as general statistics, and, possibly, more personally by their home-town newspapers. Somewhere in America there were sad Christmas-times in the homes of these men who died in a Belgian forest. Somewhere wives and mothers wept for those who would be home for Christmas no more. Children asked childish questions and grandparents answered with tearful eyes. There were empty places around the table, and empty hearts around the Christmas tree.

Events of this day in the Fourth Combat Wing, first over Europe, over-shadowed much of the other mission news of that Christmas Eve in the headlines of the American press. Heading the Third Division formation was Brigadier-General Frederick Castle, commanding Fourth Wing. Though our take-off weather was excellent, there was morning fog at some of the fighter bases, and escort fighters arrived late to support the Fourth Wing. Messerschmitt Me-109s hit the formation over Liège. Castle turned his B-17, on fire, out of the combat line, and baled out his crew. He refused to drop his bombs for fear of hitting Allied troops below.

Before Brigadier-General Castle could jump himself, a wing burned off the Fortress, and Fred Castle went down with his ship. He became the highest-ranking man in Eighth Air Force ever to win the Medal of Honor (posthumous), and the last. Castle Air Force Base – nowadays Castle Airport, a local airport with an air museum – was named for him.

The *Luftwaffe* shooting down a young and highly competent brigadier-general like Fred Castle was worthy of headlines. It was different with Giesen. No one but his friends, family, and his squadron clerk had ever heard of Charlie Giesen. Besides, Brigadier-General Castle was riding in a B-17, the War's only heavy bomber of any consequence to newsmen.

I felt bad that I had picked on Charlie Giesen in the hospital, and had complained because he voiced his fears of death in combat. We all had such fears. But some unknown power gave Charlie Giesen the ability to see into his own future, brief as it was to be on earth.

Giesen's terrifying fears had been well grounded.

CHAPTER 17

THE BUZZ BOMB

M ajor Fred Vacek, the Group Bombardier, needed an assistant. He
and I both concurred that Eddie Gniewkowski would be excellent
at the job, so Vacek asked Eddie, and he agreed. That meant that,
unless Eddie was flying the mission, he got up in the middle of the night every
mission day, and carried out the bombardier's briefings, both for lead crews
and for wing crews.

Like an idiot, I was doing my own navigation briefings. Gniewkowski
suggested that I appoint an Assistant Group Navigator so I could get more
sleep and rest, and be more alert to do the big load of daily paperwork that
the Group Navigator always had. He suggested that his good friend,
Lieutenant Theodore Zelasko, could do the job very well.

Teddy Zelasko had finished his tour of missions, but he had no particular
desire to go home at the time, so I made him my assistant. He did a great job
of handling the pre-dawn briefings, giving me some greatly-appreciated time
to sleep in once in a while.

Gniewkowski and Zelasko were both Americans of Polish parentage, and
I used to enjoy getting up prior to briefing and wandering into the joint office
that Vacek and I shared. There I would watch Eddie and Teddy preparing
their briefing materials. They conducted a little language lesson each
morning by reading off the route numbers to each other in Polish:

'*Osiem trzydiesci szesc! Dwanascie Piecdziesiat jeden! Cztery siedemdziesiat
dziewiec!* . . .' went the litany of the mission numbers.

I wondered if the Nazi high command knew they were plotted against daily
in the mother tongue of their vanquished victims.

In the early months of 1945, the War was obviously in its final phases. The
Luftwaffe had almost ceased to exist as a fighting force. It had been decimated by the overwhelming strength of our American fighter forces
organised by Major-General William E. Kepner. The Eighth Air Force
ranged the daylight skies of Europe at will, and without noticeable opposi-
tion. We flew every day when weather would permit, pounding the
transportation systems of Germany, and bombing those few strategic indus-
tries not yet reduced to oblivion.

But as the Germans lost their *Luftwaffe*, they struck back with other
weapons. The German V-1 weapon, known fondly as the buzz bomb, was
launched at London in impressive numbers.

The buzz bomb was a small pilotless aircraft. It had a rudimentary gyro-
scopic guidance system that directed it to its target area. The whole nose of

the buzz bomb consisted of one thousand pounds of high explosive, triggered by an impact fuse.

The buzz bomb was propelled by a pulse jet engine, mounted high on the tail assembly. Its usual target was a large urban area, such as London, and its accuracy was typically only good enough to make it useful against such a widespread target. When the bomb had flown out to its assigned distance, the engine cut off, the tail surface flipped to put the bomb into a steep dive, and it plunged into its target to explode on impact.

With its straight flight course, the buzz bomb was a simple target for British anti-aircraft fire and many of the bombs were brought down by British gunners. With a good dive to gain speed, the British defence fighters could overtake a buzz bomb.

Shooting them down could be exciting, since they often exploded when hit, but some particularly gutsy British pilots (of whom there were many) developed the technique of flying close alongside a buzz bomb, hooking a wing under its wing, and tipping it. This confused the gyros of the bomb's rudimentary guidance system, and it spun in and crashed, usually exploding harmlessly in some open space.

We had become familiar with the buzz bomb through many missions to bomb the weapon's launching sites on the French and Belgian coasts, and we were also familiar with it from trips to London on leave. When a buzz bomb got through the British defences, the air-raid sirens went off in London. However the British sat stolidly in their chairs, reading their newspapers as the voiced warning to take shelter resounded through the Regent Palace Hotel. Often we heard the staccato cough of a bomb's engine as it cruised across London. Then there was the sudden, awesome silence, followed by a loud explosion somewhere in the great city. On one of our trips to London, a buzz bomb struck near Liverpool Street Station about an hour before we caught our train back to Norwich. We observed the damage with minor interest as our taxicab drove by it, but buzz bombs in London were a long way from Norwich.

One morning as Gniewkowski and Zelasko completed their Polish language practice, having checked out their work, Major Fred Vacek came into the office. He told Eddie Gniewkowski that he had decided to take the lead crew briefing. Eddie and I both elected to attend the briefing. Though we were not scheduled to fly, we were wide awake anyway, and going downstairs to the briefing was less effort than going back to the sack to try to sleep some more.

Twelve combat aircrewmen were present, the lead and deputy lead navigators and bombardiers from each of the three squadrons of B-24s that the 458th would put up that day. Vacek and Zelasko sat at the table in the front of the room with Major Davis, the Group G-2 (Intelligence) Officer. In a chair up front, but at the side of the room sat Lieutenant-Colonel James Hogg, the Air Executive.

Hogg stood up. He raised the curtain from a huge map of western Europe at the front of the room.

'Well, men, it's Stuttgart today,' Hogg said. There was quiet muttering from the aircrewmen. 'Oh, shit!' someone said, an obligatory remark often heard at any target briefing.

Stuttgart was not an extra-deep penetration. It was not far behind the friendly lines at the Rhine and was not overly defended by flak guns. German fighter attack was probably a very remote possibility. All in all, Stuttgart should be more or less of a milk run.

'I'll be going out with you today, men,' Hogg said, as though that offered extra assurance of safety.

We looked at the long, red tape on the map that marked the penetration route. It went south over the Thames at Southend-on-Sea, out to the channel coast at Dungeness, over the French Coast near Berck-sur-Mer, south of the Belgian border to cross the Rhine near Strasbourg, to an initial point at the small German town of Ebingen, then north on a bomb run to Stuttgart, followed by a right turn off target towards Ulm. The route rejoined its inbound flight pattern near Strasbourg to return homeward along the same path taken going in.

Colonel Hogg went over the details of the mission. The First Air Division B-17 aircraft would lead the Eighth over Europe this day, followed by the Third Division bomb groups, also Fortress-equipped. The B-24 Liberators of Second Air Division would bring up the rear of the parade. Division fighter escort was defined; the little friends were to meet the bomber stream off the coast at Dungeness, staying with the big ships till they left the coast of Europe on return.

Lieutenant Zelasko took over as Hogg went back to his chair. Zelasko gave the lead navigators all their times and routes, and their positions in the line of Division assembly. Gee codings for the day were given, as were updated maps for troop front line positions, bomb lines, and new emergency airfields.

Next Major Vacek gave his share of the briefing, and his detailed description of target characteristics took up appreciable time. The target was a heavy machinery assembly plant in the industrial section of Stuttgart. The intelligence photos showed it clearly, its sawtooth roofs looming up beside the Neckar River. Railroad spurs, the surrounding factories (some of which were bombed out) and, most of all, the River itself, made it an easy target to spot from a long distance, provided there was no cloud cover.

The aiming point was the centre of the roof of the main factory building. Bombs were to be dropped at minimum intervalometer setting in the hope of getting the maximum number of hits within the factory itself – the famous 'pickle barrel' concept of the United States Strategic Air Forces.

If the weather was bad, the target was not to be bombed by radar. The factory was too small to be a good radar target.

No secondary target was designated for the day. If, for any reason, Stuttgart could not be bombed, then any suitable target, typically a city inside Germany should be bombed. This was an action preferable to hauling heavy explosives back home again and trying to land safely with them.

However, and this point was heavily stressed, no bombs were to be dropped west of, or even near the bomb line. This line was drawn on the map well ahead of the farthest advance of Allied troops. Its presence was known, even above complete cloud cover, by the radio beacons which the gutsy men of Signal Corps kept in place at, or even ahead of the front lines.

By this time in the War the German battle and industrial capacity was staggering badly. The Bulge attack had been tried, and pushed back; the *Wehrmacht* had been driven from the Calais area back across Belgium and well into the Netherlands in some areas. Their launching sites for V-1 buzz bombs along the Channel coast had all been abandoned, and they had only a few sites left in the Frisian Islands, out of range of London. A few V-2 rocket weapons were being launched from inside Germany, but the supply was apparently sparse. There had not been a serious German aircraft attack on England for well over a year, though an occasional loner might penetrate British airspace, usually to be shot down promptly.

So it was a matter of considerable surprise during this target briefing of the 458th Bomb Group that the air-raid sirens went off all over Norfolk. Major Vacek paused momentarily in his target description, then went on. The eerie wailing of the sirens carried through the night, a strange soprano over the steady background rumble of the B-24 engines on the flight line.

Vacek went into considerable detail about the landmarks along the bomb run. The attack on the target was to begin over the *Schwarzwald*, the Black Forest of Germany, where there were few definitive checkpoints on the ground. The route went near to the towns of Pfullingen and Reutlingen on the right, between Neuhausen and Boblingen, and over the suburbs and central city of Stuttgart to cross the River Neckar at an angle.

The pictures of all these places were remarkably big and clear. Once again we had ample reason to respect the expertise of our photointelligence aircraft, manned by those fliers who went out alone with no guns and no bombs, only cameras, cunning and speed. Such pictures were particularly useful to the lead bombardier who needed all the information he could get about where he was going on the bomb run.

As Vacek talked the air-raid sirens stopped and their wailing faded away into the night. Then, after a time, there was a new sound above the rumble of engines on the flight line. It was a strange, steady, coughing rattle, both penetrating and insistent in its harshness. The sound grew steadily louder – a buzz bomb in flight.

The noise made by a buzz bomb's pulse jet was very loud. As long as one heard this penetrating noise, things were safe, but when the noise stopped suddenly, that was an indication that the bomb had begun its dive, and would strike nearby.

The insistent growling of the bomb over Horsham St Faith grew louder and louder. A certain tenseness was evident among the men in the target briefing room – the bomb sounded as though it was headed precisely for our headquarters building.

Suddenly the noise stopped. Major Vacek stopped talking, Colonel Hogg stamped out his cigar. No one said anything. No one moved. There was only silence.

After fifteen seconds there was still silence. Everyone braced for an explosion that would cave in the walls or blow in the blacked-out windows. The explosion never came.

After about thirty seconds there was an appropriate comment from an unidentified bombardier in the back of the room:

'Holy cow!' he said.

The target briefing continued.

Some days later we found out that the buzz bomb had landed, unexploded, in a vacant field just past the Headquarters Building. It was a dud.

754th Bomb Squadron aircraft P – Peter dropping bombs.

CHAPTER 18

ODD EVENTS

Just as huge as General Kepner was small, was Brigadier-General Walter Peck, who commanded 96th Combat Wing, and who shared the head-quarters building with the 458th Bomb Group. The General had the downstairs and we had the upstairs. After I moved up to my exalted job at headquarters I shared the same latrine that General Peck used. I would encounter him there at times, but I was always afraid to speak to him. He was such a majestic and fearsome figure, and he did not offer to speak to me, even when we stood at adjoining urinals.

General Peck seldom came to our briefings as General Kepner did, but he was an omnipresent force on our base. To have the Wing Commander in residence may have kept us a bit more shipshape than we would have been otherwise.

Brigadier-General Walter Peck, left, congratulates Captain Weber on award of his DFC.

Peck had a son who was a flier in the Eighth, in a B-17 group. Naturally the General was proud of his son and would sometimes sneak up in a fighter aircraft during a mission if he knew his son was flying.

General Peck's son finished his tour of missions with the Eighth and went back to the States. There he was killed in some stupid accident in a training flight, which took a lot of the starch out of Walter Peck. He aged twenty years in a few hours when he got the news.

Peck was the only high-ranking officer we knew who was bigger than Colonel Jim Isbell. Isbell once commented that Peck could slap him on the back in friendship and knock him down, but I doubt that statement.

General Peck had attended all the sessions of the court martial of Private George E. Smith, accused and convicted of murder. It is certainly understandable that Peck was upset that such a terrible event had taken place in the Bomb Wing he commanded.

As he observed that Court, General Peck became favourably impressed with the work of the Defence Counsel, First Lieutenant Max M. Sokarl. Some time after Private Smith was hanged by the neck until dead, Peck signed the orders transferring Sokarl from his lengthy series of nothing jobs with the 458th Bomb Group to the wheeling and dealing position of aide-de-camp to the Wing Commanding General.

No longer was Sokarl the in-house clown to Major Manley. He moved into

Lt-Colonel Walter Williamson, Operations Officer, 458th Bomb Group, is awarded the Distinguished Flying Cross by Major-General William E. Kepner.

the General's quarters where the food was great, the cumshaw out of sight, and the perks magnificent. As they say down in Arkansas, Sokarl had cut a fat hog in the ass.

It was about this time that Lieutenant-Colonel Frederick O'Neill left to be replaced as Group Operations Officer by Lieutenant-Colonel Walter Williamson. Williamson came up to Headquarters from the 752nd Bomb Squadron where he had been Commanding Officer for a while. I now had an old friend for a boss, for Williamson had been in phase training at the same time as my crew.

Colonel O'Neill had been a very interesting boss. I enjoyed him a great deal – he liked to take time off to go fishing, or to relax out in the world. One day he was gone somewhere without having signed out, apparently. Colonel Isbell looked into my office about five times that day.

'Granholm, have you seen O'Neill?' he would ask at each visit.

'No Sir.'

O'Neill came back late in the afternoon, I was standing in his office talking to him when Isbell found him. The Colonel strode in briskly, filling the whole doorway as he passed through it:

'O'Neill,' he said, 'One of these days you'll go out somewhere to goof off, and when you come back someone else will be sitting at this desk!'

And with these brief words, Colonel Isbell departed.

The fastest I ever saw Fred O'Neill move was on one day in March 1945. Our mission of the day had taken off, assembled, and departed. I was standing in O'Neill's office when *First Sergeant*, our garish Group assembly ship which had replaced its predecessor, the *Spotted Ape*, came in for a landing. It touched the runway and rolled out of sight behind a hangar. It appeared on the other side of the hangar sliding in a great cloud of dust, its main gear collapsed.

'Sir, the assembly ship just crashed out there,' I said.

'What?'

'I say, the assembly ship just crashed out there.'

'No crap?' O'Neill dived for his desk phone. He called the tower. 'Did the assembly ship just crash?' he demanded, as though I were a blind idiot who couldn't accurately see a bent B-24 at a quarter-mile.

O'Neill slammed the phone down, grabbed his hat, and ran out. He was despondent for a week. He loved to fly the assembly ship. It was a high-performance buggy with no guns or bombs. He lost an old friend when it slithered in.

There was never a German fighter attack on the 458th Bomb Group during any combat mission I flew. The *Luftwaffe* left us alone, which I figured was because of Jim Isbell's continual demanding that his men fly tight defensive formations. He liked to stand in the control tower and watch his people come home 'flying with pride' and socked in there tight. I grew to be grateful to him for it; his hard-nosed edicts had saved lives.

On 9 March, 1945, Colonel James H. Isbell went home to the States for rest and recuperation. He was the first bomb group commanding officer in Eighth Air Force to have led his Group through over two hundred consecutive combat missions.

Command of the 458th was taken by Colonel Allen F. Herzberg who moved down from Wing Staff. Herzberg projected a different image from Jim Isbell. So impressive was Isbell's physical presence that you were awed by his size and demeanour. Allen Herzberg was a man of average size, quiet, and competent. We were a fortunate Group, both men were excellent commanders.

Major Chuck Booth also went home. We missed his smiling face and warm personality in the briefing room – at times he had been the only bright spot in an otherwise crappy day. Booth's chair as Assistant Group Operations Officer was taken over by Major Maurice Speer, who was well-liked and easy to get along with.

Our experience on our first combat mission with the instructor pilot had made me realise that not all our compatriots in Second Air Division, Eighth Air Force, were totally sane. In fact, some of them were downright crackers, to use an apt British term. Our military term for such an addled mental state was flak happy. In retrospect, considering the job we did, and the pressures of doing it, it is not surprising that some folks got a bit off track at times.

Some of our bomber pilots were frustrated that they had been assigned to fly formation in a big, four-engined monster and worry about a crew – they would rather have flown a fighter. A fighter pilot was a lone wolf, endowed with killer instinct. He could fly low and fast, and engage the enemy in heroic combat. There was no flying formation through the flak and over the target, and none of the discipline of a formation commander yelling over the horn for the wing men to shape it up. Flying fighters was the wild blue yonder with a scarf around your neck. It was the image of von Richthofen and Fonck and Mannock and Rickenbacker. It was pure euphoria in a P-51.

Or so some pilots imagined. There were some so patriotic, or so mad, that they volunteered to fly fighters, having just completed a mission tour in heavy bombers. They came back to visit us from time to time, and to report the grisly facts: no matter what your job in the wartime air, someone out there is trying damn hard to shoot your ass off.

But a noticeable aberration of some bomber pilots was found in their trying to fly like fighter jockeys. One pilot I recall got into bad trouble that way – I attended his summary court martial.

He had gone out on a shakedown flight with a B-24. When he returned, broken portions of tree limbs were found lodged in the damaged bomb doors of his aircraft. In his testimony at the court, he alleged that he had no idea how the limbs got there. Maybe they were there when he took off, and he had somehow overlooked them. Certainly he had not been out buzzing. He could not, in fact, recall having ever flown below 1,500 feet above the terrain except on take-off and approach.

When he talked to me about his trial, he was most indignant that the United States military would waste valuable time on such a witch hunt. No one had been injured, he alleged, and try to find the pilot who doesn't occasionally bend or dent his aeroplane. It was all very unjust in his mind.

As a result of action taken by the court, he was removed from duty, and sent off somewhere unknown to us, allegedly to be retrained as a mess officer.

Or, possibly, he had been assigned to help the cavalry shovel shit in South Dakota – not necessarily a bad job considering what the rest of us did.

Over fifty years later I still shudder when I remember the wild look in the glazed eyes of a pilot named Jim. His actions varied from odd to totally screwball, and there were various bets on among aircrewmen as to whether Jim's troubles were real or affected, aimed at a medical discharge for mental problems.

Jim sat looking out of the window of his room at the combat officers' mess one day, apparently observing the world with equanimity and pleasure. He got up and walked slowly over to the closet and took his John Roscoe 45-calibre service automatic out of its holster and walked back to the window.

Opening the window, he began carefully shooting the blossoms off the rose bushes in front of the building. People were diving for cover all over the front lawn.

This episode of Jim's was ended by his squadron commanding officer demanding the return of his weapon. Jim gave it up willingly and with a charming smile, he was apparently all right without his rose-destroying sidearm.

In his next notable episode, Jim was on his way to his plane out on the flight line. Suddenly he stood up in the jeep. Yelling 'Flak!' he jumped out, popping his parachute as he went. He was badly skinned up by his contact with the asphalt taxiway.

Jim recovered from his taxiway bruises, and was still kept on flight duty. One night the Colonel gave a big party for all hands, and when the festivities were at their height, Jim stood up abruptly. Stepping up on top of the table, he undid the fly of his uniform trousers and strolled nonchalantly along the table, urinating at random on food and diners.

We didn't see Jim again after that. There were rumours about where he went, but none were verified.

Pilots were not the only ones to suffer mental quirks. Jake was a likeable young bombardier who was assigned to lead ship duty. He made a sloppy drop, and was called in and reprimanded by his squadron bombardier. At the second sloppy drop he was reprimanded by Major Vacek, our Group Bombardier. Since Vacek and I shared the same office, I was a witness to the chewing.

That's how I met Jake. For some reason he seized on me as his particular friend. After Vacek ate him out, Jake's world seemed to crumble, he confided to me his terrible worries. He would lie awake at night, seeing himself missing the target again and again. He would sleep for an hour, then wake up with the sure knowledge that out on the flight line was a bombsight for him to use, and its gyroscopes had just tumbled, throwing the aircraft off course on the bomb run.

The Norden bombsight was a 'precision instrument' but it could be a bitch to operate. The bombardier was under considerable pressure. Through most of the mission he sat around, watching all the mayhem of flak and fighter attacks, then, at the initial point, he had to get over his bombsight, cramped in the aircraft nose and jammed under the front turret. He had precious little time to identify his target, set his telescope cross hairs on the precise aiming point, get the correct wind and drift cranked into the bombsight, and let the sight motors run out, dropping the bombs correctly.

While he did all this, the bombardier was staring down at all the flak guns below, each manned by someone trying desperately to shoot big holes in him and his aeroplane, and to kill his whole crew.

Jake went over and over the bombing procedure in his mind. Despite the fact that he was a highly intelligent and well trained bombardier, the whole process came to seem impossible to him.

Jake was given one more chance. He got assigned as squadron lead on a 'milk run'. The 458th was to bomb by squadrons, hitting all the German railroad traffic in the marshalling yards at Strasbourg in occupied France.

Major Vacek called Jake in for a pre-mission pep talk. I cringed at my desk as I listened, watching the strained expression on the kid's face.

'This is no sweat,' Vacek said. 'You can do this. What the hell! You've got one of the best records I've ever seen on your practice drops in school. Just pretend it's back in the old desert there. Set the cross-hairs, stabilise her in, and let 'em drop. No sweat at all.'

'Yes, Sir,' Jake said, sweating profusely.

So he went forth in the lead ship of his squadron. It was a calm, quiet mission. The visibility was clear all the way, about a hundred miles or so. There was no flak and there were no fighter attacks. Strasbourg was easily visible all the way from the initial point.

Jake set his cross hairs and synchronised on the railroad yards. Things seemed to be going very well indeed.

But he apparently suspected things were going too well. Jake began to fiddle with his bombsight and fiddled till the gyros tumbled and he lost sync. Then, in his frantic efforts to recover, he failed to shut the bombsight off, and to ask the pilot to bring the formation around for a second try.

The Norden was controlling the lead ship in a big, banked turn when the bombs cut loose under control of the bombsight timer. The wing ships dutifully dropped their loads, the bombs slammed into the downtown area of the city, narrowly missing the unique mediaeval Cathedral of Notre Dame de Strasbourg, and probably killing a number of friendly Frenchmen.

Jake was sent off to other duties where his nervous state would not exact such a high price.

About the same time that Colonel Herzberg took command, Fred Vacek finished his tour of missions and went home, so I had a new office mate. Major Gehringer came down from wing staff to take over Vacek's desk as Group Bombardier, somewhat to the disgust of various squadron bombardiers, none of whom was moved up.

Flight-rated officers were not the only ones to suffer from an up-tight state of mind. The problem was shared by enlisted men. A sergeant waist gunner provided an unwelcome baptism of fire for Allen Herzberg a few days after the Colonel assumed command of the 458th.

Standard procedure, in the absence of any firm orders to the contrary, was to charge and test-fire the bomber's guns over the sea during climb-out to Europe. This gunner got on board a bomber of the 752nd Squadron readying for a mission. He went to his station at a 50-calibre waist gun, made sure the ammo belt was properly in place, charged his gun, and pulled the trigger, discharging a few rounds into the concrete of the parking revetment. The 50-calibre slugs ricocheted into the bomber on the next pad, bursting the fuel tank of the auxiliary power unit. The tracer rounds set the spilled fuel on fire, and the crew of the burning aeroplane evacuated quickly. Everybody stood around, waiting for something to happen. The fire trucks rolled up rapidly to pour foam all over the burning bomber, and put out the fire.

Colonel Herzberg was in the control tower, with some others of his staff, expecting to see the impressive take-off of his fighting force of the day. He heard the 50-calibre fire out on the field, saw the fire engines roll out, and wondered what was happening.

Just then Captain Joe Tanahey, our Group Ordnance Officer, came speeding up in his jeep. He jumped out, ran over to the foamed bomber, and stuck his head up inside the bomb bay to see if his bomb load was all right.

The blazing putt-putt fuel had spilled all over the 2,000-pound bomb in the left front bomb bay. Joe Tanahey told me later that when he stuck his head up inside the bomb bay, about fourteen inches from the nose fuse of the bomb, he saw liquid TNT, hot and under pressure, squirting out around the fuse socket.

Tanahey came out of the bomber like a man insane, setting an all-time record for speed running. He forgot his jeep, running for the wide open spaces, and yelling wildly at everybody to get the hell out of there.

Just as the last person got clear, all four bombs went off, followed by the topped-off main fuel tanks. There was a horrendous explosion, and it took that squadron out of service for a while. All the bombers parked nearby were riddled with flying pieces of the blown-up aeroplane.

Up in the control tower, the Colonel and the others heard the explosion. Simultaneously they saw debris flying overhead, so everyone ducked behind the parapet till the aeroplane pieces came to rest elsewhere. Military decorum was temporarily abandoned in favour of personal safety.

The site of the explosion presented a memorable picture: there was a great greasy smudge on the concrete and the surrounding burnt grass. Little pieces of aluminium rat crap were scattered far and wide, and four great blackened lumps marked the spots where the engines fell. Far out in the field, at least fifty yards away, was a single propeller, one of its three blades stuck in the ground up to the hub.

The gunner who initiated this mess did not fly again. He had done more damage than a German fighter attack.

A short time later Colonel Herzberg got a phone call from a local Norfolk farmer. The farmer wanted to know what the American military was going to do about the flak holes in his chicken house, and the dead and traumatised chickens. Major Manley, borrowing the Wing Commanding General's Aide temporarily, gave the problem to Lieutenant Sokarl to mediate. Max Sokarl sent out his usual copious reports on the progress of the investigation.

There were a lot of important things to be done in the Eighth Air Force. Not the least among these was the need for a constant effort to keep your sanity in the midst of bedlam, but in the 96th Bomb Wing was one officer who cared nothing for sanity, his own or the world's. He marched to his own drummer, and piped his own tune. That officer was the remarkable paddle-foot, First Lieutenant Max Sokarl.

Sokarl often told us of his amorous adventures, and usually we considered these far-out tales to be pure fables, but occasionally Sokarl would stage a demonstration.

Shortly after he went off to his important job on General Peck's staff, Sokarl invited Irving Goldman and me to meet him at the Bell Hotel in downtown Norwich one evening, saying that we were to meet some noted English philosophers. Like idiots, we went. I had never been in a Norwich hotel before and after seeing inside this one, I was happy that I had no need to stay there. Not that it was an unpleasant place, but one would surely not confuse it with the Hilton, nor even with the London Regent Palace.

It transpired that the true reason for the evening's invitation was so that Goldman and I could meet Sokarl's paramours in person – not one, but two. Max introduced them to us with considerable amusement. These two, neither a candidate for a beauty contest, seemed to hold the view that there was nothing at all unusual in both of them sharing a room with the 'American Lieutenant'. To go one better, they issued a thinly-veiled invitation for Goldman and me to join them.

Irving and I were both a bit embarrassed by this session. We thought up a good excuse to leave as early as possible, and took the bus back to the air-base. I'm sure that as we drifted off to sleep that evening, *sans* the dual companionship that Sokarl was doubtless enjoying, we each prayed in our own fashion that God would help us keep our sanity, and that we would not wander away into a flak-happy state, likely candidates for a section eight release and a free room at the funny farm.

CHAPTER 19

HOLE IN THE CLOUDS

About nineteen miles due west of Horsham St Faith was the air-base of Wendling. There the 392nd Bomb Group, a part of the 14th Combat Wing, Second Air Division, Eighth U.S.A.A.F. was stationed.

The 392nd had been the fourth Liberator group assigned to Eighth Air Force, beginning combat operations out of Wendling in September 1943. It was the first group of the Eighth to fly B-24H model aircraft, built in San Diego, and factory-equipped with Emerson electric nose turrets, which replaced the old-style greenhouse noses. These nose-turreted Liberators first rolled out of San Diego in June 1943 and all but the first twenty-five B-24Gs, built in Dallas, had these nose turrets.

The first nose-turreted G models did not hit the ramp until November of 1943, although some B-24s were modified in the field earlier. Consolidated hydraulic turrets, cannibalised from the tails of wrecked aircraft, were fitted as nose turrets. The first such hermaphrodite Liberator was built at Hickam Field, Hawaii.

The air-base of Wendling at Beeston Parish, not far from the Norfolk town of East Dereham, was a typical Eighth Air Force station, equipped with Quonset huts, coke-burning stoves, and mud. Today, in a small, fenced plot at the one-time site of the military police station, there stands a nine-foot granite obelisk, a gift of the men of the 392nd. The obelisk's inscription reads:

> DEDICATED TO THE MEN OF U.S. ARMY AIR FORCES STATION NUMBER 118, WHO, THROUGH THEIR EFFORTS, DEVOTION AND DUTY, AIDED IN BRINGING VICTORY TO THE ALLIES IN WORLD WAR II.

All around is green countryside, farmland, and small villages. The air-base at Wendling has returned to peaceful uses.

During the War we often saw the bombers of the 392nd joining our Air Division combat line as they flew in from the south-west towards Splasher Five. They came that way when we had a mission into northern Germany, or went out to Europe over the North Sea. We recognised their white-painted tails with black horizontal stripes, the aircraft letter painted white in the stripe centre. Frequently we saw them in the target area during a concentrated attack when there was much weaving and bobbing of different groups, sometimes splitting themselves into squadrons to bomb in assigned order.

The men of Wendling did their part in the great air war over Europe. The Group turned in distinguished performances on many occasions. In February 1944 the 392nd Bomb Group flew its forty-first mission. The target was the Wagenfabrik Werke at Gotha, largest production centre of the twin-engined Messerschmitt fighter. The 392nd sent thirty-two heavy bombers to Gotha on 24 February, and its attack won the Group a Distinguished Unit Citation. The 392nd lost seven bombers and seventy-three aircrewmen in that attack.

Some of the missions of the 392nd produced results spectacular in other ways. By April 1944 radar-equipped lead ships, those with 'Mickey' sets, were in limited use in the Eighth Air Force. Such a bomber was assigned as lead ship to the 392nd by Second Air Division Headquarters. The target for 1 April 1944 was a chemical works at Ludwigshafen, which, with its twin city, Mannheim, sits astride the confluence of the Rhine and the Neckar west of Heidelberg. A command pilot and a dead-reckoning navigator of the 392nd augmented the crew of the radar pathfinding ship.

The 392nd cranked up out of their assembly area over North Pickenham on time, but as they left the English coast the lead ship radar set began to malfunction. However, the command pilot elected to continue the mission. Over the continent the Group encountered a storm front with cloud tops four miles and more high. The ground was totally obscured by undercast. They could not locate Ludwigshafen and its chemical plant.

A fortunate break appeared in the clouds below, however, and through this break a city could be seen. Consensus identified it as Freiburg, Germany, so the 392nd opened bomb doors and unloaded which resulted in 1,184 hundred-pound bombs being dropped on the Schaffhausen salient of Switzerland. The 392nd had been an incredible 130 miles or so off course.

This attack on a neutral country was not viewed in very happy fashion by the U.S. Government nor the high command of the U.S. Army. Disciplinary action viewed as appropriate was taken. However, this unfortunate episode had been forgotten by March of 1945. Bombing Axis targets in Europe had become pretty routine by that time.

On 4 March 1945 the 392nd Bomb Group put up a formation of twenty B-24s, commanded by Major Myron Keilman, Commanding Officer of the 579th Bomb Squadron. Because weather was bad at assembly altitude in England, assembly was scheduled over France, north of Paris.

Weather in the French assembly area proved to be little better than that left behind in England; clouds and condensation trails were all over the place. Bombers wandered everywhere in the sky and, in desperation, tacked onto the formation of any group they could find.

Keilman got part of his group together and headed east for the target of the day which was a tank factory at Aschaffenburg, south-east of Frankfurt am Main. The weather scouts were on the horn, reporting to Division command, indicating weather solid from the deck to thirty thousand feet. Keilman was not encouraged. He was flying through cloud tops and trying to hold formation. The contrails wrapped around each other, thicker than a staff sergeant's head.

In spite of appalling weather, Major Keilman was happy with the mission's progress, and the performance of the lead ship radar set seemed good, but then a recall message came from Division as they flew south of Stuttgart. Keilman gave the word over the horn, then ordered the flight engineer to fire the Very pistol loaded with recall colours.

Flying just ahead of the 392nd, and heading the 14th Combat Wing for the day, was the 44th Bomb Group. That group began a big, sweeping turn, and disappeared into heavy cloud tops, the 392nd was all alone out in the clouds over Germany. They began a long turn to head back for England and maybe to find the rest of the wing. Keilman left his seat at the co-pilot's station and went aft to talk to the radar operator. They agreed that Pforzheim, Germany, a city on the Enz River halfway between Stuttgart and Karlsruhe, would make a good target. Keilman ordered the attack.

When Major Keilman sat down and looked out his window again the high squadron ships were missing from his formation – they had been lost in the clouds in the turn.

The lead squadron of the 392nd bombed Pforzheim by radar through cloud cover, and returned home to Wendling. All the way home they looked in vain for their missing squadron.

Flying as lead ship pilot of the disconnected high squadron of the 392nd was First Lieutenant William R. Sincock. With him that day were Co-pilot First Lieutenant Norman F. Johnston, Navigator First Lieutenant Theodore Balides, Bombardier First Lieutenant Alfred R. Williams, Radar Operator Second Lieutenant Murray Milrod, and Pilotage Navigator First Lieutenant George W. Barger riding the nose turret. No assigned command pilot was on board.

Lieutenant Sincock had earned an A.B. degree from the University of Michigan in June of 1941. Thirteen days after his graduation he was called to active duty as a Second Lieutenant, Infantry, and was sent to the Infantry School at Fort Benning, Georgia. From there he went to Camp Wheeler where he was assigned as an instructor in communications and radio. He was promoted to First Lieutenant, then sent to the Amphibious Training Command at Camp Edwards, Massachusetts, where he served as a staff instructor.

He then went to the Signal School at Fort Monmouth, New Jersey, for an advanced course in radio and returned to Camp Edwards as Assistant Signal Officer and Regional Communications Officer.

In December 1942 Sincock applied for pilot training in grade. He was sent in April 1943 to the Classification Center at Nashville, Tennessee. He went on to pre-flight at Maxwell Field, Primary at Lakeland, Florida, Basic at Courtland, Alabama, and Advanced Training at Freeman Field, Seymour, Indiana. From the Distribution Center at Westover Field, Massachusetts, he went on to Phase Training at Chatham Field, Georgia. From there he transferred to Langley Field, Virginia. There he and his crew picked up a bomber and flew it to England in July of 1944, joining the 392nd Bomb Group.

When Sincock found himself alone in the cloud tops he looked around. Only two other bombers of the 392nd Bomb Group had come with him from the weather-plagued assembly over France. However, as he muddled along through the cloud tops, he had been joined by three assorted B-24s from other bomb groups. There was one belonging to our 96th Combat Wing neighbours, the 466th Bomb Group at Attlebridge, and two from the 491st Bomb Group, North Pickenham. One of the 491st bombers was apparently a lead ship, since it had its radar dome down and locked. Sincock must have looked like he knew where he was going, for he was leading a six-plane impromptu formation.

They had lost sight of their own group lead squadron, but, coming out of some cloud tops, they saw the 44th Bomb Group. Sincock manoeuvred his six-plane squadron into a high left position on the 44th formation.

The wing command pilot was riding with the 44th. Sincock called him on the horn and asked what was up. The plan of the 44th was to make a radar run on Stuttgart and bomb it as a target of opportunity. Sincock elected to tag along, dropping on their lead, since his own radar was so crapped out. About ten miles out of Stuttgart, more or less, the 44th went into a sharp right turn, and once again disappeared into a cloud bank. Sincock got left behind, paddling air on the outside of the turn and did not see the 44th Bomb Group again that day.

It was pretty lonesome up there. No buddies of the Eighth Air Force were to be seen. There were no escorting fighters, just a lot of giant clouds, and six B-24s with pregnant bomb loads, looking for somewhere to go. Sincock led his formation through a wide turn, almost a full circle.

They saw no one.

The full circle searching turn was certainly no help to the Dead Reckoning Navigator, Lieutenant Balides. He was shut up inside a blacked-out area, the better to see his gee scope. The Germans were jamming the gee reception like mad; Milrod could give Balides no reliable radar positions, and Barger up in the nose turret could see nothing but clouds.

Sincock's navigator, Lieutenant Theodore Balides had graduated from high school in June 1939. In September 1942 he enlisted in the U.S. Army Reserve as a private. After six months he was called to active duty. In March 1943 he was selected as an Aviation Cadet and assigned to the Classification Center at Nashville, Tennessee. He went from there to pilot training at the Primary School at Camden, South Carolina. There he washed out, was reclassified for navigation training, and was sent to Selman Field for Preflight.

Next he went to Gunnery School at Fort Myers, Florida, then back to Selman Field for Navigation training, being commissioned as a Second Lieutenant in February 1944. At Westover Field, Massachusetts, Balides was assigned to Sincock's crew, and had stayed with it since that time.

Sincock gave up trying to find the rest of his Group formation. He decided to find any target of opportunity, if possible, and dump on it rather than carry the bombs home. Landing with a bomb load was no fun, and dumping them in the Channel contributed nothing to the war effort.

Briefing instructions for lead crews described targets of opportunity at the time as 'Any military objective positively identified as being in Germany, east of the current bomb line, and west of twelve degrees (east longitude, approximately the longitude of Leipzig)'. But for Sincock's crew finding a target of opportunity was not a simple job. They had relinquished the first ship in which they began the mission because its gee-H bombing equipment was faulty. Aircraft number 577, the ship which they flew, proved to have a faulty navigation radar. Range was a maximum ten miles, and the definition was very poor. Below them was total cloud cover, so a visual position fix was impossible.

Sincock asked Co-pilot Norm Johnston to get the 491st radar ship on the horn to see if they could help with a position fix. Johnston tried several times. There was no answer from the green-tailed monster alongside. The waist gunners waved out of their windows and the gunners in the 491st bomber waved back.

Lieutenant Milrod on the radar set reported that he thought he saw a city dead ahead, but he could not be certain. The radar was performing too poorly to be sure.

Lieutenant Balides' chart, derived from such dead reckoning as he could summon up in a very confused situation, showed them to be headed west somewhere in the vicinity of the headwaters of the Danube River in the Black Forest. In a gee-H ship such as they flew, equipped with a modification of the British gee navigation system, the lead navigator rode in a blacked-out compartment for better visibility of the gee scope. Balides might as well have been in a photographic darkroom for all he could see of the world outside.

Lieutenant Barger up in the nose turret reported a break in the clouds coming up below. He looked more intently. There was a part of a big city visible down through the hole in the clouds.

Barger checked signals with Balides and Milrod, and gave his opinion: The City was Freiburg, Germany, biggest city in the Black Forest.

'Let 'em have it!' Sincock said.

Williams crawled down in the nose, got over his bombsight and opened the bomb bay doors. The wing ship bomb doors all opened in dutiful reply.

Williams squinted down through the Sperry bombsight. The hole in the clouds was like a big well with steep sides. Not all of the city was visible, but enough of it was visible for Williams to see a big railroad yard full of freight – a good target. Williams went hastily into his bombsight synchronisation procedure. He had to hurry while he could still see down through the hole in the clouds; wisps of white vapour kept drifting through the field of vision.

There was a very strong wind. Williams wondered if the navigators knew how strong the wind was. It was hard to synchronise all the drift out. He got the cross-hairs steadied as well as he could, considering the haste and the short bomb run, and the general nervous condition of the whole damn mission.

The sight timer ran out and the racks opened. Sincock's ship lightened suddenly as the load of half-tonners cut loose. All the wing ships dropped on the lead ship's release.

Down the bombs went – 48 thousand-pounders whistled earthward, their deadly screech audible below. The bombs hit, exploding in row houses, streets, and out in a patch of woods. It had not been a particularly good drop; no rail traffic was damaged. But at least a few more dwellings for German workers had been made uninhabitable. Quite a bit more plumbing leaked, and several more shit pots were cracked. It was better than carrying the bombs home.

Sincock and his companions went home, arriving safely back in England, glad to be out of the crummy weather and done with a stupid mission. The bomber from 466th and the two from 491st went their own way. The three ships of the 392nd landed late at Wendling.

The deputy lead ship carried the mission cameras and the film of the strike on Freiburg was turned in for development. Later that evening Major Percy B. Caley, chief intelligence officer of the 392nd, got a phone call at his quarters. It was from his photo interpreters. They were having a problem matching Freiburg landmarks.

Caley went down to his office to see if he could help. He stood looking at the strike photos on the light box.

'What the crap!' he said, 'This is Zurich, Switzerland! There'll be Hell to pay for this one!'

CHAPTER 20

HIGH-LEVEL RHUBARB

Three minutes before Sincock's squadron hit Zurich, nine B-24s bombed the railroad yard at Basel. Eight of them, including the lead ship, were from the 466th Bomb Group at Attlebridge, the ninth plane was from the 392nd.

It was a bad day in Switzerland. This small, neutral country had just been attacked by a powerful and major combatant nation.

The bombs which Sincock's squadron dropped on Zurich hit in the Milchbuck quarter of the city. The residence at 16 Hub was blown all to rat crap, leaving only a white bathtub sitting upright on the lot where the house had been. At 184 Frohburg Street both sides were blown out of the building, leaving it like some gigantic doll's house with furniture in place, albeit broken and bloody. Next door the very old 'Schlossli' at 186 Frohburg had disappeared, leaving a large rubble pile where it had stood. All about in adjoining houses were broken windows, leaky plumbing, shifted foundations, and other results of American 'precision' bombing.

Five Swiss citizens were stone cold dead in the rubble. Twelve more were rushed to the hospital with severe injuries. Numerous others, unfortunate enough to be nearby, had wet their pants or temporarily lost their hearing. Fortunately, however, about twenty of the bombs from the lost squadron landed out in the woods, otherwise the carnage and wreckage might have been much greater.

When the strike photos were properly identified by the intelligence officers of Second Air Division, a great flood of telephone and paper conversation began. All over Eighth Air Force group bombardiers sat up all night in order to prove that they were not the ones who did it.

I may have been very lucky on that day. The 466th Bomb Group headed up the 96th Combat wing on 4 March 1945. When the recall and order to select targets of opportunity came, the Wing command pilot elected to make a 'Mickey' run on Stuttgart. As he started a turn towards Stuttgart he almost ran into the 20th Combat Wing turning in another direction. In the cloud tops and the resulting confusion the 458th Bomb group lost sight of the wing-leading 466th, and went off to do its own thing, dropping, allegedly, on the Stuttgart railroad marshalling yard with unobserved results. Two of our bombers, lost in the God-awful cloudy murk over Germany, bombed with some other group of confused aircraft. There, but for the grace of God and his weather, abetted by good luck, went my navigators, leading our formation off to dump its bombs on Switzerland.

As it happened, the 458th came out of the event as pure as Caesar's wife. In fact, we received a commendation in 1945 for flying forty consecutive combat missions with no gross navigational errors. This was a commendation for which I was pleased to accept all possible credit, undeserved though it was.

Many of the written reports and notes of phone calls of the time are interesting in retrospect. There was a clear flood of communication aimed at establishing that the writer or the caller was not guilty of anything, had never made a mistake, and was in no way affiliated with any bombs that might have hit Switzerland.

The reaction in Switzerland to the damage in Basel and Zurich was hardly one of loving forgiveness for American airmen. There were quite a few people who believed the attacks were intentional.

They thought up various reasons. Language was one. The people of this area of tri-lingual Switzerland spoke German, and German was the language shared by the Nazi enemy. Various factories in Switzerland made goods which were sold to Germany. As neutrals the Swiss had every right to do this. To have refused would have been a violation of their neutrality. The allegedly neutral Swedes sold their flak guns to the Germans and their ball-bearings to both the Germans and the English. Could the Swiss be denied the same kind of trading rights?

Some Jews who escaped to Switzerland had been sent back to Germany. Technically, this may have been correct action, since they were German citizens. Nonetheless, they were doubtless sent to certain death. But at that time those of us who were ordinary civilians and soldiers were not aware of Hitler's mad plan of total extermination of his Jewish citizens.

Swiss soldiers found a German flag in the debris of one of the houses destroyed in Zurich. A Swiss newspaper ran the headline,

'American Fliers Hunt Nazis in Switzerland'

It is true that the Nazi party had workers and organisations in Switzerland, and there were German sympathisers there, but it is also true that the Swiss Government trod a very thin line to remain neutral. The Swiss much feared that Hitler would decide to 'protect' the Swiss German-speaking nationals as he had done for Czechoslovakia, and there was great fear and distrust of their large neighbour with its massive military power.

Such distrust of the Nazis does not mean that the Americans were loved. Forty innocent civilians had been killed in the 392nd Group attack on Schaffhausen in 1944. The Swiss remembered this incident vividly.

The reaction in Washington D.C. and in higher commands of the American military was not one of instant joy. Word came to General Eisenhower from General Marshall that President Roosevelt was damn unhappy, and that the State Department was most displeased. Marshall's message indicated that something useful should be done about this mess, and promptly.

The phone rang in the office of Lieutenant-General James H. Doolittle,

Commanding U.S. Eighth Army Air Force. The call was from General Carl (Tooey) Spaatz, Commanding U.S. Strategic Air Forces in Europe. General Spaatz wanted to see Lieutenant-General Doolittle right away.

In early 1944 the United States Strategic Air Forces in Europe (U.S.S.T.A.F) had been set up under command of General Spaatz. General Doolittle was transferred from North Africa to head up Eighth Air Force, allegedly at Eisenhower's request. Under Doolittle's command the Eighth Air Force became the largest air armada ever assembled. It was the primary chosen instrument to prove the concept of daylight precision bombing set forth by the aerial military planners of the United States.

The Eighth took on a good deal of the personality of its leader. Jimmy Doolittle was a hero and a public figure long before World War II. Born in Alameda, California, Doolittle spent much of his boyhood in Nome, Alaska where he lived from 1900 to 1908 while his father was involved in the Nome gold rush. Doolittle enlisted in World War I, and was trained as a flyer, being commissioned a second lieutenant in 1918.

Jimmy Doolittle was an excellent pilot and was retained in the United States as a pilot instructor. This griped him, because he wanted to go to France and become an ace, like Eddie Rickenbacker. But aviation proved to be Doolittle's lifetime fascination and career. He earned a doctorate in Aeronautical Engineering at M.I.T. (Massachusetts Institute of Technology) in 1925.

Superb and spectacular performances in aviation became Doolittle's trade mark. In 1928 he won the Schneider Trophy Race in England, flying a seaplane. In 1930 he was awarded the Harmon trophy for his work in the development of blind flying. In 1931 he won the Bendix Trophy Race, a transcontinental derby. In the 1932 Thompson Trophy Race Doolittle won and set a new world speed record flying a Granville Gee Bee. This superbly dangerous aeroplane had killed a number of pilots. It was a tiny craft with minimal aerodynamic surfaces built around a monstrous radial engine. When Doolittle was asked how he flew the Gee Bee, he replied, 'Very carefully.'

Jimmy Doolittle was President of the Institute of Aeronautical Sciences in 1940 when he was recalled to active duty in the U.S. Army. Probably his most famous military exploit was the raid on Tokyo which he planned and led. Sighting of a Japanese ship caused Doolittle's formation of B-25 bombers to take off early from the deck of an aircraft carrier in the Pacific. The damage to Tokyo was not vast, but the boost to American morale was miraculous.

The Tokyo raiders could not find their assigned landing spots in China on a dark and stormy night. Doolittle, having run out of fuel, baled out his crew, then jumped himself. He landed in a muddy rice paddy, crawled out onto the bank, wrapped his chute around himself, and went to sleep. His action demonstrated his monumental state of cool. I'd have been wide awake for a week after such an adventure.

Much of Doolittle's combative spirit was characteristic of Eighth Air Force. Operations of the Eighth were not modified by caution. No inferiority complex dominated command thinking. All was driven by vigour to get things done, and to keep the show on the road. Even the loss of over six thousand men in combat in our Second Division alone was no deterrent.

Confidence permeated the Eighth from high command to the lowliest waist gunner. The men of every operational bomb group knew themselves to be part of the best damn fighting outfit in the world.

When he got the message from General Spaatz, Jimmy Doolittle hopped into his P-38 and flew down to Headquarters, U.S.T.A.A.F, and strode into the office of the Commanding General.

Both Doolittle and Spaatz had been around for a while. Neither had fallen out of a tree in the last rainstorm. Spaatz graduated from West Point in 1914, transferred to the Air Corps in 1915, and in 1918, with the rank of Major, commanded an air squadron at the Western Front. Doolittle was five years younger than Spaatz. Though Doolittle was always more of a civilian than a military man, his service in World War II was outstanding. His prior aviation exploits had made him an authentic American hero at an early age.

Tooey Spaatz was noted as a man of few words and pithy statements. As Lieutenant-General Doolittle stood before him, Spaatz spoke sternly:

'The President is very unhappy. The State Department is very unhappy. General Eisenhower has called me. He has ordered me to go to Switzerland immediately to explain how this happened. What I want to know from you is, what the hell do I say?'

Whatever he decided to say, General Spaatz did go to Switzerland. He spoke with the Swiss authorities about the measures that would be taken to avoid such glitches in the future, and eventually substantial reparations were paid to the Swiss Government for the damage done in these mistaken attacks. However, some peevish Swiss politicians complained that they had not been paid interest from the time of the attacks to the time of the reparations.

A TWX to General Doolittle from Major-General William E. Kepner, Commanding Second Air Division, indicates that Sincock and his crew were taken off lead crew duties on 5 March 1945. The same action applied to lead crew personnel of the 466th for their damage to the rail traffic of Basel.

One of the more hallowed of human practices is, when anything goes wrong, to seek someone to blame. In the instance of the bombing of Switzerland, there was a wide choice of candidates. First of all, of course, were the aircrewmen of the bombers themselves who misidentified their targets of opportunity, and who made navigation errors significant enough to back up the misidentification. Then there were the formation command pilots who were charged with making sure that the mission went off as well as possible. In the instance of Sincock's ship, however, no command pilot of rank had been present. Sincock had been lost from two group formations in the impossible weather. In searching for those to blame one must not forget the weathermen of the military who failed to predict such flying conditions and the resulting debacle. Their work was clearly suspect. However, weather prediction in World War II was more of a black art than a science. One might as well blame the chaplain as the weatherman if God did not smile on our flight operations on 4 March 1945. Then there was the Division command pilot of the day. Keilman heard the weather scouts telling him that it was socked from the deck all the way up – why not turn back with receipt of that information? But none of us liked to turn back once we were committed.

There was always the possibility of losing mission credit if we met no enemy action and dropped no bombs. Also there was always the feeling that to turn back for any reason was a chicken thing to do, not in keeping with our image. So Division command was not to be put down for perseverance. And, finally, there were the people back in England – the big brass – those who flew the desks and planned the missions. We sometimes had the feeling that they sat there stupidly and sent us out on poorly-conceived expeditions, doomed to be poorly executed. But in the Eighth Air Force, this was really not so; there were no flight-rated desk jockeys. Everybody flew except the paddlefeet, and the biggest brass frequently flew some of the toughest missions. Brigadier-General Walter Peck, who commanded 96th Combat Wing for most of the time I was in it, was ordered by General Kepner to quit flying so many missions, and to go out only when told to. The top brass of the Eighth had the biggest balls in the bowling alley.

One thing we knew about this dumping of bombs on Switzerland. It's one of those things for which you develop a military gut feel. We knew that someone would be handed the 'green weenie' for this screw-up. We just didn't know who.

458th Bomb Group at bomb drop. Smoke pots are from the lead and deputy-lead aircraft.

CHAPTER 21

A TRIP TO GERMANY

On 6 March 1945, two days after our Second Division bombers led by the lost lieutenants from Wendling dumped on Zurich and our Attlebridge Wing neighbours pasted Basel, the American Armies captured the Rhine Bridge at Remagen. Our ground troops crossed into the heart of Nazi Germany. We could see the end coming soon in Europe.

When Major Chuck Booth was Assistant Group Operations Officer, we saw little of him except at briefings, which he conducted with great class. He didn't come around to the navigation office to ask pertinent questions or to bug us, he left that to Colonel O'Neill. But now that Major Maurice Speer had replaced Booth, we saw him frequently. He apparently believed in close co-ordination with the Group Navigator and Group Bombardier, for Speer was always popping into the office, if only to wish us well.

Shortly after the Americans secured the Rhine crossing at Remagen, a request came into Headquarters for the 458th to transport an Eighth Air Force liaison officer. The Signal Corps had people who kept radio beacons at (or sometimes ahead of) the front lines. Our lead ships could receive the signals from these beacons and (hopefully) drop bombs only beyond them, even on targets of opportunity. Eighth Air Force kept a knowledgeable officer, usually a pilot, with the Signal Corps on the continent to advise about beacon placement and other matters related to strategic bombing. The man currently on duty in Europe was scheduled for rotation, so we were asked to take his replacement in, and bring the rotating officer out.

The TWX carrying our personnel transport order came across the desk of Major Maurice Speer. He came running into my office.

'Granholm,' he said, 'how about a trip to Germany?'

'What?' I said, 'What for? I've already been there.'

'This trip is different.'

Speer showed me the TWX. 'I've assigned myself as pilot. I'll put you down as navigator if you like.'

'Let's go,' I said.

General Peck, among the various aeroplanes suited to his exalted rank, had a Norseman. This ship was a single-engined, high-winged monoplane built in Canada for puddle-jumping and bush-piloting. Speer arranged to borrow it for our tour to Germany.

The day following, our replacement liaison officer showed up at Horsham, and the three of us loaded our baggage into the Norseman. Since we did not know what we might find in recently occupied Germany, Speer and I each carried our John Roscoe 45-calibre automatic pistols. I also checked out and loaded aboard a Thompson sub-machine-gun – a 'Chicago tattoo machine' – just in case. Having loaded all our essentials, we took off into the afternoon.

The range of the Norseman was too short to make it all the way into the Rhineland in one hop. We crossed the Channel without event and put down at Lille, France, to gas up and spend the night.

We got up early the next morning and went out to the air-base. Everything looked fine, so we took off in our little puddle-jumper, headed for some obscure destination in Germany called Brühl, which was where we were to deliver our liaison officer.

Brühl is a suburb, a wye in the railroad, about ten miles south of Cologne. It was alarmingly close to the Rhine, and the German Army was just on the other side of that river. At least, we hoped they were all on the other side by the time of our arrival.

When we arrived at Brühl there were farms and green pastures all around, but no airfield. We checked the maps and the orders. This clearly was where we were to go, but where were we to land? Speer circled the place about five times. Each time he flew on the Rhineward side of Brühl, I yelled at him to look inconspicuous. I expected a flak shell through the Norseman momentarily, remembering how well *panzer* troops could shoot at aeroplanes.

Finally we gave up. We went west again till we found an impromptu airfield out in the boonies which had P-38 fighters parked all over it. It had to be a Ninth Air Force operation so we called the tower, and came in to land.

The whole airbase was made of pierced steel track. This remarkable material, laid on the local mud, made runways, taxiways, and aeroplane stands for a whole tactical fighter group. It was the bright idea of some inventive genius.

We asked how to find the airfield at Brühl. Nobody knew, so they took us to their leader.

The commanding officer of the P-38 outfit was a light colonel. He was in his command tent with his mess kit out, just ready to eat lunch. He invited us to have lunch with him and we accepted. It was good chow, served up on a G.I. tin plate.

I commented to the colonel that our information was a little out of date so his steel airfield was not shown as an emergency landing opportunity for a B-24 in trouble. I said that I intended to add it to my navigators' lists of good places when I got back to Horsham.

'Don't bring any of your goddam bombers in here!' the colonel said. 'They'll mash my track so deep we'll never be able to dig it out. We'd have that big ugly motherfucker stuck in the mud here forever. I'll shoot the son-of-a-bitch who brings a B-24 in here!'

The colonel told us that the place we were expected to land our Norseman was a green cow pasture just to the south-west of downtown Brühl, and he drew us a little map of the correct pasture on a page of his notebook. He said that if we looked closely, we would see that some thoughtful person had stuck up a windsock alongside the fence.

After lunch we went back to our Norseman. We had to sit there for a while. A bunch of P-38s were landing from a strafing mission. They were taxying, each to its assigned steel parking area. A G.I. mechanic was walking towards us along the steel planking, carrying his mess kit. He stepped off the plank taxiway to avoid a P-38 taxying towards him. There was a sudden sharp explosion. The G.I. had stepped on a land mine – a booby trap – one of many left behind by the retreating Germans in their thoughtfulness. The kid's leg was blown off above the knee.

The medics were with him in an instant, hauling him off to the field hospital. I exercised skill to keep from vomiting at the sight. We had walked down the same steel planking ten minutes previously. I hoped that the land mine victim would survive, but I knew it would be quite a while before he walked again.

A bit shaken, we fired up the Norseman, and took off when the runway was clear. We found our cow pasture at Brühl and landed, more or less expertly. But taxying was a problem. The place was very muddy.

We found our Signal Corps people and got a jeep ride downtown where we found quarters and bunked in for overnight. That evening, we discovered, there was a movie to be shown at the G.I. theatre, appropriated by the Americans for the purpose in downtown Brühl. Speer and I decided to go and watch Jimmy Stewart, or whomever, on the silver screen.

My John Roscoe 45 automatic was government issue for all flying officers. It came with a shoulder holster, just like the ones worn by Capone torpedos, but I shortened the strap and wore it on my hip, like Gary Cooper or Tom Mix would have done. We were walking down the main street of Brühl at dusk when I sensed an upstairs window open opposite us. Thinking immediately of a German sniper, I pushed Speer into a doorway. I had (fortunately) left the Thompson gun under the bed in our quarters, so I unlimbered my John Roscoe. Across the street was a pretty girl, hanging her sweater out to dry on the window shutter.

The girl did not know the frightful danger she was in. Of course, my expertise with the John Roscoe was such that I could never have shot her, but I surely would have hit the building she was in.

We delivered our liaison officer to the local honcho of Signal Corps. This person was a captain, a gutsy little guy, who ran around the battle lines in his jeep, moving his signal beacons. We had a particular love for the men of Signal Corps, for we knew that they had been the first home of Army fliers.

Our captain invited us on a trip the next morning. He had, he said, to go into Cologne, and we were invited to go along. Speer and I piled into the back of the captain's jeep, and he drove expertly into the very middle of the city. I was astounded at the damage our bombing had done to Cologne – there was no building in the place intact. I doubted that any plumbing worked, or any utilities at all. Particularly impressive were the gigantic craters where the RAF had dropped their five-ton 'block-buster' bombs in their night saturation raids.

Our captain drove his jeep into the central square of Cologne. There was the great cathedral of Cologne, known around the world from its postcard pictures. Built to the 1300-vintage plans of architect Gerard, a designer of Amiens Cathedral, this great building had not been finished until 1880. The nave and choir vaults of Cologne are the highest of any Gothic church in the world, exceeding in altitude by one foot those of the half-cathedral of Beauvais.

I decided that I had to look inside the cathedral, but the vast church is on the river-bank and the Germans were on the other side of the Rhine. I crouched and scooted across the square, trying to look totally inconspicuous, and went into the cathedral. With devastation all around, the damage was remarkably slight. There were a few holes in the vaults and all the glass was shattered, but the main fabric was essentially intact. I was filled with admiration for mediaeval building methods.

When I got back to the Signal Corps jeep there was a lieutenant-colonel of infantry standing there.

'Will you flyboys kindly pack up and get the hell out of here,' he said, 'The damn Germans are right across the river there with their artillery, and I don't want any more fire drawn over here than we have to get. So please go!'

I was embarrassed. We got in the jeep to drive off, but our little captain of Signal Corps was not intimidated.

'We're fightin' this war too, you know, buddy,' he said, 'I'll drive where I damn well please, or where I'm ordered to!' He put the jeep in gear and took off, leaving the lieutenant-colonel standing in a cloud of dust.

Next morning Speer and I decided that we better get back to Horsham and keep running the store. We went out to our cow pasture with our returning liaison officer, climbed on board, fired up the Norseman, let the brakes off, and shoved the throttle to the firewall – nothing! The wheels were totally mired in local German mud.

We got out to discuss the problem with the little captain.

'Hell, that's no problem,' he said. He ordered four G.I.s to help us. Two got hold of the wing struts on each side and pushed while we revved the engine. The Norseman pulled out of the mud reluctantly and taxied with two men pushing on each side. We got it rolled into take-off position.

Speer pushed the throttle full open, the G.I.s shoved like mad, and we began to roll slowly. When the G.I.s got up to their full running speed they gave a mighty shove and ran clear. We gathered speed slowly and ponderously as the tyres sloshed through more mud. The ditch at the end of the cow pasture was coming up rapidly – I figured we would leave the wheels in it, but Maurice Speer gave a mighty heave backward on the stick as we got to the ditch. We jumped it and continued rolling through the next cow pasture full of mud. There was a ditch at the end of that cow pasture. We had enough speed to jump that one more easily.

I looked ahead. Instead of a ditch there was a big hedge at the end of the third cow pasture. About halfway through the pasture Speer hauled back on the wheel. The Norseman staggered into the air in a semi-stall, dipped a bit gaining airspeed, and cleared the hedge by about a quarter of an inch. We were on our way back to England.

We had a strong headwind going across France. Speer worried that we would not have enough gas to get to Lille. So did I, but we made it without mishap. We refuelled, took off, crossed the Channel, and headed north. Our returning liaison officer was a pilot of the 392nd Bomb Group, so we delivered him to the air-base at Wendling and headed east for Horsham.

458th Bomb Group formation peeling off to land at Horsham St Faith.

Bishop Losinga built his Cathedral in Norwich in 1096, thirty years after the Norman conquest. The people of the middle ages built gigantic churches in the centre of their cities. Today we build tall bank buildings. 'Render unto Caesar . . .'

Norwich Cathedral once had a wooden spire which blew down in a big storm, taking a part of the original wooden roof with it, so in the 1300s the cathedral was topped with stone lierne vaulting. In 1490 a stone spire, rising three hundred and fifteen feet into the sky, was built on the old Norman foundations. This spire was our constant navigational landmark in coming home to Horsham St Faith. We could see it for miles in any direction, and as we skimmed the treetops with the little Norseman, the cathedral spire of Norwich was an especially welcome sight – it told us we were safely home again. We swung around it, lined up on our runway, put down the Norseman and taxied into the hangar.

We were back in England again after a brief adventure in the enemy's land.

CHAPTER 22

THE ACCUSATION

After I became the Group Navigator my relationships with my crew suffered a good deal. I spent more and more time in headquarters wheeling and dealing, and time at the club with Group and Wing staff people. My bout with strep throat which sent me to the hospital had put me a couple of missions behind everybody else, and my crew now often went out on missions with a different navigator.

Eddie Gniewkowski was such a proficient bombardier that he was borrowed to fly with other crews for a few special missions. On 31 January 1945, he had flown his last required mission out of a tour of thirty. A few days later word came that Eddie's father had died, leaving some of Eddie's minor siblings home alone. With the help of the Red Cross, Eddie left us and hastened home to Michigan. I was not to see him again.

Over the months of our combat flight duties I had watched Bob Hayzlett grow less and less enamoured of Eighth Air Force strategic bombing. And our duties, in spite of what the American newspapers said of us, had an exceedingly black side. The thrill and excitement, which no one could deny, was countered by the omnipresent stress of a highly dangerous job. Also there was the continual shock of the loss of friends – people like Charlie Giesen – with us one day and gone the next.

With Gniewkowski gone home, and me preoccupied with desk duties, Hayzlett commanded a lead crew which had to borrow front office people to fly a mission. He sampled the opinion of his crew's excellent enlisted men, they could not care less whether or not their bomber flew leading the formation.

So, what remained of Hayzlett's crew, minus three of the four original officers, flew its last mission, hanging out in a wing ship position at the side of the formation, on 15 February 1945. They went, of course, off to bomb Magdeburg. That job done, they went home.

In the high command levels of Eighth United States Army Air Force, the mills of the military gods grind slowly, but exceeding fine. Lieutenants Sincock and Balides of the 392nd Bomb Group had been taken off lead crew duties the day after their distressing visit to Switzerland.

Meanwhile continual discussion went on among the mighty about the 4 March attacks led by the 392nd and 466th Bomb Groups on a neutral country. That not all of this discussion may have been happy is indicated by the recollection of Brigadier-General Leon Johnson. He commanded 14th Combat Wing on the day we bombed Switzerland, and the 392nd Bomb Group was a part of that wing.

B-24 *Final Approach* taking off for a raid on Berlin in February 1945. (*Courtesy Memorial Library, Second Air Division, USAAF – Norwich, England.*)

General Johnson was one of the first four flight-rated officers assigned to Eighth Air Force, and an authentic hero. He was awarded the Medal of Honor for his outstanding performance commanding 44th Bomb Group, 'The Flying Eightballs', during the attack on the oil refineries of Ploesti, Rumania, on 1 August 1943. He recalled that General Spaatz suggested that he and General Walter Peck, commanding 96th Combat Wing (which included the 466th Bomb Group), be relieved of command and sent back to the States as a result of the 4 March 1945 attacks on the Swiss. Johnson remembered that General Doolittle defended them both successfully. General Doolittle did not later specifically remember Spaatz asking that Johnson and Peck be set down, but he did recall that both were highly competent officers and worthy of his full support.

Whatever went on in high command, one can hardly blame General Spaatz for being a bit bent out of shape. Chances are most of the yelling from the Home Office echoed in his ears.

The rumbling in the volcano's throat eventually burst into the open. On 8 May 1945, Colonel Lorin L. Johnson, commanding 392nd Bomb Group, signed a formal paper, charging Lieutenant William R. Sincock and Lieutenant Theodore Balides with violation of the 96th Article of War. The fat was in the fire.

The specific charges against Sincock read:

'In that First Lieutenant William R. Sincock, 576th Bombardment Squadron, 392nd Bombardment Group, while in command of and piloting a B-24 type aircraft flying in the position of a squadron leader on a combat operational mission, did, at or near Zurich, Switzerland, on or about 4 March 1945, wrongfully, negligently and contrary to the provisions of Field Order Number 618, Second Air Division, APO 558, U.S. Army, dated 3 March 1945, cause the planes of the formation he was then leading to drop bombs upon and near the city of Zurich, Switzerland, which territory belongs to Switzerland, a nation friendly to the United States of America and to the United Nations.'

The specific charges against Balides read:

'In that First Lieutenant Theodore Balides, 579th Bombardment Squadron, 392nd Bombardment Group, while dead reckoning navigator in a B-24 type aircraft flying in the position of squadron leader on a combat operational mission, did, at or near Zurich, on or about 4 March 1945, wrongfully, negligently and contrary to the provisions of 2nd Bombardment Division Instructions No. 55–16, Headquarters 2nd Bombardment Division, APO 558, U.S. Army, dated 3 August 1944, fail to maintain a complete and accurate log and chart and did negligently and incorrectly determine the then existing geographical position of his aircraft to be in the area of Frieburg [sic], Germany and convey such incorrect information to the officer commanding said aircraft, who, in reliance thereon, caused the planes of the formation he was then leading to drop bombs upon and near the city of Zurich, Switzerland, which territory belongs to Switzerland, a nation friendly to the United States of America and to the United Nations.'

Chances are that Sincock had never heard of Field Order Number 618, and Balides had never heard of 2nd Bombardment Division (the predecessor organisation to Second Air Division) Instructions Number 55–16, and that neither one of them had ever read the 96th Article of War. These charges demonstrate, if nothing else, that military lawyers write with just as much excess verbiage as do civilian lawyers.

There is some self-contradiction in the way the charges are drawn up. Careful reading of the charges against Balides seems to show that, if he is guilty, Sincock is innocent. Nonetheless, these two young officers were in a highly unnerving position and the charges were serious enough to call for a general court martial.

Colonel Lorin Johnson did not execute the affidavit associated with the formal charges against Sincock and Balides, which is an indication that he believed the accused to be innocent. Colonel Johnson, in fact, was later to offer to testify in the defence of his two lieutenants. Whether Johnson was under pressure to file these charges, and from whom, is not recorded. However, Lieutenant-Colonel Birney van Benschoten, Acting Judge Advocate General of the Eighth Air Force, wrote in a memo the understanding that General Spaatz had suggested that the charges go to trial. The 'suggestion' of a four-star general usually gets a lot of careful attention.

Sincock and Balides were not arrested nor confined as a result of the charges filed against them. The charges were investigated by Lieutenant-Colonel James W. Wall, commanding the 465th Sub-Depot, stationed at

Wendling. Captain Olen F. Levell, Jr signed the results of the investigation of charges against Sincock. Major Myron H. Keilman, who flew group command on the day of the Zurich bombing, approved the investigation report of the charges against Balides. In further approving the investigation report regarding Sincock, Colonel Lorin Johnson wrote:

' . . . I recommend that in the interests of the service as well as for his own protection, the accused be tried by general court-martial.'

On 10 May 1945 Lieutenant-General James H. Doolittle stepped down from command of Eighth Air Force. He returned to the States to plan the movement home again of the Eighth, its equipping with B-29 bombers, and its actions against the Japanese homeland.

Major-General William E. Kepner moved up from Second Air Division to command the Eighth Air Force. Replacing Kepner in command of Second Air Division was Brigadier-General Walter Peck.

The charges brought against Lieutenants Sincock and Balides were not minor. In 1945 the 96th Article of War read:

'General Article. – Though not mentioned in these articles, all disorders and neglects to the prejudice of good order and military discipline, all conduct of a nature to bring discredit upon the military service, and all crimes or offenses not capital, of which persons subject to military law may be guilty, shall be taken cognizance of by a general or special or summary court-martial, according to the nature and degree of the offense, and punished at the discretion of such court.'

Lieutenant-Colonel Birney M. van Benschoten set forth, in a memo to General Kepner, the punishments that could fall on Sincock and Balides if they were convicted of the charges levied against them. Such punishments included dismissal from the U.S. Military Service, forfeitures of all pay due, and confinement at hard labour for life. The two young officers did not face a pleasant prospect in their forthcoming trial.

On 21 May 1945 Major Burnis Archer, assistant Eighth Air Force Adjutant-General, signed the endorsement, by command of General Kepner, naming Major Richard M. Krannawitter, Air Corps, as Trial Judge Advocate in the general court martial of Lieutenants Sincock and Balides. Two days later, on 23 May, Krannawitter personally delivered to Sincock and Balides a copy each of the court martial orders.

We had not heard much of our flamboyant friend, Lieutenant Max Sokarl, since he went off to Second Air Division Headquarters to serve there in his position as aide-de-camp to General Walter Peck, now commanding the Division. We missed Sokarl's ex-cathedra pronouncements around the club, and his wonderful tales and fables about the state of the world in general, and sex in particular.

But now that Sincock and Balides were to be led forth for potential keel-hauling, it was decided that their general court martial would be held at Ketteringham Hall, Second Air Division Headquarters. Hence it would fall to General Peck to order up and organise the court. He gave this entire awesome responsibility to Max Sokarl.

The job could not have come to anyone who would appreciate it more. Sokarl manifestly enjoyed making maximum drama out of almost any mundane situation. Now he could get his teeth into what was apt to, and did, turn into the biggest general court ever held in Eighth Air Force.

My job at Horsham St Faith had changed. The Eighth Air Force dropped its last bombs on Germany on 25 April 1945. The 458th went out that day to drop bombs on Bad Reichenhall, and there was no resistance at all from the Nazi defences.

On 7 May 1945 the War ended in Europe.

At last our job of hauling death and destruction was over – there would be no more air war over Germany for us. It was a great relief, but it was also a great sadness. Something memorable had gone out of our lives, never to return.

Orders came down from high command that all bomber navigators be given refresher training in celestial and trans-oceanic navigation. Following these orders, and passing them on to squadron navigators, I set up a programme for each navigator to go through a rehash of his celestial navigation practices, a discipline not used in combat flight over Europe.

This change of pace gave me a little time for personal recreation. I went downtown in Norwich and wandered through the castle and the cathedral, the old curved and narrow streets were fascinating. In the castle museum I read of how many times the fearsome Danes had come up the Wensum River in their longships to steal the chickens and rape the women. Norwich had seen warfare many times before the Eighth Air Force arrived.

One evening, having tired a bit of club conversation, I went into Norwich to the theatre. While vaudeville may have been dead in the United States in 1945, it was very much alive in England. I found English vaudeville to be quite entertaining. Among the favourite topics of the vaudevillian's jokes were the American troops who had been all over England for the last three years or so. Lines like 'There's so much chewing gum in Trafalgar Square the pigeons are dropping rubber balls!' never failed to bring down the house. I had no objection to being an American cousin and the butt of British jokes. I figured the English had been through enough tough years and that they deserved something to laugh at.

The vaudeville troupe touring Norwich at the time had a dancer listed on the programme as Valerie Forde. She did a wonderful spoof act in which, among other things, she rolled herself up in the curtain (apparently inadvertently) then unwound to skid across the stage on her butt.

There was something about this vaudeville troupe that sent me. I went back to see the performance several nights in a row, so often that soon I could unravel all the magician's tricks, and I laughed every night at Valerie Forde. She was a pert little blonde, cute as a bug's ear.

So one night I waited at the stage door till Valerie came out with two of her dancer friends.

'How about a date?' I asked.

'Too late, Yank,' she said, 'I got to get my sleep.'

'I mean tomorrow,' I said.

'Well, maybe. What's on your mind?'

'How about lunch?'

'Sure. Meet me here at noon.'

I felt silly standing outside the theatre stage door at high noon. Somehow I confidently expected to be stood up. Probably my dancer just said 'noon' to get rid of me.

However, Valerie Forde showed up right on time, so we went to a little tea shop a couple of blocks away and had lunch. It was not a particularly exotic place, but Valerie said she had never had lunch in such elegant surroundings before. I didn't know whether theatre people were too poor to eat, or she was putting me on.

Then we toured the old Norman castle, now converted to the museum. Valerie alleged that she had never been in a museum before. She was fascinated with the displays, the ancient armour, and the battle weapons. Apparently for the first time she had discovered that England had a history. We spent hours in the place.

Two days later I met Valerie again. We had lunch in a different restaurant, and walked the parks of Norwich, the river-bank, and the cathedral close. Valerie was fascinated; she must have spent most of her life on the road or on stage. I didn't go back to watch her comic dance again after that evening. When the sets were struck after the last show, Valerie's troupe took the night train out of Norwich, and headed off for the next theatre at which they were booked.

The day following I was in my office going over the progress reports on celestial navigation training, when the phone rang.

It was Max Sokarl.

'Jack, I have superb, magnificent, wonderful and exciting news for you!' Max said.

'I see.'

'You will be absolutely overwhelmed by what I've done for you. You'll be famous!'

'I don't need to be famous, Max. What's up?'

'Are you ready for this? Are you sitting down?'

'I'm sitting down, Max. How's it going up there, polishing the General's boots?'

'The General and I get along just fine. He does his thing, and I do mine. And I always remember my old friends. I take care of my friends.'

'What the hell are you up to, Max?'

'You may recall that a couple of high-ranking lieutenants from the 392nd Bomb Group took an impromptu tour and unloaded their bombs on downtown Switzerland.'

'I've heard something to that effect, yes.'

'Well, Jack, they've got to stand before a general court martial. It's very serious.'

'Yes. No doubt.'

'And, Jack, General Peck has just appointed you to be their defence counsel.'

'He what?'

'I say, he's appointed you to be their defence attorney.'

'Have you gone crazy, Max?'

'Certainly not. I'm as sane as I ever was.'

'That's not saying much. What have you done to me, Max? This is your half-baked idea, isn't it?'

'You should be honoured that the General has confidence in you.'

'The General doesn't know who the hell I am. You did this! I can't get mixed up in this mess, Max. I don't know anything about military law.'

'Relax. The General has provided you with highly competent help.'

'Who?'

'Well, Yours Truly, for instance.'

'Yes. Anyone else?'

'Yes. Goldman will also assist you.'

'He's the radar officer.'

'He's also about the best attorney you'll ever meet. He's excellent. He'll be our one-man brain trust.'

'Goldman is a captain. Make him the defence attorney.'

'Your date of rank preceeds Goldman's. You outrank him by military rules. We need an expert navigator on this defence. You're it, and because of your superb high rank, you will be the defence attorney.'

'I can't do this, Max.'

'The General has already signed the order. Are you going to tell him to shove it?'

'No. I guess not.'

'Great. This will be a magnificent case. You'll be world famous!'

'Yes. I bet.'

Sokarl was not kidding. He had named me as defence attorney for Sincock and Balides. General Peck had signed the order. A copy came for me the next day, naming the entire board of the court martial with my name on it.

I was trapped.

CHAPTER 23

GETTING READY FOR TRIAL

Navigation training for overseas flight was going well for navigators of the 458th. However, now that Sokarl, with his Machiavellian mind, had got me appointed as a defence counsel for Sincock and Balides I had no time to refresh my own navigation skills. Presumably, though, if we went somewhere, I could ride as a passenger. My crew had already gone home so I had no regular crew assignment.

It was about two days after the first disturbing call from Sokarl that I got a second.

'We need to have a big conference tomorrow,' he said, 'the General has ordered it.'

'Yes, Max, I'll bet he has.'

'You'll enjoy this. No need to fuss. I'll send transportation over there for you and Goldman. Can you be picked up at headquarters building at eight a.m?'

'I'll write out my excuse, Max. I'm sure the Colonel will approve it, since General Peck has ordered it.'

'Yes. Well see you tomorrow. I'll be looking forward to it!'

'You bet.'

Captain Irving Goldman was the opposite of Max Sokarl, while Sokarl exuded garrulous bombast, Goldman was thoughtful and quiet. He was exceedingly polite and considerate and had genuine concern for people and their welfare.

Goldman and I were standing in front of headquarters building at eight a.m. when the transportation arrived. Sokarl had sent the gigantic black limousine belonging to General Peck. The flag on the front bumper was covered, but it was still one of the most impressive vehicles in petrol-starved East Anglia.

As we drove out of the gate at Horsham, the M.P. on duty racked to rigid attention. Goldman and I solemnly returned his salute. Our drive to Headquarters, Second Air Division, took us directly across the city of Norwich. Ketteringham Hall was in roughly the same relative location south of Norwich that Horsham St Faith was to the north. At the gates of Ketteringham Hall, we were met with another remarkable reception. The guards racked to rigid attention and we returned their salute with brisk military precision, smiling all the while.

We were led into Sokarl's office. As aide-de-camp to the Division Commanding General, Sokarl, a high-ranking first lieutenant (as he would say), had an office roughly equivalent to that occupied by Colonel Herzberg, our group commander. The whole place reeked with ancient British opulence. There was no doubt about it, Max Sokarl was a highly professional *macher*.

Sokarl introduced us to Major Richard Krannawitter, Trial Judge Advocate for the court assigned to try the charges against Lieutenants Sincock and Balides. I was amazed. There was no doubt that someone had picked a worthy opponent. Krannawitter was an older, higher-ranking, sort of out-west and down-south version of Sokarl himself. The verbiage flowed from Krannawitter just as smoothly as it did from Sokarl. If anything, he was even more fluent, only the style was a bit different. Whereas Max Sokarl was somewhere between Brooklyn and Boston, Richard Krannawitter was somewhere between Big-D and Yuma – more of the Judge Roy Bean personality. He exuded good-ole-boy and steer manure philosophy all over the place.

With Krannawitter was his assistant, Captain Albert Mason. Mason was quiet and studious and was a rated navigator. His job was that of a duty navigator in operations at Headquarters, Eighth Air Force. Mason said very little, but there was no need for him to talk. Krannawitter said it all.

Sokarl and Krannawitter opened up with some preliminary sparring that indicated this was apt to be a memorable trial indeed from the standpoint of flowery statement. As they approached paragraph three hundred and six, Goldman interrupted with a pertinent question.

'Is this a put-up job?' he asked.

Sokarl took on a horrified look. 'What do you mean?' he asked.

'I mean is the result of this court martial cut and dried and a foregone conclusion? Are we just putting on a show here to make high command look good?'

'You cut me to the quick,' Sokarl said, placing his hand over his heart. 'Surely you do not cast aspersions upon the character of General Walter Peck, commanding Second Air Division, or upon the character of General William Kepner, commanding Eighth Air Force. These gentlemen have ordered up this trial in order to see that justice is done. There is no other reason. To suspect so is unthinkable.'

'I understand, Max,' Goldman said, 'But is it a put-up job?'

'Certainly not!' Krannawitter broke in, 'I don't mess around with put-up jobs. The young gentlemen on trial here have their reputations and their whole future on the line. This is a terrible thing that's happened, this bombing of a friendly and neutral country. Conviction could lead to these officers having their hides hung out to dry.'

'O.K.', Goldman said.

Sokarl and Krannawitter continued with their discussions of the forthcoming trial. Occasionally Goldman put in a telling point, but Mason and I had little to contribute to this discussion. About mid-morning, the learned attorneys expressed their wish that Mason and I go over the navigation records that Balides had kept on the ill-fated mission to Switzerland. We should all, they indicated, be intimately familiar with what had happened, and with what had probably gone wrong.

So Mason and I spent the balance of the time looking at Balides' work, and seeing if we could organise a plan of attack towards rebuilding the actual path of the lost high squadron of 392nd Bomb Group on that fatal fourth of March, 1945.

By the end of our first session at Ketteringham Hall we had all agreed on our approach. Mason and I were to meet, going over the records kept by Balides in detail, but there was no reason for Krannawitter, Goldman, and Sokarl to meet so often until we had the navigation story in hand.

In the early afternoon Irv Goldman and I rode the General's limousine back to Horsham St Faith. We got the same V.I.P. treatment from the gate guards that we had going south.

Max Sokarl apparently never tired of an exciting project. That evening he was at Horsham St Faith, rounding me up along with Goldman for an impromptu conference.

Sokarl and Goldman had a long, involved, and legal-technical discussion about the upcoming trial of Sincock and Balides. Since I was nominally the defence counsel, they included me in all of it which gave me considerable insight into the way they worked together. Goldman was the deep thinker, the introspective one, the one who knew every fine point of the law. Sokarl would lean heavily on Goldman for guidance, then translate that insight into his own unique kind of presentation, guaranteed to make the listener cry in sympathy.

Like many of Sokarl's conferences, this one eventually degenerated into one of his philosophy and fable sessions.

Sokarl's current paramour was an English lady. She was single, a doctor of psychiatry, or some such; very learned, very British, and very cultured. Because he liked to show off his victories in the love department, Sokarl had arranged that Goldman and I be invited to this lady's home for tea and crumpets, or whatever. I recall that it was a somewhat stiff session for us. Goldman and I felt as though we had just dropped from Mars into this lady's parlour.

But Max was charm itself in caring for the whims of his English girlfriend. We got some insight into how smooth his line really was, and why almost any woman would have been flattered by Sokarl's attentions. He could be Mr Romance, personified.

Max's later detailed description of his success in getting repeatedly into this lady's panties was so fascinating that we could not stop listening, but basically so unseemly that we wished we hadn't heard.

Captain Albert Mason and I set up a series of study sessions at Horsham St Faith. The location was good from my standpoint, since it kept me near my office in case anything important in Group navigation might happen, which it did not.

Mason brought with him Captain Benjamin Foote. Foote was a navigator who had completed a tour of thirty missions over Europe, whose current assignment was Assistant to the Director of Intelligence, Eighth Air Force. In his job at Air Force Headquarters, Foote plotted the briefed route and the actual track flown by all wing lead aircraft of the Eighth on each mission. Clearly he was a valuable man to have around on this case.

When we began to dissect the records kept by Balides, it became clear that there had been ample difficulties in navigation on the mission to bomb

Switzerland. For a period of eighteen and a half minutes, beginning at 9.51 a.m. on 4 March 1945, there were no entries in the navigation log. That was the time period during which Sincock took his squadron on a long, full-circle turn through the cloud tops, looking for the 44th Bomb Group formation.

Probably few navigators in the Eighth Air Force could accurately track a bomber formation through a wide, wandering turn. With the terrible weather conditions at flight altitude it was not possible for the pilotage navigator in the nose turret to help, and the malfunctioning Mickey set was apparently not putting out reliable information.

The air position indicator was a brand new development at the time, and there were none in operational use in the Eighth, to our knowledge. Air position indicators integrated instrument inputs to display longitude and latitude from some initial position, assuming no wind. They later proved to be valuable in navigating aircraft through complex manoeuvres.

Balides had recorded nothing during the period of the long turn. There may well have been frustration and upset on board Sincock's ship while everyone wondered what the hell to do and Balides may have been preoccupied with a long discussion, or so we surmised. Riding the lead ship of a formation of six bombers, lost in the weather over Germany with no fighter escort, was not an enviable position in which to be at any time in the War.

At 10.09 a.m. Balides had logged a fix apparently given to him by Lieutenant Milrod at the Mickey set. This radar fix, from a bearing and distance on Stuttgart, was logged as eight degrees, fifty minutes east longitude – forty-eight degrees, forty-three minutes north latitude. But in plotting the position on his chart, Balides fixed the point at eight degrees, forty three minutes east longitude – forty-eight degrees fifty minutes north latitude. He had reversed the minute readings for latitude and longitude. Hence his chart now showed him to be flying about twenty five miles north-west of where he actually was.

This was the kind of error that any navigator might occasionally make under the pressure of combat flying. Usually the error is found later, and corrected. But Balides did not find nor correct his error. He charted his position from that point and continued from there.

I began to feel a good deal of worry for Lieutenant Balides. What if the prosecution were to seize on this error as a perfect example of gross negligence, and hammer home the point? Suppose the voting members of the court were convinced? Military justice was known for inflexible toughness. Balides might be on his way to a lifetime career on the rock pile at Fort Leavenworth Federal Prison.

I looked at Captain Mason to see if I could get some idea of the prosecution view of these findings. But he was calm and non-committal. His demeanour revealed nothing.

We also discovered that the wind which Balides used was probably about seventy degrees in direction off the actual wind at operational altitude that day. This mistaken direction of high-velocity wind at flight altitude resulted in the assumed true headings which Balides had used being about thirty degrees off actual. Thus, the farther Sincock's bomber flew, the more northerly became Balides' computed position from his actual position. These errors accumulated till Balides was deluded into concurring with the mistaken identification of Zurich as Freiburg.

To make matters look even blacker, we had the flight log and chart of Lieutenant Damerst who flew navigator in the right wingship next to Sincock on 4 March 1945. Insofar as we could determine the actual track of the lost squadron, it seemed that Damerst was within five or ten miles of the correct position throughout the mission. We wondered why his pilot had not called Sincock to ask what the hell was going on.

Knowing that we would need to tell this story in detail in court, we undertook a time-consuming project. We mounted a large chart of Europe on a big display board and on the chart we plotted three routes. The briefed route for the day we plotted in green; the route according to Balides we plotted in black, the route that we believed the squadron to have taken we plotted in red. The red line was the one that went over downtown Zurich.

Several days were taken up in this reconstruction of the path of the 392nd's lost squadron, and when we were done we got together with the legal eagles to go over our findings.

Mason briefed Major Krannawitter on what we had done, and using the same chart, I briefed Sokarl and Goldman. It was an interesting session.

It came out in the conversation that Sokarl did not know what navigational co-ordinates were. When I tried to explain longitude and latitude, it developed that he did not know the earth was a sphere. He seemed fascinated when I imparted that information to him. He had no inkling whatever of planetary motions, the positions of the Sun and Moon relative to the Earth, or any rudimentary facts of the kind commonly taught in grade school. It was as though he had been born in the dark ages.

Goldman began berating him. 'Good grief, Max,' he said, 'I can't believe what I'm hearing here. I hope you're kidding us. Is it actually possible that you are such an ignoramus you don't know the world is round?'

'Who cares?' Sokarl said.

'Many people care. You should care!'

'I don't care. I'm a damn lawyer. What the fuck good does it do me to know the world is round or square or whatever the hell it is? If it has nothing to do with the practice of law this week, piss on it!'

'But an attorney should be familiar with facts of the case in hand. If you don't know that, how can you possibly understand the rudiments of navigation? And clearly this present case, a hell of an important one, hinges mightily on a knowledge of navigation.'

'That's why we've got Granholm here. He knows all the navigation I need to know. Let him figure out what shape the world is. All I've got to do is tell the court convincingly after he briefs me.'

'My aching back!' Goldman said.

Thus it became apparent that we were fated to go into court with a mouthpiece attorney who was a flat-Earth thinker.

CHAPTER 24

COUNSEL FOR THE DEFENCE

Captain Irving Goldman undertook an in-depth study of the accusations against Sincock and Balides. He read the statements of charges and the 96th Article of War, and prepared his own analysis of what might happen, and what we should do. He went over his notes and findings in great detail with Max Sokarl.

I was a party to these proceedings. I felt somewhat like a camel among the giraffes, snowed with legal terminology, and trying to think clearly in an area in which I had no background nor training, and even less experience.

Goldman was good at getting to the heart of the matter, and in reducing legal terminology to speech of the common man. Sokarl could not tear his mind away from the utter drama of the situation. He was clearly enjoying himself a great deal, but I felt more comfortable with Goldman's down-to-earth realism than I did in depending on Sokarl's dramatics to get us through the coming ordeal. I asked Goldman's opinion of the probable outcome.

'It's probably a toss-up,' he said. 'We can assume that the high command is pretty irked at this whole episode, or we wouldn't be having a trial in the first place. Can we get an acquittal? I frankly don't know. Military courts are noted for being tough. Mercy is not a word found in the military manuals. And we're organised differently here from a civilian court. You won't, for example, find any enlisted men on the court roster. Maybe that's a good thing. Their natural inclination might be to send any accused officer to Leavenworth. The board also acts as the jury. They have powers and responsibilities different from those of civilian jurymen. All of us in military service are subject to reprimand and punishment of one kind or another from higher command. That spectre has got to sit on the court members also, no matter how independent they may think they are. These two guys may just go up the river without a paddle, and there may be nothing that we can do about it. Don't be too disappointed if they get hung.'

As a part of the duties of the defence, we met with our clients, Lieutenants Sincock and Balides. The first session was in Sokarl's office at Ketteringham Hall, and as usual, Max sent General Peck's car to Horsham St Faith so that Goldman and I could ride across town in it. We got the V.I.P. treatment going both directions.

If ever in my life I saw two worried young men, it was Sincock and Balides. They were each scared silly, and who could blame them? They stood accused of heinous crimes against the Government of the United States, and of having launched a wanton and unprovoked attack upon a neutral country. They had a good chance of losing all, and being locked up and forgotten on the rock pile till Hell froze over.

The very atmosphere of Ketteringham Hall with its British posh, contrasting so vastly with the Nissen huts and mud of Wendling, was enough to make them nervous, and the situation they were in was totally unnerving. We did our best to make them feel comfortable with us, but I would not have blamed them for wondering who were these three inept characters in whose hands their lives had been placed. Sokarl tried to relax them with a bit of high-level and friendly bullshit. He was able to be so charming that their diastolic pressures may have possibly dropped below a hundred or so.

Sincock and Balides had the right to ask for and get separate trials, and we discussed this with them. They elected to have a common trial. In retrospect, this decision was probably wise. Why not choose a common trial? At least there would be one known and friendly face in the courtroom and just as they had faced being shot out of the sky on many occasions, if they went down this last time, they would go together.

Sokarl went over in detail the statements that Sincock and Balides had given to Lieutenant-Colonel James Wall, who investigated the incident. Sokarl told Sincock what it was that he should have said, which seemed to me a fruitless exercise, since Sincock and Balides had never heard of Sokarl at the time Wall interrogated them, and Sokarl knew nothing at that time of the details of the bombs dropped on Zurich.

In his statement to Lieutenant-Colonel Wall, Sincock said that he had been briefed to lead the high right squadron of the 392nd on a mission to Aschaffenburg where they were to bomb a chemical plant. If the plant was obscured by clouds, they were to bomb it by gee-H, and if the gee-H was out they were to dump on the railroad yards by radar (Mickey). As a final resort they were to attack a target of opportunity. Sincock stated that he was well aware of the locations of all briefed targets.

This last statement possibly should not have been made. Sokarl's view about it had some validity. It was my experience that many bomber pilots had really only a vague idea of geography. Before getting their wings they all underwent some navigation training, which they promptly forgot, and they tended to depend heavily on their navigators. There was nothing wrong with that: that's what the navigator was there for.

Sincock stated that the assembly over the continent was ordered, as he understood it, because the weather over England was predicted to be bad. He took off in aircraft number 385 and was up to six thousand feet, and climbing, before he discovered that both the H2X radar and the gee set were not functioning properly. He stated that Major Keilman in the Group lead ship instructed him to go back to base and get another aeroplane.

So Sincock and his crew (he said) returned to Wendling, climbed aboard lead ship number 577, and took off again. They were up and flying towards Europe when they discovered that the H2X was malfunctioning on that bomber also, but the gee seemed to be all right, so they continued on course.

The assembly over France was 'very difficult', as Sincock described it, due to dense condensation trails. The difficulty was concurred with by just about everyone who flew that day. Assembly altitude was 23,000 feet above sea level. After assembly, the formation descended to 18,000 feet which was their briefed altitude for the attack that day. Why they had been ordered to descend into what was bound to be worse weather I could not understand.

Sincock noted that, after they crossed the Rhine, Balides told him that gee reception was very poor. Others were to testify that it was a heavy jamming day for the Germans, trying to block out the British navigation aids. Milrod was getting only ten miles of range at the Mickey set. The navigation equipment was functioning very poorly indeed.

Sincock told how he lost the 392nd Group lead squadron when they made a turn to follow the 44th Group which was flying Wing lead position. He found the 44th Group, and then lost them in another turn through the murk. On the horn (so he testified) he heard that all the other groups were attacking targets of opportunity, so he proceeded with bomb bay doors open looking for a target along what he and his crew believed to be the briefed withdrawal route.

If this was true, as described in Sincock's recorded statement to Wall, it was not a particularly brilliant manoeuvre. The B-24 with a bomb load had little extra performance at 18,000 feet. Bomb bay doors added a lot of drag when open, and unnecessary cruising with them so stowed was not a standard manoeuvre. But the lost squadron may have been looking for a target to hit in a hurry, then get out of there to go home. One can hardly blame them.

They broke out of dense clouds into thick haze, according to Sincock. The haze gave them downward visibility, but that was restricted to 'five or six miles'. Balides reported their position as in the vicinity of Freiburg, Germany, and Milrod picked up a city ahead which Sincock presumed might be Freiburg. Sincock then asked Williams and Barger to see if they could identify the place, if at all possible. Both concurred it was Freiburg. They dropped their bombs, aiming at a single-track railroad in the area, and then they went home.

Sincock offered these comments as a statement sworn before and witnessed by Captain Franklin W. Dawson, Summary Court Officer for the 392nd Group. Sokarl took the view that Sincock should have said none of this, and that it might be viewed as an admission of guilt. What Sokarl thought Sincock should have said when being officially interrogated by a lieutenant-colonel was not specified.

The Statement of Lieutenant Balides was much briefer. He described the take-off and the return to get a ship with more operable equipment. He described computing a wind at 6,000 feet while climbing out over the English Channel. But he assumed (no doubt correctly) that this wind would be invalid at flight altitude, so he used the winds provided by the meteorological briefing. Using the briefed wind was probably a big mistake. Such were the unknowns of weather prediction at the time that the weatherman often did not know the wind blowing outside his office door, let alone at flight altitude. The jet stream was not known nor understood in 1945, though, in retrospect, it is obvious that some of the bomber formations of the Eighth flew through the jet stream, sometimes with startling effects on ground speed and resulting in confusion of navigators.

Balides reported his gee set as 'useless' because of the heavy German electronic jamming. Lieutenant Balides described the various manoeuvres of the formation and his squadron, and his attempts to follow them by dead reckoning alone. He told of being asked by Sincock for a 'heading home', and of directing the squadron 'south' for ten minutes to 'get to a flak-free area', then ' . . . west to get out of Germany.'

Balides described their bombing of the target, his getting a gee fix over France and their trip home. He told how Barger had identified the target as 'Freiburg', but did not say that he agreed with the identification. He did not mention having transposed longitude and latitude minutes in transferring his H2X fix from his log to his chart. In fact, his testimony did not mention the fix at all.

In contrast with his view of what Sincock had said and sworn to, Sokarl seemed to be a bit happier with Balides' statement to Colonel Wall. While he still took the view that neither should have said anything, that was clearly wishful thinking. Besides, both statements were now history, and it would hardly do to go back and deny them.

I failed to see the damage done by the statements, which seemed to agree with all the other facts about the incident, including the whole state of confusion on the day of this ill-fated mission. But then, I had not been trained to think like an attorney.

After berating the two young lieutenants for having said anything during the official investigation of the bombing of Switzerland, Sokarl became very chummy. This, he told Sincock and Balides, was going to be one very tough ordeal indeed. They were going to have to exercise all the cool they could summon up, keep a stiff upper lip, and be prepared to go through Hell.

But, they had friends. In fact, they were looking at them.

Sokarl pledged himself to do the best possible job in defending them. Captain Irving Goldman, he described as ' . . . the best lawyer in Eighth Air Force.' He told them that I was ' . . . the best navigator in Eighth Air Force,' able to figure out what catastrophe had really overtaken them. This was, of course, a crock. Sokarl would not have known a good navigator if one parachuted on top of him. But he surely sounded impressive saying it and I was too enthralled to disagree with him.

Goldman gave them a few simple words of comfort which were, somehow, more soothing than Sokarl's blatant assurances. I said nothing, not knowing what to say that would be comforting. What should I say? 'The General has given you a totally inexperienced dolt as your defence counsel?' Elementary pride precluded such self-effacement.

Sincock and Balides were still scared, or so one would discern from their demeanour. They were up the military shit creek, and we were the only paddles available. After this skull session at Ketteringham Hall, the young officers departed, looking little more relaxed than when they had arrived for their meeting with us.

Goldman and I got together again, while Sokarl was off engaged in high level political boondoggling for General Peck. We went over in some detail the military paperwork on which we expected the Trial Judge Advocate, Major Krannawitter, to hang his hat when we all got into the court room. Things did not look too promising for our defendants, based on a raw reading of the military orders purporting to define what they should have done. According to A.A.F. training standard Number 20-2, pilots of heavy bomber crews, along with being able to fly an aeroplane, had to be skilled in such things as bombing and navigation, enabling them to ' . . . function efficiently on the bomb run.' This Training Standard had been set forth in Washington D.C. in July of 1944, signed by General Henry Arnold. In actuality it would have been hard to find a pilot in the European theatre who was 'skilled' in bombing and navigation, but the requirement was on the books. Such are the wartime gaps between wishful military paperwork and the real world. The whole Eighth Air Force had about twenty 'highly experienced' pilots.

According to Second Bomb Division (the predecessor organisation to Second Air Division) Instructions Number 55-16, each navigator was to 'maintain an accurate log and chart on every operational mission.' It was manifest that Balides had not done this in the instance provoking the pending court martial. The same Instructions indicated that the navigator should rely primarily on dead reckoning, using available aids such as radar, radio, gee, and pilotage. When General Kepner had signed this document in August 1944, he failed to state just how 'accurate' a navigator's work should be when he was shut up in a dark closet on board a bomber with all electronic navigational aids malfunctioning and weather such that the pilotage man could see nothing of the ground.

Second Bomb Division Instructions Number 55-15 of 3 July 1944 stated that 'Each Navigator will notify his crew by means of interphone (the horn) as all international boundaries are crossed on all operational flights.' This document was set forth over the signature of General Hodges, predecessor to General Kepner. It was published shortly after the great 392nd Bomb Group attack of April 1944 on Schaffhausen, the one that had killed a number of Swiss citizens.

We found no evidence that anyone had ever paid any attention to this order. First of all, except for those escaping to internment, no lead navigator had ever knowingly taken his formation across the Swiss border; and there seemed to be little point in announcing the crossing of the French–German or Dutch–German borders, for instance, when all the territory below was occupied by the *Wehrmacht*. The same flak guns were down there trying to shoot your butt off whether you were over Hamburg or Rotterdam.

Nonetheless, these orders were there on paper, and signed by purportedly cognisant authority. Presumably everyone on duty in the affected organisations, down to the yardbird in Sokarl's latrine of the performance coefficient, should be aware of the documents. As Goldman pointed out, we might well have to face these orders in court.

Those of us selected to defend Sincock and Balides had a common worry. The viewpoint of the high command regarding these charges and this forthcoming trial was enigmatic to us, though we did have the inkling from the memo of Lieutenant-Colonel van Benschoten that General Spaatz, by God, wanted somebody tried for this mess. High command had all the marbles, since they could appoint the members of the court.

The real question was, were Sincock and Balides going to be handed the 'green weenie', and, if so, was there anything we could do about it?

CHAPTER 25

GERMANY CLOSE UP

An order from Brigadier-General Peck, now commanding Second Air Division, came through Wing HQ to the 458th. This order called for low level aerial photographs to be taken of bomb damage to various strategic and tactical targets which the Eighth U.S.A.A.F. had hit in Europe. The area to be photographed was bounded roughly by Hamburg, Leipzig, Munich, and IJmuiden in the Netherlands.

The assignment to carry out this picture taking over Germany was sent on by Light Colonel Walter Williamson, Group Operations Officer, to Major Valin Woodward, commanding the 755th Squadron. Captain George Chimples was Operations Officer on duty at the time. After some discussion with Williamson, Colonel Herzberg, and those of us on Group Operations Staff, Woodward assigned George Chimples to fly the photo ship missions.

A test run was flown on 7 May 1945. This confirmed Chimples' opinion that the work should be done by an experienced combat crew who had been over Germany numerous times, and that all these photo missions should be done by the same crew. Herzberg concurred.

Chimples and his crew went out on their first mission of Second Air Division Hollywood, as the photo flights were called, on 8 May 1945, flying to Cologne, Dusseldorf, Mannheim, Bonn and Koblenz. They brought back film which yielded very impressive pictures.

On 10 May 1945 an emergency request came into my office. Lieutenant A. B. Guest, Navigation Officer on Chimples' crew, had become sick, and was not able to fly the photo mission that day. I was asked to assign a capable navigator to Chimples.

Thinking that this might be a fun trip, and a welcome change from paperwork associated with trying to save the buns of Sincock and Balides, or with preparing all 458th navigators for flying across the Atlantic, I assigned myself to go along as navigator with Chimples' crew.

We loaded up and took off. Chimples' aeroplane was a visual lead ship with no radar and no navigation desk on the flight deck, so I rode the nose, working at the fold-down desk, just like in the early days. With no bombs and no ammo, loaded only with cameras, film, and gas, our B-24 flew like a hot rod. Chimples made the most of its performance. He flew the big, ugly mother like a fighter pilot.

We went east out of Horsham St Faith and hit the North Sea at Great Yarmouth. Chimples dropped it down to about ten feet. The backwash from our churning props left a wake on the water befitting the Queen Mary as we ran slightly south of east towards the Netherlands.

We pulled up at the coast to photograph the submarine pens at IJmuiden. These had been built by the Germans (with Dutch slave labour) to service the German Navy's U-boat fleet. Our photography done, we flew down the main street of IJmuiden. The Dutch people heard us coming. Citizens of IJmuiden were out in the street waving bedsheets, Dutch flags, dish towels and suits of long underwear – anything to signal their welcome. Some of them were banging on pots, kettles, dishpans, and old bass drums. They lived in a free country again after too many years of captive serfdom enforced by the German military. They were clearly grateful to American flyboys, and they showed it.

We went on across Amsterdam and the south end of the IJsselmeer, crossing the German border near Bentheim. We flew on over Minden, looking at the canal aqueduct which we had destroyed a few months earlier, bombing through ten-tenths cloud cover by radar.

At Braunschweig (Brunswick) we flew over various assigned target locations, photographing each from very low altitude. What I could see of the damage, looking out of the nose blisters, was enough to make me happy I had had a job dropping bombs, not running around on the ground trying to dodge them.

From Braunschweig we went on east to Magdeburg. May 10 was a bright and sunny day over Europe, and we had pleasant weather and unlimited visibility all the way. The bomb damage to Magdeburg was appalling. The whole city looked like a cratered mud hole, and in the centre of this old place was the ruin of the mediaeval cathedral. In one 1944 night of ferocious bombing by the R.A.F. all five of the great old churches along the River Elbe went up in explosion and flames. The cathedral of Magdeburg was never rebuilt.

Rebuilding of cathedrals was not to be a priority of the post-war government of East Germany. Today the ruin of the cathedral still stands and before it is a plaque whose English translation reads:

> 'We mourn that person who learns nothing from the past, and sows further hatred and division.'

It was a bit difficult to pick out our photographic targets in the midst of the total mess that was Magdeburg, but we did it, shot our film, and turned west for home. Our route outward from Germany paralleled the one we took flying in, but was a bit farther south. We took photos of whatever looked interesting along the way.

The steel truss bridge across the Weser River at Rinteln had been bombed; the north end of it was in the water with the south end still on its piers. Chimples was doing such a buzz job flying west up the river that he had to pull up to clear the wrecked bridge. On this warm spring afternoon in Germany with the war over, no jobs, and little to do, many people were apparently taking a needed holiday. The bridge structure was covered with boys climbing on it and when our massive bomber appeared, apparently about to strafe them, or crash into the bridge, the boys scattered in all directions, some of them diving briskly into the river.

We continued on our tour across Germany, circling several times at Osnabrück to take pictures of those ruined facilities on our list of targets.

Then we headed back across the North Sea to Horsham St Faith and supper.

Lieutenant Guest had recovered enough to make the next trip on 11 May, so I went on no further such joy rides, but the trip I made was enlightening and fascinating. The opportunity to see the results of our bombing efforts at ground level was impressive, and I was thoroughly impressed with the ability of George Chimples as a pilot. The B-24 had a reputation, especially among those who had never flown in one, for handling like a ruptured hippopotamus. George Chimples made his aeroplane perform like a graceful swan.

On 19 May 1945, George Chimples and his crew flew the final mission of Second Air Division Hollywood. General Peck signed a letter of commendation for their excellent work. Chimples told me later that, flying along happily at fifty feet above the terrain, he would often see little red flashes of light on the ground. People were taking pot shots at him with rifles.

I was pleased he hadn't told me this before the trip I took with his crew. Apparently, even though the war was over, there were some in Germany who resented a gigantic American aeroplane buzzing their livestock. Certainly, at the time, the Germans had nothing as huge as a B-24.

Some weeks after the photo missions, an operation was set up, at the instigation of higher command headshed, to run tours to occupied Germany in order to show Air Corps people, especially ground support folks, the results of our combined efforts.

The 458th loaded up bombers with anyone who wanted to go along and we flew excursions into the Rhineland for the day. There people could wander around and look at the bombing results.

Feeling the need to goof off a bit, I booked on a flight to Koblenz. This was a place I had flown over numerous times, and now I got to see it on foot. The tour made me happy that I didn't live there.

Koblenz is situated where the Mosel flows into the Rhine. While not one of the major cities of Germany, it had been well plastered with bombs. The confluence of the Rhine and the Mosel is at a point in the centre of Koblenz somewhat like that triangle where the Allegheny and the Monongahela join to form the Ohio in Pittsburgh. On this point was the statue of some past great emperor astride his war horse. The statue had been hit and toppled so it hung upside down from one side of its pedestal. It could well have represented the state of Germany at that time.

We had been instructed, on orders from some high-ranking command decision maker, not to speak to German people under penalty of court martial. Apparently someone at the upper level of military asininity had determined that this would punish the civilians of Germany and show them how mistaken they had been to obey their misguided government.

I could speak German acceptably well from my language studies at the University of Washington, and I chose to ignore this order, believing that I was unlikely to find any American military tattle tales among the depressed inhabitants of Koblenz.

I picked out a boy of about five years old.

'*Wie heissen Sie?* [What is your name?]' I asked.

There was no answer. I had embarrassed this lad by using the formal term,

'*Sie*', usually reserved for adults. I should have said, '*Was heisst Du?*'.

But I was able to carry on a minor and halting conversation with his mother. The boy asked his mother why my uniform looked different. I was wearing dress greens, different from the usual G.I. battle fatigues, and I had my navigator's wings pinned on the blouse.

'*Sie sind Grenadieren*', the mother told him, identifying me and my associates incorrectly.

The people of Koblenz were subdued and unhappy. Who could blame them?

As we flew back to England that afternoon I counted my blessings. I belonged to the winning side.

CHAPTER 26

SWINGING INTO ACTION

O n 22 May 1945 Brigadier-General Francis H. Griswold, Chief of Staff to General Kepner, issued special order number 142 naming the Court Detail to try Lieutenants Sincock and Balides. The document was signed by Lieutenant-Colonel Bert A. Arnold, A.G.D., Assistant Adjutant-General. It listed the following:

Colonel Elvin S. Ligon, A.C.
Lt. Colonel Louis E. Kearney, J.A.G.D., Law member
Lt. Colonel Edward L. Sheley, Jr., A.C.
Lt. Colonel Walter C. Stroud, A.C.
Major Eugene T. Simonds, A.C.
Major Guy W. Murrie, A.C.
Major Theodore G. Gerringer, A.C.
Captain James R. Steeg, A.C.
Captain Raymond W. Sullivan, A.C.
Captain Leroy H. Bothwell, A.C.
Captain John H. Caldwell, A.C.
Captain Wilbur C. Bryson, A.C.
Captain John R. Moseley, A.C.
Captain Fred J. Eisert, A.C.
Major Richard M. Krannawitter, A.C., Trial Judge Advocate
Captain Albert L. Mason, A.C., Assistant Trial Judge Advocate
Captain Jackson W. Granholm, A.C., Defense Counsel
Captain Irving Goldman, A.C., Assistant Defense Counsel
First Lieutenant Max M. Sokarl, A.C., Assistant Defense Counsel

While, in theory, in a civilian court one is tried by a jury of peers, Sincock and Balides were outranked by everyone on the Court Detail except Max Sokarl. The officer selected as President of the Court is listed first. Since 17 February 1945, Colonel Ligon had commanded the 466th Bomb Group, our Wing neighbours at Attlebridge. The 466th was the group whose squadron attacked Basel on the same day Sincock's little formation hit Zurich, so maybe we could expect some sympathetic understanding from Colonel Ligon.

But it was not to be. On 29 May I got a phone call from Max Sokarl, it was obvious he was brimming with excitement at some dramatic development.

'Mr Counsel-for-the-Defence, Sir,' he said, positively spewing entrancing verbiage into the horn, 'Colonel Ligon can't serve. Guess who I've got now for president of our court!'

'Gargantua the Gorilla?'

'No, dammit, Colonel Jimmy Stewart. Isn't that just wonderful?'

'Colonel who?'

'Colonel Jimmy Stewart!'

'You mean *the* Colonel Jimmy Stewart?'

'Yes.'

'You're kidding, Max. You're putting me on.'

'No, I'm not. General Kepner's already approved it.'

'You're absolutely too much, Max.'

'You're kind to say so, Sir.'

'Thank you for the news, Max. That's nice.'

'We'll have a blast!'

'I'm sure you will. Thank you, Max. I have navigation work to do. See you later, right?'

'Right!'

I have always wondered how much influence Sokarl had on the picking of the Court Detail. At any rate, on 31 May 1945 General Griswold sent Special Order number 151 forth from Eighth Air Force Headquarters, also over the signature of Colonel Arnold. It made two changes in the Court Detail: Colonel James M. Stewart, A.C., was named to replace Colonel Ligon and First Lieutenant Harvey Karlin, O.R.D., was named to replace Captain Mason as Assistant Trial Judge Advocate. Sokarl later explained that Major Krannawitter had decided to have Mason testify for the prosecution. Having him also serve as Assistant T.J.A. would be a military no-no – a conflict of interest. While our relationships with Major Krannawitter during preparation had been friendly, I now had retrospective misgivings about my many meetings with Mason, and our joint reconstruction of the events of the bombing of Switzerland. Maybe all this friendliness was about to backfire.

Colonel James M. Stewart was Chief-of-Staff of the Second Combat Wing. Second Wing headquarters was at Hethel, an air-base near Wymondham, south-west of Norwich. The 389th Bomb Group of Second Wing also operated out of Hethel.

The black-tail-with-white-stripe bombers of Second Wing groups were familiar sights to us; we had seen them many times in the Division line on a mission day.

Stewart had served in Second Air Division since November 1943. In that month he flew the Atlantic with his crew and took up his first job as C.O. of the 703rd Squadron, 445th Bomb Group of Second Wing, stationed at Tibenham. But he was doubtless better known as a motion picture actor of considerable fame and ability. His face and tall, lean frame were known to everyone from repeated showings on screens around the world.

Jimmy Stewart's talents were clearly not limited to acting. His number came up early in the draft and he gave up his Hollywood career to serve in the U.S. Army as an ordinary G.I., being inducted as a private. Stewart had a relatively high number of flying hours from his training as a civilian pilot, and he had applied, and was accepted, for Army flight training. He became a rated pilot and a second lieutenant and in time he had moved up through the ranks to his present position.

All who knew Jimmy Stewart agreed that his military advance was based on good performance, not on some kissy-assed version of pull, his personality off-screen was much the same as on. He was a likeable and dependable ordinary American guy.

On 7 January 1944 the 389th Bomb Group went out on a mission to Ludwigshafen, to attack the great chemical plant of I.G. Farben Werke. The formation hit the plant successfully, but the 389th, leading Second Combat Wing, got off course and out of the Division line while returning to England. South of Paris, without fighter escort, the Group was attacked repeatedly by Focke-Wulf 190s and Messerschmitt 109s. The lead ship was shot down and the formation scattered over the sky like a flock of confused geese. They were prime targets to be decimated by German fighters.

Seeing this pending disaster, (then) Captain Jimmy Stewart, flying command chair of the 445th Group that day, moved his whole formation over the top of the scattered 389th, protecting them from fighter attack from above, and giving them time to collect their wits and reassemble a tight defensive formation. Both groups went home with no further battle losses.

Colonel Milton W. Arnold, Commanding Officer of the 389th Bomb Group, wrote a letter of thanks and commendation to the 445th Bomb Group, and to Captain Jimmy Stewart in particular. He cited this brave action, based on quick thinking, that had saved his men from further disaster.

In March 1944 Stewart was transferred to the 453rd Group of Second Wing, stationed at Old Buckenham, near Attleborough. There he served as Group Operations Officer till his reassignment to Wing Headquarters.

So we had our Court Detail assigned and ready. There was one more key person required, a vitally important one, in fact.

On 31 May Sokarl, Goldman, and I met with Major Krannawitter and Lieutenant Karlin, we wanted to make sure that there were no loose ends lying around for us to trip over.

'We do have one problem,' Krannawitter said.

'What's that?' Goldman asked.

'The court reporter,' Krannawitter said, 'I had a ring-tailed doozy lined up, I mean fully experienced at this kind of thing and all that, but she's been appropriated elsewhere. However, we have a replacement.'

'The court reporter is a she?' I asked.

'Yes,' Krannawitter said, 'A WAC, a superb court reporter. You know, a secretarial expert.'

'Really?' WACs were rare items indeed in the operational bomb groups of the Eighth. The 458th had one or two, and I never did know what they did – worked in intelligence or some such.

'Yes,' Krannawitter said, 'Now this sub we have is not all that vastly experienced, but she's a good scout, willing and all that, you know.'

'Oh, for corn sake!' Goldman said.

'What do you mean?' Krannawitter asked, looking startled.

'I mean we've got enough trouble here without having to slow up for the court reporter. Why weren't we consulted about this?'

'Dear boy, have no fear. All will be well!' Krannawitter said.

'It's all right, Irv, we'll muddle through.' Sokarl said.

'You go ahead and muddle. I'll be happy enough just to be through,' Goldman offered.

I learned many years later, from reading the trial records, that Corporal Dolly Palmer, our WAC court reporter, was paid, in addition to her regular pay, $87.20 for recording and typing up the 87,200 words of testimony in the forthcoming court – a rate of one tenth cent per word. At that rate of pay, we should have been happy if her competence included the ability to sharpen a pencil.

On the first of June, 1945, the court to try the charges against Lieutenants Sincock and Balides convened in the early morning at Ketteringham Hall. One of the opulent rooms there had been set up to serve as a courtroom.

The officers of the board filed in and took their seats. I glanced over them. They were an impressive bunch. None of them was smiling. Colonel Stewart sat right of centre and Light Colonel Kearney, the Law Member, sat to his left.

These officers of the court – the decision makers – looked very uncomfortable in their present seats. One got the distinct impression that several of them would rather have been almost anywhere other than where they were.

Sokarl, Goldman and I shared a table at the left as we faced the members of the court. Krannawitter and Karlin had the table to the right and Sincock and Balides sat in the middle, facing the court.

I looked at the two defendants. Neither appeared to be well; Sincock looked like a statue carved of petrified wood and Balides looked as though he didn't know whether to crap or go blind. They had my sympathy. I'd have looked worse in their predicament.

I looked at our court reporter, Corporal Dolly Palmer. She was a trim and neat person, a pretty American girl, one of the sort we dreamed about, but practically never got to see any more. She evoked visions of home and main street and the corner drug store – the Saturday night dance, and the senior prom. Looking at her was a trip into nostalgia and homesickness.

But here I was, many thousands of miles away from home, wearing a uniform, sitting stiffly in a British manor-house, and pretending to serve as defence counsel for two young men whose lives might be flushed right down the military toilet with this major event. I had Max Sokarl to thank for this current flap – he of the wild imagination and the warped sense of drama.

Sokarl, confidant and legal counsel to the Division Commanding General – he was the far-out wonder who had got me mixed up in this. I wondered what the penalty might be for choking him to death in the courtroom.

Colonel James M. Stewart called the proceeding to order. He spoke in his famous, halting, midwestern drawl, familiar to us from the sound systems of many motion picture theatres. Corporal Dolly Palmer looked as though she would probably swoon. Here she was in the very same room and at the very same trial with a handsome and famous movie star, and they were actually going to collaborate on the same legal proceedings.

Major Richard Krannawitter, the Trial Judge Advocate, stood up and gave the suffering defendants a warm and friendly smile. His uniform was clean and superbly pressed. He bespoke neatness, confidence, and capability in his whole appearance and with his every move. He strode across the room and stood smiling at the members of the court board.

'May it please the court . . .' he said.

It was a phrase we were to hear many times during the trial.

Krannawitter continued his statement:

'The Prosecution is ready to proceed with the trial of the United States against First Lieutenant William R. Sincock and First Lieutenant Theodore Balides. The case on hearing this morning will be a common trial, with the consent of the accused. I would like to have each of them right now state to the Court that they consent to be tried on a common trial this morning, and the counsel also consent.'

Sincock stood and spoke: 'I, Lieutenant Sincock, consent to a common trial.'

And then Balides: 'I, Lieutenant Balides, consent to a common trial.'

They did it solemnly and well, just as we had briefed them.

I stated for the defence that we had no objection to common trial. The court reporter so duly recorded, as directed by the Law member and the defendants were then allowed to sit once more.

Upon query by Colonel Stewart, both Sincock and Balides said that they desired to be defended by me and my learned associates, the regularly-appointed defence people. I thought this might have been their big mistake of the day.

The charges against each were then read to the Court in detail and Krannawitter alleged that he had delivered the charges to the defendants on 23 May 1945. The Trial Judge Advocate then advised both defendants that, if they had any special pleas or motions, such were to be made at this time. Sincock and Balides each stated that they had none.

Krannawitter asked them to plead to the charge. Each pleaded not guilty, exactly as we had instructed them and they were then asked to plead to the specification of the charge. Again each pleaded not guilty.

Advocate Krannawitter told the court that he had no particular citing of military manuals or legal authority to make in this case. His statement was duly noted. He asked if the defence had any such citing of legal authority, we had none, and our response was duly noted.

Krannawitter asked if the Court had any such authority to cite. Colonel Stewart said that there was no wish to cite authority.

Krannawitter then launched into his opening statement:

'If the Court please,' he said (and I wondered what the hell would happen if the Court didn't please), 'in the nature of an opening statement, I wish to state that the fact situation in this case has been agreed upon by the prosecution and the accused. I will recite to the Court the facts we will seek to develop through the medium of the witnesses' testimony: this hearing concerns the mission of 4 March 1945, in which two hundred and seventy-seven B-24 aircraft, in accordance with Second Air Division Field Order 618, were dispatched on a combat mission over southern Germany . . .'

Krannawitter went on with a full description of the mission. He recited the positions that Balides had logged, mentioning, in sepulchral tones, the fix

logged at 10.09 a.m. which had the minute figures transposed between latitude and longitude when it was plotted on the chart.

A good deal of this mission route reconstruction was possible because
Mason, Foote and I had available the lead squadron mission logs of the
392nd and 44th Bomb Groups, and we knew the times that Sincock said he
had these groups in sight.

Krannawitter then pointed out (and this was a telling point against the
defence of Balides), that the log of the navigator flying in deputy position
alongside Sincock's ship agreed in essential detail with the reconstruction
that we had made. Why this person had apparently never opened his yap
while everybody proceeded to bomb Swiss territory was not brought out at
the trial. Sincock and Balides had apparently gone on for an hour flying
twenty-five miles and more south of the briefed course, and no one had
offered a second opinion.

Having summarised what we had found in looking over the mission
records, Major Krannawitter then offered the typed copy of his lengthy statement in evidence, subject to objection by the defence. We declined to object.
Somehow I doubt that the opening statement of a prosecutor would be
accepted as 'evidence' in a civilian court, whether or not the defence objected.

Light Colonel Kearney, the Law member, looked puzzled. He asked
Krannawitter if he were offering the typed record of his opening statement
as an exhibit. Krannawitter replied that he was not so offering it; he merely
wanted it to be a part of the record. Since presumably Corporal Dolly
Palmer had just finished recording all of Krannawitter's extensive
recounting of a relatively simple story, there was some understandable
wonder about his wanting his typed version also included in the record. But,
there seemed, at the time, to be no particular reason to exclude it, and his
request was allowed.

Major Krannawitter then proceeded with his rather long definition of the
meaning of the charges. His voice took on a deeper tone, and his face wore
a serious look. He was getting well into the nitty-gritty of why we were all
there.

'May it please the Court, from the evidence in the case it will be necessary
for you to find whether either or both accused were culpably negligent by
their acts on this mission on 4 March 1945. The degree of negligence required
is universally recognised as being greater than that which would ordinarily
be required in a civil tort action.

'In criminal law, a different degree of negligence must be found. Only a
finding of culpable negligence in the conduct of the accused on 4 March 1945
will support a finding of guilty.

. . . the accused must have entirely departed from care, prudence, and
concern. A proper understanding of culpable negligence, of necessity, rests
upon the assumption that the accused knew the probable consequences of his
act, but was reckless, intentionally or wantonly indifferent to the results.'

Krannawitter was able to say the word 'culpable', with approximately the
same inflection that a revivalist preacher might use saying the word 'God'.
But I felt happy with the definition he was putting forth. I doubted whether,
in the wildest stretch of anyone's imagination, Sincock and Balides had been

that negligent. On the other hand, no one on the court board was smiling, and I could not read their minds.

Krannawitter then told how he would present his case. He would call forth the men who had conducted the briefing of the 392nd Bomb Group crews on the early morning of 4 March. These men would brief the court board, flight-rated officers all, except the Law member, as if they were actually going off on the mission.

Krannawitter promised to bring forth the testimony of the other officer members of Sincock's crew on the day of the Swiss bombing. I doubted that these men would make telling points for the prosecution: members of a combat crew tended to stick together through thick and thin. But, of course, there was always that possibility that, unknown to us, there was bad blood among the various members of Sincock's crew.

Trial Judge-Advocate Krannawitter then summed up his lengthy recitation by saying as follows:

'... The final question which will then be left for you gentlemen to decide is whether either or both of the accused were culpably negligent ... Does the defence counsel wish to make an opening statement at this time?'

The courtroom was chillingly cold with that cold that only a British manor-house in the English climate can achieve. It was an all-permeating cold. I looked at Sincock and Balides, both of whom were sweating profusely.

Lieutenant Max Sokarl rose majestically to speak for the defence. He smiled at all present and nodded reassuringly at Sincock and Balides. With resounding voice and magnificent gesture he addressed the Court:

'May it please the President and members of the court martial: I am certain it must be obvious to all of you that we convene here this morning faced with a most serious and a most grave responsibility.'

It soon became obvious that Sokarl's remarks were apt not to be brief.

'... I have a duty to perform here this morning.' Sokarl's voice deepened. He looked deadly serious. His tone took on a confidential quality, as though each member of the court were his personal friend, and he had a deep secret to confide.

'It is my sworn duty as an officer in the Army of the United States, and my solemn duty as a defence counsel for these two accused. My duty throughout this hearing is to make certain that no fact compatible with the innocence or the defence of these accused is overlooked.

'And, obviously, in view of my limitations (did we hear a sob in Sokarl's voice?), it may well be that my approach may not be as capable as I should choose, so that it will enable you from a full and fair consideration of the evidence to render a verdict compatible with the evidence and the ends of justice!'

I glanced over at Goldman who looked pleased. Sokarl was only into paragraph twenty-three, just warming up, as we damn well knew, and already he had hammered home the concepts of innocence and justice, speaking as though he were Moses reciting them from the Mount.

'The Trial Judge-Advocate, gentlemen, has read to you an agreed statement of fact with which the defence is in complete harmony. He has also stated what he, as well as I and all competent authority (Sokarl always managed to include himself among the competent authorities) consider to be a correct statement of the law applicable in this case. I would, however, be delinquent in my duty, and I know that you will grant me the premise, gentlemen, if I did not restate to you the conditions precedent to an adverse finding on your part against these two young officers at the conclusion of the evidence.'

Sokarl then launched into a definition of culpable negligence some four times as long as the one Krannawitter had just given.

'I believe you know, gentlemen (and they damn well should have known it, since they had just heard Krannawitter explain it at length) that we have two branches of the law; we have the civil law and we have the criminal law . . .'

'A tort is known as a breach of legal duty for which an action for damages will lie. For example . . .'

Sokarl went into a lengthy illustration of having struck someone with an automobile because of his negligence. Then he cited the example of striking someone with his automobile, but not because of his negligence. He cited an explosion which injured people, but for which no one could be found responsible. He cited the example of a guest falling down the stairs in his house where he had negligently failed to maintain the stairway in proper condition. He told of a doctor performing an operation. The patient died, but the death was not due to the doctor's negligence.

Members of the Court were beginning to yawn. I wished that Max would get off this irrelevant kick of civil negligence. Just then he changed the subject slightly:

'Now when we come to the criminal law, which is a separate branch of the law, we are not now concerned with your effort to indemnify yourself for harm or injury which you may have sustained by my failure to exercise due care in a given situation. We are now concerned with the effort of society to punish for a criminal thing that has been done. The act must be anti-social in its concept, an act which is to be condemned!'

I looked at Sincock and Balides. They looked about as non-anti-social as anyone I had ever seen, though I could not be sure that their actions were not about to be condemned.

'In the criminal law,' Sokarl continued, 'whether it be in a Federal court of the U.S. Government or one of its sub-divisions – this court martial, or in a state criminal court, it is not the law that if you fail to exercise due care, the Court will fine you or put you in prison. In the criminal law, there must be something more, and that something is known as criminal negligence . . .'

Sokarl now sounded as though he were reading from the Declaration of Independence.

'. . . when we speak of criminal intent, we mean a state of moral turpitude.

' . . . Gentlemen, you must find in this case more than ordinary negligence. You must find culpable negligence!'

And the word, culpable, came out like a whispered threat. At least one of the Court members shuddered at its baleful syllables.

'Such a wanton and wilful disregard of consequences, such an abandon-ment from the normal standards of care and caution to be expected of a human being, negligence so gross that you can infer an intent to do harm – not to the enemy, Gentlemen – obviously, there is an intent in war to do harm to the enemy, but an intention to harm the land and the gentle, kind people of Zurich, Switzerland, a people friendly to the United States.'

Through Sokarl's words we could see the cows lazily grazing in a tranquil Swiss meadow; we could smell the golden cheese melting on crusty bread over an open fire, and see lovely blonde girls in native dress skipping through fields of alpine flowers. We wanted to leap up and shout a warning because bombs were falling on their heads!

Sokarl stopped. He took out his handkerchief and wiped his eyes. He had been overcome with the excellence of his own oratory. When he began again, it was in a new and quiet tone.

' . . . let us assume that you find a want of due care on the part of either one of these accused . . . let us say that there are errors in calculation on the part of this navigator – let us go even further and say that their performance was not compatible with recognised standards in the Army. Let us assume that you find all that, Gentlemen, and if you merely denominate that as ordinary negligence, then there cannot be a finding of guilty! You will have to go even further and say it was gross, wilful, a disregard of consequences, in fact, culpable negligence! . . . criminal intent!'

I found myself wishing that Sokarl would quit saying 'criminal intent'. It had an ominous sound. I liked 'innocence' and 'justice' better. But he kept right on hammering away:

'I leave you with one thought, Gentlemen . . . I mean it with all sincerity . . . that thought must dominate our minds throughout this entire trial . . .'

Sokarl walked to where the defendants sat and put his arms around Sincock and Balides.

'These two gentlemen, Lieutenant Balides and Lieutenant Sincock, walk into this courtroom free and innocent Americans. The very and complete cornerstone of . . . civilisation is equality before the law. These gentlemen wear a mantle of protection . . . their inalienable, constitutional right, which they carry with them throughout this entire hearing . . . They have the presumption of innocence!'

' . . . I know you will grant me your indulgence, and I feel certain that you will understand, with me, that I am trying, as well as my brothers, to carry out our duty as best we can in a very difficult and complex matter.'

Sokarl returned to our table and sat down. There were tears in his eyes. I felt like saying 'Amen!' out loud. It seemed to me he had clearly out-emotioned Krannawitter, which was no mean accomplishment. Even Goldman was prepared to admit that it was an 'effective bunch of bullshit.'

After such terrific ear-bending, we all had to adjourn for lunch.

CHAPTER 27

THE TESTIMONY BEGINS

T he dining room at Ketteringham Hall was tended by Englishwomen. These waitresses came totally unglued when Colonel James Stewart came in for lunch with the rest of the participants in the court martial. The Limey ladies stood in little clusters, giggling among themselves, and smiling self-conscious smiles. The one who actually got to serve lunch to the famous Colonel Stewart blushed beet red with excitement.

During the dessert course, one dapper little dark-haired girl of the serving staff summoned up more nerve than the rest. She asked Jimmy Stewart for his autograph. I was impressed with the friendly graciousness with which he granted her request. I'm sure she became the heroine of the kitchen.

My own wonderful Grandmother was an Englishwoman. She died while I was in high school. She had been an indentured servant girl at age thirteen in Kent. I thought of her, a young lady of long ago, as I watched the little waitress talking, shy but bold, to the noted American movie actor.

When the Court reconvened after lunch, Major Krannawitter introduced into evidence A.A.F. Training Standard 20-2 and Second Bombardment Division Instructions 55-15 and 55-16. These were some of the documents which we had previously studied, and which we expected the prosecution to introduce. The defence did not object and the Court took judicial notice of the papers.

The prosecution then swore in its first witness, Captain Henry W. Hofmann of the 392nd Bomb Group. Hofmann had been Briefing Officer for the Mission of 4 March 1945.

Under questioning, Hofmann stated that he knew the defendants. He correctly identified Sincock and Balides and said that he had known each for about eight months. The details of Hofmann's Army career and his flight rating (he was a pilot) were set forth. He had completed a combat tour of missions and testified to that fact. He also testified that he now served as an Assistant Operations Officer, and that he gave the briefing on 4 March 1945, based on Field Order 618 of Second Air Division. The original of the Field Order, as it had arrived by teletype at 392nd Bomb Group Operations, was admitted into evidence.

Captain Hofmann then proceeded to present the briefing as he recalled having given it to combat crews of the 392nd on the morning of that day when bombs fell on Switzerland. He presented the briefed primary (and secondary by gee-H) target correctly as the tank depot at Aschaffenburg. In his statement of 24 March to Captain Dawson, Sincock had said that the target was a chemical plant. This statement did not now look encouraging, since it was

followed in the record of the investigation by Sincock's statement that he was
'. . . well aware of the location of all targets'. Sokarl may have had a good
point in advising Sincock, *ex post facto*, that he should have shut up and said
nothing.

In giving his reconstructed briefing from the day of the fatal mission,
Hofmann made use of the chart which Mason, Foote, and I had prepared.
He described and identified it correctly. It was to come to the court's atten-
tion many times during this trial.

When Hofmann had finished his direct testimony, Sokarl stood to cross-
examine him. He began with inconsequentials, asking Hofmann's age, the
number of combat missions required to complete his tour (the same for
everyone at any given time period), and whether he was briefed for every
combat mission he flew.

On his eighth question, Max began to dig into pay dirt. He asked if
Hofmann had specifically briefed the combat crews of the 392nd that their
flight route went within twelve nautical miles of the Swiss border. We chose
the distance in nautical miles because it was the measure used by all aerial
navigators of the Eighth, and, as we had coached Sokarl to realise, it sounded
smaller than its equivalent in statute miles.

Hofmann was a bit taken aback. Obviously he had not thought the briefed
route to be that close to the border. After fumbling around a bit for the
proper words, he said he had not so briefed his people.

Sokarl asked if such information was included in the Field Order.
Hofmann countered somewhat evasively, by saying the information was not
'specifically' contained in the Field Order. Sokarl was on him like cat on a
mouse, asking what was meant by 'specifically'. Hofmann replied that, in
order to get the information, one had to plot the route of the Field Order on
a chart and then it could be seen that the briefed track went close to the Swiss
border, assuming that border was depicted on the chart used.

Sokarl, smiling his most charitable smile, asked which bombers out that
day had gee-H and H2X equipment and what briefing information was given
on targets of opportunity.

Hofmann testified, quite correctly, that no information was given on
targets of opportunity other than general location (in enemy territory) and
kind of installation. There were no target photos, no briefed bomb runs. The
rule, more or less, was 'drop 'em where you think they'll blow up something
that might be important.'

Max had thus established that crews got an abject minimum of information on selecting targets of opportunity. I thought this was pretty good
establishing.

Max went on through a series of seemingly inconsequential questions and
then he asked Hofmann to quote directly the exact words used in the Field
Order to describe a target of opportunity.

Hofmann quoted as requested:

> 'Last resort – any military objective positively identified as being in
> Germany east of the current bomb line and west of twelve degrees (east
> longitude).'

Sokarl asked if the phrase 'positive identification' was used typically in every such briefing and if Hofmann had heard it before. Hofmann admitted that he had heard it in every briefing he had given and attended.

Sokarl asked if, during all these briefings, anyone had explained what was actually meant by the phrase 'positive identification'.

'No one did,' Hofmann said.

Sokarl asked if Hofmann had tried to explain the phrase at the briefing of 4 March 1945.

'I did not,' Hofmann replied.

Sokarl asked if Hofmann had ever seen a memorandum, order, or any other military document purporting to set forth rules for 'positive identification' of a target.

Hofmann alleged never to have seen such a document.

Had Hofmann ever personally flown on a mission which bombed a target of opportunity, Sokarl asked. He had not. There followed a long and extraneous discussion about what Hofmann probably would have done or might have done had he ever had occasion to find a target of opportunity.

Lieutenant Sokarl then asked Captain Hofmann if he had heard the phrase, 'Any bomb on Germany is a good bomb!' Sokarl put this question in a tone of voice that indicated Hofmann was apt to go out deliberately seeking a hospital or a P.O.W. camp as a target. Hofmann said he had heard the phrase.

Sokarl asked Hofmann to describe the characteristics of the targets briefed for 4 March 1945. Hofmann said they could be described as 'transportation and communications.'

Sokarl wanted to know if a railroad would fit this broad category.

Hofmann admitted, somewhat unenthusiastically, that it would be a 'fair' target.

'What if,' Sokarl asked, 'this railroad were combined with a marshalling yard and a major highway?'

Hofmann noted that such would be ' . . . an excellent target.'

Sokarl's description fitted, as he damn well knew, the photos of the ground below their bombers taken by Sincock's squadron over Zurich. There were two minor problems not mentioned in the testimony, however:

The bombers of 392nd high squadron had missed the railroad and dumped into a residential area, and Sincock, in his statement of 24 March to Dawson, had said that they aimed for 'a single track railroad'.

With a few more minor thrusts, Sokarl finished his interrogation of Captain Hofmann, and released him from the witness stand.

Krannawitter, apparently having thought of some things he should have asked and did not, asked permission of the Court to recall Hofmann at a later time. Lieutenant-Colonel Kearney conferred with Colonel Stewart, and finally they gave Krannawitter permission to recall Hofmann later, ' . . . subject to objection by any Court member'. It was becoming obvious that this trial would be going on for a long time.

'Ah, folks, we just sat through a pretty long session here, not that it wasn't interesting, of course,' Colonel Jimmy Stewart said. 'I think we better take about a ten minute break or so – give us time to relax for a while – so we'll see you all back here pretty soon.'

When we came back to the courtroom, Major Krannawitter put on the stand as a witness Captain J. A. Folkert, also of the 392nd Bomb Group. Folkert, Weather Officer of the 392nd, was a relatively old man among us, having achieved the advanced age of twenty-eight.

Folkert testified that he was a school teacher prior to being metamorphosed into a weatherman by the Army. Folker's testimony brought forth the interesting fact that the weather brief for the mission day by each local bomb group weather officer was whatever the teletype from Second Air Division said it was. In other words, Ketteringham Hall determined the briefed weather which insured that the execution of the mission itself was highly democratic and everybody flew according to the same screwed-up guess as to what the weather for the day would be. The job of each group weather officer was essentially that of teletype message reader or 'parrot'.

The weather teletype of the day for 4 March 1945, as received at Operations, 392nd Bombardment Group (H), was presented as evidence, and sworn in to lie among the other exhibits in the growing pile of papers attendant upon the trial.

Captain Folkert told how the weather maps were prepared locally for display with an epidiascope (a projection device used to show incomprehensible and illegible copy on an under-illuminated screen). His original map was presented in evidence.

Folkert could not positively recall that Sincock and Balides were present at weather briefing, but this was a statement with legal implications only, for no one present doubted that they had been there, for all the useful information it might have given them.

At Krannawitter's request, Folkert gave a repeat of the weather briefing he had presented to the crews of the 392nd on the day Second Air Division bombed Switzerland. The forecast clouds were much less severe than actual, and condensation trails were predicted as 'moderate' and 'semi-persistent'. Actually, they had been so thick you could almost get out and walk around on them.

Having testified as to the briefed weather, Captain Folkert was then asked to testify as to the actual weather. Though it was manifest that this was hearsay, since he had not flown the mission, the testimony was allowed. We did not object for the defence.

There followed a long and boring description of types and heights of cloud layers, which could have been summarised pretty well by saying that hardly anyone could see anything, including the adjoining aeroplane in the formation, for most of the day.

Folkert was then asked to testify as to the difference between briefed weather and actual weather. His summary was a magnificent example of professional plonk:

' . . . as I see it, there was more middle cloud in the assembly area than forecasted. Consequently there were more contrails in the assembly area. Contrails were more dense and persistent than forecast, both in the assembly area and over the target area. Also cloud tops in the target area were higher than forecast. Associated with those cloud tops were more contrails. In the main, I think contrails being worse than forecast was the main difference from the forecast as given.'

Krannawitter finished with the witness and Sokarl stood to fire the big cannons for the defence. He bored into the probable validity of the weather teletype from Ketteringham Hall.

When, Sokarl wanted to know, was the forecast from Air Division compiled that, according to the testimony of Folkert, formed the basis of the poop passed out at each group to all crews. Folkert was of the opinion that the Division teletype was taken from the Division weather map, and that it would be a maximum of three hours old before the messages went out to groups. Sokarl asked Folkert to describe the function of the weather scout aircraft that went out alone over Germany, flown by gutsy young men with expendable lives, to report back the actual conditions seen. Captain Folkert testified that he did not know all the responsibilities of the weather scouts.

In response to Sokarl's extensive queries, Captain Folkert gave a learned definition of a contrail. He said it was ' . . . a vaporous condensation caused by disturbance of moist air by some object moving through it.' The source, Folkert said, in the instance of an aeroplane, was ' . . . either the wing tips or the exhaust.' This statement was rather at variance with the observed facts. As every aircrewman knew, condensation trails originated chiefly at the tips of propeller blades. There they could be seen, even when the plane was on the ground, under some weather conditions. There were a few snickers among court members.

The discussion of contrails went on through numerous questions and answers, not many of which added a great deal to the total store of man's knowledge.

Sokarl then led Folkert, in his testimony, into recognising that the forecast given to the crews showed that 'middle clouds' were actually predicted over France at 14,000 feet, at the place and altitude chosen for assembly. In other words, the 392nd had been deliberately sent out to assemble in the clouds. Folkert took objection to Sokarl's revealing goading by offering the opinion that 'middle cloud is not necessarily the cloud worst for flying,' as though there were important degrees of not being able to see a damn thing out of an aeroplane window.

Sokarl asked Captain Folkert if he, personally, had he been the decision maker, would have sent the formation out to assemble there under the forecast conditions. Folkert alleged that he was not qualified to answer. Sokarl, turning his voice up to full snotty remark level, countered that it was the Court's job to rule on the ability of the witness to answer.

Krannawitter, somewhat purple around the gills, jumped up to object, noting that Folkert was not the person who ordered aircrews out on a mission. Kearney sustained Krannawitter's objection, but Sokarl had made his point.

My admiration for Max Sokarl went up a couple of notches. For a guy who didn't know the world was round, he did pretty well finding his way through quasi-technological double talk.

Sokarl got in one last dig by asking Folkert if he had personally forecast the weather over Switzerland on 4 March 1945. Folkert said he had not, he was dismissed from the stand after Colonel Stewart noted that no member of the Court had further questions. Captain Folkert looked very happy that he had left Lieutenant Sokarl behind as he departed.

The gratitude was general when Colonel Jimmy Stewart offered us a five-minute recess. 'Ah, yeah, I think we better recharge our batteries a little bit,' he said.

Outside on the steps I talked with Sokarl and Goldman. 'How's it really going?' I asked my legal eagles.

'It's about a toss-up,' Goldman said.

'Don't be modest, Irv,' Sokarl offered, 'I've got the prosecution by the balls!'

CHAPTER 28

DID THE BRIEFING TELL ALL?

As its next witness the prosecution put on the stand Captain Marvin Felheim of the 579th Squadron, 392nd Bomb Group. The 579th was the lead-crew squadron of the 392nd. Felheim was Squadron Intelligence Officer and also served as a duty briefing officer.

Felheim had been in charge of giving the combat lead crews detailed target information. He identified Division Field Order 618, now prosecution's exhibit one, as the document that had guided his work on the day that Zurich was bombed.

He also introduced a map 'similar' to the one he stated he had used at the briefing and which he said showed the correct briefed route to the primary target at Aschaffenburg. This map was admitted in evidence as prosecution exhibit seven. Felheim stated that he also used two R.A.F. night target charts, and high and low altitude photographs of the Aschaffenburg Tank Depot and these also were introduced into evidence.

Using these documents, Felheim then gave the target briefing to the Court, allegedly as he had given it to the lead crews on that fateful day. He had to explain to Krannawitter the meaning of his term 'M.P.I.', the 'mean point of impact', or the place that should be in the centre of the bomb pattern when the bombs hit and exploded.

Felheim's testimony covered all the aspects of the assigned target in long-winded detail. He told of his work in the briefing for lead crew members, and the subsequent briefing for officers of all the crews to fly that day.

Krannawitter, a bit upset by Sokarl's skilled hammering on Captain Folkert, asked Felheim how targets of opportunity were specifically described to the crews. Captain Felheim quoted the now-familiar phrase about ' . . . any military target positively identified . . .' Krannawitter asked him how he had interpreted to the lead crew members the words, 'positively identified'.

Sokarl was on his feet like a shot out of a cannon, objecting.

'The witness has not stated if he made an interpretation,' Max said.

'I asked him if he did,' Krannawitter said, a bit miffed.

'You asked him how he did!' Sokarl barked, smiling a pleasant sneer.

Sokarl's objection was sustained by the Court.

Krannawitter continued, changing tack ten degrees:

'Did you discuss what was meant by the words, 'positively identified?'

'No, Sir.'

'Did they ask you any questions with reference to that?'

'No, Sir.'

'Did there seem to be any misapprehension about that?'

Sokarl was up again, trumpeting, 'Objection!'

'Sustained,' said Lieutenant-Colonel Kearney.

Krannawitter gave it up.

Now the questioning of Felheim turned to maps and documents supplied to each bombardier and pilotage navigator. Krannawitter wanted to know whether such input was complete and usable by a reasonable person. Trial Judge-Advocate Krannawitter also asked whether there was a large map at the briefing that showed the front lines, the bomb limit lines, and other information on where people were not to bomb. Felheim's answer was 'Yes'.

Krannawitter then asked, 'Did you have mapped out on that map for the crew the route that was to be flown on this mission?'

'If it (meaning the teletype with the mission route detailed) had arrived in time, it was.' Felheim said.

'Do you remember whether it was (on time) on this mission of 4 March 1945?'

'I would have to check the time of arrival of the Field Order.' And Felheim stood up to sift through the exhibits.

Sokarl was on him in an instant: 'The question is,' Sokarl said, 'does he remember?' May it please the Court, . . . the witness is trying to refresh his recollection by looking at the instrument, and the question is whether or not he remembers and that should be answered without reference to the instrument!'

Colonel Kearney spoke directly to Felheim: 'Refresh your recollection all you please so that there will be no misunderstanding.'

Sokarl sat down, a terribly wounded look manifest on his face.

Krannawitter put the question again after Felheim had looked at the teletype: 'Do you (now) remember . . .'

'No, I do not.'

It was obvious that Max Sokarl was beginning to enjoy himself greatly with the progress of this trial. His alternately pained and triumphant looks were clear evidence of that fact. He was making numerous opportunities to indulge in balloon-pricking: one of his favourite pastimes.

Krannawitter asked if the big bomb-line map at the 392nd Bomb Group showed Switzerland, and Felheim testified that it did – it covered areas south clear into Italy.

There were no further prosecution questions put to Captain Felheim.

Sokarl rose to cross-examine Felheim. He was almost saccharin in his polite friendliness. Those of us who knew Sokarl knew of his remarkable ability to put people on. We also recognised that Max believed that he himself should hold the rank, at least, of bird colonel, based on his unusual abilities. But this egotistical belief of Sokarl's could be manifested as over-respect for people who outranked him militarily, a satiric super-politeness that was intended to disguise contempt. I hoped that Max would not go too far here in the trial, for it could have most serious results for the young officers we were trying to defend.

Sokarl established that Felheim held an M.A., earned at Harvard (something else for Sokarl to sneer at after hours). He then began to enquire into the purpose and contents of the lead crew target folders. The target folder was a set of information given to each lead bombardier and navigator, which typically included maps, drawings, photos, and detailed written descriptions of the target area.

Sokarl asked if any similar information was given about targets of opportunity, and Felheim responded that such information was not given. Sokarl asked if any definition other than 'positive identification,' was given to describe targets of opportunity. Felheim stated that no such definition was given.

'No maps covering the topographical pattern of all the available targets of opportunity within the bomb area are given?' Sokarl asked.

'The navigator has them in his possession,' Felheim answered.

Those air-crew members present knew that this was an exaggerated answer. To describe the navigational charts which everybody carried as giving the 'topographical pattern' of every target of opportunity in Germany was stretching belief too far. The charts showed major checkpoints such as big rivers and rail centres, but in no way did they give intimate detail of particular factories, buildings, or installations of the kind the 8th Air Force typically said it could, and often did, hit 'with precision'. It seemed to me that maybe we were getting a leg up here, for one could detect a tendency among the paddlefeet testifying for the prosecution to set forth the view that nothing they had ever done was in error, or even if it had been, it could have had no effect on the outcome of a bombing mission.

Felheim, when asked if he had specifically stated at the briefing that the route passed within twelve nautical miles of Switzerland, replied that he didn't remember, but he didn't think so. He admitted, for what it was worth, that a target of opportunity, 'might lie' within such a distance from the Swiss border.

Needling the Law member a bit, Sokarl said, 'Referring to your notes, if necessary, will you indicate to the Court what list of maps was given (to the lead crews) that morning?'

'I don't have my notes from that briefing,' Felheim replied.

Sokarl, by his whole demeanour and his knowing smile, indicated broadly to all present that he found it startling that we were expected to believe anything in the testimony of a prosecution witness, an officer, so absent-minded as to show up to testify in Court and to forget to bring his notes with him.

'Do you remember what maps were indicated in this list?' Sokarl asked in a tone of voice that showed clearly that he knew damn well Felheim didn't remember.

'No, Sir.'

'Can you state whether the Berne map was included?'

'I cannot.'

'Isn't it a fact that it was not included, Captain?' Sokarl's sneer could have been detected as far away as London.

Krannawitter was turning purple as he stood to object. 'The witness has stated that he doesn't know!' he shouted.

'Overruled!' Kearney said.

Sokarl fired the question again: 'Isn't it a fact, Captain, that the Berne map was not included in the list that was compiled.'

'It is not a fact! I don't remember!'

'You can't state that it was included, can you?'

'No, Sir.'

'Now let me ask you this . . . Has there been, to your certain knowledge, any official criterion given as to what is considered a proper target of opportunity with respect to H2X bombing?'

Here Sokarl was attempting to show that combat crews were allowed to dump on almost anything that looked big enough in Germany.

Felheim did not look comfortable with the question. 'As I remember – ,' he said, 'a teletype coming in – stating that an H2X target – any target could be considered a legitimate target which made a return on the "Mickey" scope.'

'But do you remember?'

'Yes, Sir.'

Shrugging a bit, Sokarl gave Captain Felheim his famous smile of warm charity, reserved typically for those who suffered mental deficiency, but couldn't help it. He indicated that the defence had no further questions and Captain Felheim was excused.

The Trial Judge Advocate then recalled Captain Henry W. Hofmann to the stand. He admitted that he was the same Captain Henry W. Hofmann who had testified previously in this same trial. Since he had carried on with the briefing at 392nd Bomb Group after Felheim's part, he was now asked to continue to brief the court with essentially the same poop that had been passed out on the morning of the day of the Swiss bombings.

We listened to Hofmann's completion of the briefing, and elected not to cross-examine again. We figured we had scored pretty well with Sokarl's questions to Felheim about the Berne map. Our intensive briefings of Max on Swiss geography – not easy learning sessions – were beginning to pay off, we thought. In this respect, Sokarl yielded to Goldman's suggestion that he shut up for a while when he was ahead.

The next witness for the prosecution was Major Kenneth Q. Paddock who was Group Navigation Officer of the 392nd Bomb group. Paddock testified that he had not been present at the briefing in question. The navigation portion of the briefing of 4 March had been given by Assistant Group Navigator Captain Roy M. Swangren who cashed in his chips later on the mission of 22 March 1945.

The episode which had taken the life of Captain Swangren was one of those weird events which should not have happened, but did.

The 392nd that day had made a successful visual attack in excellent weather on the jet airfield at Schwäbisch Hall. The formation lead bomber was piloted by Captain R.B. Grettum with Major L.J. Barnes, C.O. of the 576th Squadron, flying Command. As that aeroplane let down into the Wendling traffic pattern, a flare gun, which had been left in the fuselage top mounting, fell to the flight deck and discharged. The flare ignited a whole box of flares which had, stupidly, been stowed behind the pilot's seat. The whole bomber was filled with smoke and flames, blinding all on the flight deck. The ship went into a dive, augering straight into the turf with no pull-out or recovery. Four crew members, miraculously, jumped clear and para-chuted down to tell the tale. So Captain Swangren was not with us to testify on his own behalf.

With no objection from us, the Court allowed Major Paddock to re-construct the details of the briefing from the records in his office files. Paddock gave a detailed recounting of the methods used in the 392nd to brief navigators, and the specifics of the briefing of the Group's lead navigators on the fateful day of the scenic tour of Swiss territory.

When it was our turn to cross-examine, Sokarl asked Paddock to define the difference, in a bomber attack formation, between 'lead navigator' and 'wing navigator'. Paddock replied that lead navigators are assigned to for-mation lead ships. Sokarl asked how lead navigators were chosen and Paddock gave a remarkably clear answer. He stated that things depended in part on how badly a lead navigator was needed versus the abilities of the man being considered. Then it depended on the skill of his crew, since command did not like to shuffle people around to break up crews.

I thought back to my own selection as Group Navigator. Clearly I owed some of the credit to my fellow crew members, yet I was the one who went to Squadron and then to Group staff. Now I was still here in England while the rest of my crew had gone home: thus did the mills of the military gods grind. Sokarl got back to the question with which he had tormented Captain Felheim and he got a clear answer from Paddock.

'And now let me ask you,' Sokarl intoned, 'from all the information at your command . . . can you state whether or not the Berne map was included in that list (of the maps the lead navigators were to carry)?'

'The Berne map was not listed on the form which was prepared for that morning,' Paddock said.

Sokarl then established through questioning Paddock that the Mercator carried that day by the lead navigators did not cover Switzerland.

I suppose that Sokarl was making some telling points from a legal point of view, but it seemed to me to be hogwash from the standpoint of navigation. Whenever I went out on a combat mission I took along every goddam map I could cram into my brief-case and a few more besides. I figured my bomber could, by George, run out of gas before I ran out of maps. Besides, I knew exactly where Switzerland was, and I assumed, presumptuously, that everyone else ought to know too.

Sokarl went on to lead Paddock into a discussion of latitude and longi-tude. He did pretty well, considering the state of ignorance he had been in on the day we informed him that the world was spherical.

Sokarl also established that Major Paddock himself agreed that, upon hearing the numbers associated with a set of geographic co-ordinates, he would not immediately think of the name of the country in which they might be located. Paddock was also kind enough to testify that, in a B-24M aero-plane, the navigator had to turn deliberately and look over his shoulder to see the compass indicator at his station. It was, in fact, one of those wonderful pieces of work for which we were always praising the designers of military aircraft.

When Sokarl had wound it down, Krannawitter elected to redirect. He wanted to establish (correctly) that the Mercator chart was intended for uses other than showing international boundaries, but that the combat navigator carried plenty of other charts which did show such boundaries.

But Krannawitter's solicitation of such testimony began to get in a bit of hot water when Paddock noted that, while boundaries were shown on the British aerial maps, the country names were not. Paddock made this seem less damning, however, by saying that the navigator 'should know' which country he flew over. When Krannawitter asked by what means the navigator should know, Sokarl objected and was overruled. I couldn't figure out why he had jumped up to object – maybe he wasn't hearing himself talk enough to be completely happy.

Krannawitter went on through many more topics and interminable paragraphs. His demeanour was most impressive throughout, but, insofar as establishing anything definite went, the most I could see happening was that we had learned without doubt that both Krannawitter and Sokarl understood nothing about navigation. Neither of them knew a Mercator from a mugwump.

Sokarl began again when Krannawitter left off. As a final item from Major Paddock he drew the opinion that the bad weather, and the difficulty in finding the Group lead squadron on the day we bombed Switzerland would probably have put Lieutenant Balides under 'considerably more strain' than he might have found on his average mission.

With this cogent remark, Major Paddock was dismissed.

CHAPTER 29

MORE GRIST FOR THE MILL

Major Krannawitter swore in Major Harold F. Weiland, his next witness. Weiland was Group Bombardier of the 392nd Group. Captain Ernest R. Morton, who had conducted the bombing part of the 392nd briefings on the fateful morning of the day Zurich was bombed, had returned to the United States. From the records of his office, Major Weiland did his best to reconstruct the bombardiers' portion of that briefing.

Little new or spectacular was presented, the Bombardiers' Briefing Form for the day was admitted into evidence.

Major Krannawitter asked, '(Was) there . . . covered in the bombardiers' briefing anything supplementing the briefing of the navigators and the general briefing of the crew members?'

Weiland asked to have the question repeated. Krannawitter repeated the question, but added ' . . . is there anything else that you should bring out here?'

Sokarl now asked that the question be repeated. For the third time Krannawitter stated his question. Sokarl objected to the question. His objection was sustained. Apparently the Law member believed the question to be too general. At least, I could think of no other reason for the objection to be sustained, and no reason was stated either for the objection or the sustainment.

Krannawitter then said he was merely trying to shorten the proceedings by asking such a question.

Sokarl then withdrew his objection. There was apparently some legal gamesmanship going on here that I didn't understand. The Law member still ruled the question inadmissible, stating that he didn't understand it. That made more than one of us who didn't.

The rest of Weiland's testimony was brief, and we declined to cross-examine.

At this point, Colonel Stewart, our Court President spoke. 'Gentlemen,' he said, 'And you of course, little lady – Oh, ah, Miss Palmer (looking at his notes). We've been sitting here for a long time in this court. Well, it's about time we all got to stand up. So I suggest about a ten minute recess. See you all back here.'

When we returned to go back to work, Krannawitter swore in Lieutenant-Colonel Carl C. Barthel, Executive to the Director of Training of Second Air Division. I knew Colonel Barthel well, for he had spent a good many months as Air Division Navigation Officer.

One thing I knew about Carl Barthel – I wanted him on my side.

Now, appearing to testify for the prosecution, he was on the other side.

Krannawitter asked Barthel to tell the Court about dead-reckoning navigation. The resulting testimony was worthy of inclusion in a textbook. It was lucid, interesting, and accurate. Barthel was in the midst of his explanation: 'You take into consideration your last known position; your track – which you determine normally from heading and drift; your distance – which you determine from your ground speed and length of time involved, and normally you use your wind to determine the ground speed and drift, as well as the instruments in the aircraft – such as airspeed indicator, compass, altimeter, and true air temperature. All this produces forecast positions expressed in terms of geographic co-ordinates . . .'

There was a soft sob in the corner of the courtroom. I looked over at Corporal Dolly Palmer. Was she crying?

Colonel James Stewart interrupted the proceedings.

'Well, just a doggone minute here!' The familiar halting tones might have come off a movie sound-track. 'Let's just hold it up here a bit. This poor lady is snowed with all this big technical talk. Yeah, Yeah, that's all right dear. Just take your time.'

Dolly Palmer blushed crimson and she looked at Stewart with a combination of awe and gratitude. The famous Colonel did know she was alive, and he cared about her problems.

'Just hold it up there for a bit, Colonel. Ah, you too, Major Krannawitter. Let our court reporter catch up to all this high-toned stuff. Then let's take it a little slower here, we've got to get this all down right for the generals, and this little lady's got to do it all. Let's help her if we can.'

And as Colonel Stewart had directed, we waited till Corporal Palmer had regained her composure.

I wondered what it was that made up Stewart's astounding human appeal. We have heard of people so insane they are brilliant and we have heard of people so brilliant they are insane. I decided that Jimmy Stewart was so ordinary he was unique.

After a sufficient time had elapsed, Barthel went on under Krannawitter's quizzing to describe the job of the pilotage navigator. He described the British gee navigation system and its gee-H variant, used for blind bombing. He told of the German ability to jam reception of both systems and spoke in detail of the operation of H2X radar and its uses both for navigation and bombing through overcast.

Krannawitter then asked Barthel to explain what VHF was. Krannawitter apparently was trying to get Barthel to say that when Sincock and Balides found they were lost, they should have called their squadron commander on the horn, told him they were lost, and asked him what to do. However this line of questioning got nowhere with Colonel Barthel, and Krannawitter rested for the prosecution.

Sokarl got up to cross-examine Barthel. He brought out the fact that the Colonel had taught chemistry, physics, and mathematics in his pre-Army career and he asked the Colonel if it was correct that he had been heard to say that dead-reckoning navigation was 'common sense'. Barthel allowed that he had said so from time to time.

Sokarl asked if the Colonel had testified that air position indicators could be used to track a bomber through a turn. Barthel, in his testimony, had said nothing about air position indicators, and he so indicated. Sokarl said he thought he had heard some such testimony. Barthel countered that, while an air position indicator might have helped Balides with his difficulties, there were only two such machines in all of Second Air Division, and Balides surely didn't have one in his aeroplane on the day Zurich was bombed.

This seemed actually to be the testimony that Sokarl wanted to bring out, and I wondered why he had arrived at it by pretending to be deaf, or stupid, or both. Actually, Sokarl was remarkably sharp, but he had devious ways of trying to disguise the fact from time to time.

Max Sokarl went on and on in his interrogation of Colonel Barthel, doing pretty well. We had taught Sokarl a good deal about navigation, or at least about its jargon, in the few short weeks of trial preparation, and the Colonel's explanations were excellent. He knew what he was talking about.

Eventually Sokarl got to a question which he had previously had me help him write out in detail. We had spent quite a bit of time studying and formatting this question:

'I am going to read you a question,' Sokarl said, 'and when I have read it I will repeat it to you, so that we may be certain that both the question and the answer are in the record: Is it correct to say that the final accuracy of dead-reckoning is a direct function of the original position – the accuracy of the ultimate determination is directly proportional to the accuracy of the fixes involved and the dead-reckoning computations? . . . Would you care to have me repeat that?'

'Yes,' Barthel said.

The question was repeated.

'That is correct,' Barthel answered.

'Will you explain the meaning of the question, and why you answered in the affirmative?'

Sokarl had to be one of the world's most unusual attorneys. I doubt that there are many who would ask a witness to explain a question they had just asked.

At any rate, he kept probing away. Sokarl went on and on, and I found myself reflecting that Barthel might think he was being questioned by a madman, or a robot with an automatic mouth. But, when the warp and woof of the questions and the answers were all woven together many paragraphs later, Sokarl had put into the record the statements of a man with a distinguished career as Air Division Navigator. These statements confirmed that Balides had worked with unreliable equipment whose functioning was highly subject to human interpretation; that any person trying to navigate under the conditions met by Sincock's squadron on 4 March might have been confused, and that, from his position in the plane, Balides could verify nothing by his own view of the world outside.

I reflected on Colonel Barthel's long testimony. It seemed in retrospect that, though he was called by the prosecution, he had done the defence as much good as anyone so far.

Captain Albert Mason, with whom I had worked closely, and who was

Krannawitter's assistant until just before the trial, was next to testify for the prosecution. He described his duties at Headquarters, Eighth Air Force, where he was the Operations Duty Navigator.

Mason was asked to testify concerning the big chart we had prepared which was now prosecution exhibit sixteen. Mason stated correctly that he had prepared it in conjunction with myself and Captain Foote. We were all in agreement as to its contents and meaning.

Krannawitter now introduced into evidence, for the first time, the log and chart that Balides had kept on the mission to Zurich. These, the original papers from Sincock's aircraft, were allowed into evidence as prosecution exhibits seventeen (the navigation log) and eighteen (the chart). I looked over at Lieutenant Balides. He flinched as he saw the papers, blushing a bit.

Mason testified, correctly, that we had used photocopies of the log and chart to make up our big summary chart of the mission.

Krannawitter then dismissed Captain Mason, stating his intention to recall him at a later point in the trial. We had no objection on behalf of the defence.

By now it was getting late in the afternoon, and everybody was tired, Colonel Stewart earned our gratitude by calling a ten-minute recess. These rests were refreshing, but it was more obvious than ever that this would not be a short trial. Krannawitter still had a long list of witnesses that we expected him to call.

We had flown combat missions all through the long dark days of the British winter. Our Christmas Eve mission – the one in which we lost Giesen's crew, almost lost Maurice Speer, and came home with hydraulics shot out – was one of those flown in the time of short daylight. But now we were in the long days of late British spring. We were at a latitude farther north than any in the United States, outside of Alaska. With double British Summer Time in effect, so that the clocks were moved ahead two hours, our days seemed endless at Ketteringham Hall during the trial of Sincock and Balides – the trial that might send them both off to a life of imprisonment.

The weather outside was pleasant and beautiful, but we saw little of it. We sat in the chilly courtroom and did our duty, looking at maps and charts and listening to droning testimony.

The story of the adventures of Sincock and Balides over Switzerland was sad and a bit confused. Why the purported responsibility for this mess had been dumped on these two young officers alone, I could not understand. In our own 458th Bomb Group, squadron lead aircraft always flew with a command pilot in the right hand seat, not the lead crew co-pilot. Such a command pilot was typically a Squadron operations officer, or higher, someone who outranked everyone else on the crew, and was there to make such command decisions as ' . . . drop the bombs.' Maybe hanging such serious charges on a couple of green lieutenants made the big generals and the important politicians happy. This trial clearly was not making the defendants happy. Through it all, those of us assigned to conduct this general court martial with great wisdom tried to be as wise as God gave us grace to be.

CHAPTER 30

THE CREW MEMBERS TESTIFY

Late in the afternoon Major Krannawitter brought First Lieutenant
Norman Johnston to the witness stand. Johnston was the co-pilot of
Sincock's crew and had been along that day when their impromptu
squadron toured downtown Zurich.

Now we would find out whether there was cohesiveness among the
members of Sincock's crew.

Johnston stated his name and rank correctly, and identified Sincock and
Balides. He testified that he held a current pilot's rating and that he had flown
as co-pilot on 4 March 1945 in the bomber commanded by Lieutenant
Sincock.

Johnston told of the first take-off and the return to base to get another
aeroplane. He described their arrival, a half-hour or so late, over France, for
assembly. Johnston told of monitoring the conversations on VHF, and how,
by the time they arrived at the assembly area, the Wing formation had moved
up to 23,000 feet from the briefed 14,000 feet because of bad weather and
terrible visibility. His description of the trip into the target area matched what
we had already heard and studied so many times.

He also added some new information. Johnston testified that though they
were lost from the rest of their Group, he had been in contact on the horn
with Major Keilman. Keilman asked Johnston if he had correctly heard the
message from the Wing Commander that they were to bomb targets of
opportunity. This testimony shot down Krannawitter's apparent
contention that Sincock had been remiss in not seeking direction from
Keilman.

Johnston also testified that he had called the Wing Commander repeatedly
after they were alone and had lost visual contact and had received no answer.
Johnston also told of his futile attempts to speak to the crew of the ship from
491st Group. This bomber flew alongside in number five position in the
squadron box. Its radome was cranked down. As I listened to Johnston, I
wondered why we had not tried to locate this ship, and talk to its crew
members, or have them testify. We should have thought of this, but maybe
we would have discovered something we didn't want to know.

Krannawitter asked who on Sincock's crew had first identified the
city bombed as 'Freiburg'. Johnston, possibly conveniently, did not
remember, nor did he remember whether there was any question as to proper
identification.

Johnston did contradict one statement Sincock had made during Colonel
Wall's investigation of the incident. Sincock had said that they proceeded

from the time of losing visual contact with the 44th Group till they bombed Zurich with bomb bay doors open. Johnston testified that they had closed bomb bay doors, and opened them to bomb Zurich, but this was an item with essentially no bearing upon the question at hand.

Johnston stated that they had first learned of their mistake in target identification about an hour after they landed at Wendling. Krannawitter asked Johnston if he 'knew of' B-24 bomber number 650 of the 392nd Bomb Group. Johnston stated that the bomber with that number was the aircraft flying in deputy lead position in their squadron on 4 March 1945. Krannawitter did not seek further elaboration, and I wondered what the motivation for the question was.

Krannawitter asked if Johnston had heard Sincock give a command to drop the bombs. Johnston testified that he had not heard such a command. In fact, he had heard no conversation prior to bomb drop; he was on the horn to the rest of the Second Air Division, not listening on ship intercom.

Johnston was then released for cross-examination.

We had decided to shelve Sokarl for a while, under the theory that all bombast makes Jack a dull boy. Irv Goldman quizzed Johnston for the defence:

Goldman asked what the weather was like on the day of the mission to Zurich. Johnston described the sky at flight altitude as full of persistent contrails.

Then Goldman got to a topic that had bothered me, but that had not been brought up previously in the Court:

'Can you tell us,' Goldman asked, 'whether or not you know that it is the duty of the deputy lead, or any other ship in your squadron, to notify you if you, as lead aircraft, are off course?'

'That is customary,' Johnston said.

'. . . And did you, in fact, ever receive any information from any other ship in the squadron to indicate that your aircraft was in friendly territory or neutral territory, specifically Switzerland?'

'Not before bombs were away.'

I flinched at this answer, for it implied that Sincock's crew had heard some such comment after bombs were away, whereas Johnston had just testified that they had heard nothing till an hour after they landed. The answer raised a question, though it may have been just Johnston's way of saying it. A few questions later, however, Goldman got the point cleared up, by inducing Johnston to testify once again that, in fact, he did not know that they had bombed Switzerland till they returned to Wendling.

Goldman continued, 'Were you . . . able to make out any terrain features that would have identified the territory as Switzerland?'

'I was not.'

'You saw no lakes which would resemble Lake Constance, or Zurich Lake?'

'No. . .'

Downward visibility from the pilot's compartment of a B-24 was notoriously poor, but none of the crew saw the big Swiss lakes. They were all covered with clouds that day.

The downward view from the pilot's compartment of the B-24 is very poor.

'... Were you ... perfectly satisfied that you had made a run, and bombed the city of Freiburg?'

'I was.'

'Isn't it true that one of the sayings, always ... was that a bomb dropped on Germany is a good bomb?'

'Yes, there is no point in carrying bombs over and bringing them back.'

That seemed to tell the story pretty well; maybe too well from Krannawitter's point of view, for he chose to redirect:

'Did you have any part in identifying the place you bombed as being Freiburg?' Was Krannawitter's tone accusatory? It was hard to tell through his good-ole-boy manner. But this question raised another as to whether Johnston should be on trial too, and if not, why not?

'I did not, Sir,' Johnston said.

'... do you know who ordered the bombs to be dropped?' Johnston had already answered a similar question.

'Not directly, Sir, I didn't hear the conversation.'

Krannawitter then established, through the testimony of Johnston, that the first pilot is in command of a bomber, and is customarily charged with having responsibility for the final decision (as though any of us previously had any doubt of that).

Lieutenant Johnston was then excused from the witness stand.

Krannawitter next called Second Lieutenant Murray Milrod, Radar Navigator of Sincock's plane on the day they dumped on Zurich.

All the customary crap was established, such as the fact that Milrod actually knew Sincock and Balides and could properly identify them, that he was an officer in the U.S. Army and therefore, by definition, a gentleman and a person who could tell right from left, count to ten, recite the ABC, and so forth.

Milrod, along with everybody else, remembered the number of the aeroplane that they had actually flown over Zurich that day. And he had been briefed with everybody else, and on and on and on. I wondered why it was essential to go over all this stuff time and time again, but apparently I had no appreciation of the ball game of trial records and their purported worth.

While testimony such as that of Colonel Barthel had suggested that airplane 577 of the 392nd Bomb Group was a B-24M, Milrod's testimony described it as a B-24H. Knowing the love of 392nd Bomb Group for the H model, I thought Milrod may have been right. Actually, one hundred and fifteen B-24M aeroplanes, produced by Ford at Willow Run, and delivered to the Army without tail armament installed, were later designated as B-24L aircraft. I don't know whether any of these actual or pseudo-B-24Ms got to England and to the 392nd. It really was of little consequence in this case, except possibly for Barthel's testimony about the difficulty of looking at the compass from the navigator's station. But, of course, as the tech orders doubtless set forth, Balides was a qualified navigator and therefore must also have eyes in the back of his head. 'Human factors', if they existed at all, were in their infancy during World War II. That war took place before we had a generation of government-funded sociologists making official excuses for all sorts and conditions of human incompetence.

Milrod remembered correctly that the primary target was a tank factory. His description of the mission was pretty much what we had already heard numerous times.

However, when Krannawitter asked Milrod where they had overtaken the Bomb Group formation, Milrod reminded him that he was in a dark and closed compartment on the bomber and could see nothing of what happened outside. In this statement Milrod showed perhaps a better understanding of hearsay than our legal eagles sometimes did.

Lieutenant Milrod described the faulty operation of his radar set. There were long periods of time when he could identify nothing on his 'Mickey' scope, he said.

Then Krannawitter got to the big questions, the ones about the fix in which Balides had transposed minutes:

'What did you say to the (dead-reckoning) navigator with reference to the accuracy of that fix?'

'I told him, "If this town is Stuttgart that I am picking up, this is our position. If it is not . . . it is not a reliable fix and you can take it for what it is worth".'

'And how many times did you give him the numbers of the co-ordinates?'

'Just once, Sir, and he read them back to me, I believe,' Milrod said.

'Did he read them back correctly?'

'Yes, Sir, I think he did.'

Milrod, in his testimony, then confirmed that, as they withdrew on a westerly heading, he saw the image of a city coming up on his radar scope. He stated that Balides said that they were in the Freiburg area. He testified that Barger, in the nose turret, reconfirmed the identification of Freiburg.

I watched Balides as Milrod testified. He was pale, sweating, and clearly uncomfortable – squirming in his chair. Balides looked as though he wished he could navigate this screwed-up mission again with a chance to do it right this time. At least, if he were ever given the opportunity again, he would surely not prompt his radar navigator with suggestions of from whence an unidentifiable electronic image came.

It was truly bad news. Here were two young men, patriotic American citizens caught up in the idiocies of war, trying only to do a good job at fulfilling their duty. Without doubt both Balides and Sincock had volunteered for the jobs they had, they had not been drafted into them. Now they faced life imprisonment for a mess originated by bad weather and failing navigation equipment. The accusations against them boiled down to claiming that they had both gone forth intending to make a mess of this bombing mission. At least, this court martial seemed to be prompted by the view of high command that neither of them cared what kind of a job he did. It was unfair, in my view.

It is interesting to compare Milrod's testimony with the statement Balides gave to the investigating officer, Colonel Wall. In Wall's document Balides is quoted as saying that Barger first identified the place as Freiburg. I could understand the desire of each of these officers of Sincock's crew not to have been first with the identification.

Milrod did not believe, as Sincock apparently did, that the bomb bay doors were open as they approached Zurich. He confirmed the testimony of Johnston that they did not know what their actual target had been till they got back to Wendling, which completed Milrod's testimony for the Prosecution.

Goldman once again did the honours in cross-examination. He sought to establish that Milrod had checked his earlier attempts at radar fixes with the fixes Balides was able to get on the gee set. These had been cross-checked, according to Milrod, and they agreed rather well. Goldman, in fact, got Milrod to agree that most of the fixes were cross-checked, and the agreement was good.

The clock had now moved around to six p.m. Colonel Stewart ordered an hour and a half recess. Goldman, Sokarl, and I took General Peck's limousine, and went into downtown Norwich for supper. There was actually no place to park the limousine in Norwich – the town had not been designed for American Cadillacs. But that was the G.I. driver's problem, and Sokarl let him solve it, telling him to pick us up in an hour or so.

Ever since Sokarl had been shacking up with the mature British psychiatric expert, he had become an amateur psychiatrist. We were treated throughout our meal to his analysis of the trial, the witnesses, and the defendants, it was better fare than the wartime food in a British restaurant.

'I have it all figured,' Max Sokarl said.

'Indeed?' Goldman commented.

'We have Krannawitter running scared.'

'We do?' I asked.

'Yes, you see, his role is miscast. His id is misplaced'.

'No crap?'

'You see, Krannawitter is actually fitted to be the defence attorney. He is great on rebuttal and fending off assaults, I recognised that in him some time ago. But he is uncomfortable in the accusatory role, it doesn't fit him.'

'He looks to me like he's doing a pretty good job Max,' Goldman said, 'He's about as full of it as you are.'

'My ever-loving friend and admirer!' Sokarl said, putting his arm around Goldman. 'What would I do without you?'

'You keep your bloodshot eye on Krannawitter,' Goldman said, 'He may step right on your fat head! I have a clear picture of these two lieutenants spending eternity on the Fort Leavenworth rock pile, assuming they are not shot at sunrise like your former client, Private George Smith.'

'You cut me to the quick, Sir,' Sokarl said, smiling, 'If I hadn't followed your legal advice in the Smith case, I'd probably have had him knighted.'

'You're lucky you weren't shot with him,' Goldman said.

'The poor son of a bitch!' Sokarl said.

'I hope you don't end up saying that about these present clients!' Goldman said.

I decided that attorneys tend to think of those they defend as things instead of people.

When we got back to the courtroom, Lieutenant Milrod took the stand once more and was reminded that he was still under oath. Goldman got Milrod's agreement that the city which was presumed to be Stuttgart could, in fact, not possibly have been Stuttgart, which seemed to me to be pretty good digging by Goldman. It meant that the transposition of minutes by Balides had been done with a position that was meaningless anyway.

Goldman now asked Milrod, 'Are you familiar with the contents of a TWX which purported to say that a target of opportunity should be anything which made a return on the 'Mickey' screen, as long as it was in Germany?'

Krannawitter was on his feet immediately, objecting: 'A target of last resort for this mission is defined by the Field Order specifically and that would be the governing description of the target!' he said.

Colonel Kearney answered. 'Overruled . . . he is merely calling attention to a document.'

Felheim had opened this can of worms with his previous testimony when Sokarl was harpooning him so gleefully. He had referred to a poorly-defined TWX from somebody, saying something or other.

'Was it your understanding,' Goldman asked, 'that the contents of this TWX were the standard operating procedure for your group in attacking targets of opportunity?'

'Yes Sir.'

Goldman, in his quiet way, was clearly able to pry out telling points as well as Sokarl could with his theatrics.

Goldman then got back to the question of identifying the target as Freiburg. He tried to get Milrod to testify that he might have said 'Could it be Freiburg?'

Krannawitter was too fast for this ploy. His objection was sustained on the ground that Milrod had already testified that he didn't know for sure what the return came from on his radar scope, so we were left with Milrod's statement that it was Balides who had suggested the city was Freiburg, Germany.

Goldman tried again, changing tack a bit. He tried to get Milrod to say that it might be 'reasonable to presume' that he had said the place was Freiburg. Again Krannawitter objected, leaping to his feet and blowing steam, but before Kearney could rule, Goldman moved to strike his own question. His motion was allowed, and he went on to other topics.

Milrod, in response to further questions by Goldman, testified that Lieutenant Barger, riding nose turret, had said, 'I am positive it is Freiburg' after calling off all the features which matched those on his map. Goldman released the witness.

Krannawitter, electing to redirect, asked Milrod 'what kind' of fix he had got when he thought it was Stuttgart he saw. The testimony indicated that it was not a clear and definitive image that was displayed by the radar of aircraft number 577 on 4 March 1945, and that concluded the questioning of Lieutenant Milrod.

The evening was wearing on at Ketteringham Hall, and we were all getting weary. Both Sincock and Balides in fact looked as though they were already dead and buried.

CHAPTER 31

AND SO ON INTO THE NIGHT

W e were well into the evening when First Lieutenant George William
Barger was called to testify. He was Pilotage Navigator on
Sincock's ship on the day when Second Air Division bombed
Switzerland. Because he rode nose turret, he was the only navigation officer
of Sincock's crew on that mission who could see what went on outside the
squadron lead aeroplane.

Krannawitter swore him in and went through his customary preliminaries.
Barger testified that his flight rating was that of bombardier. His assignment
to the nose turret was not an unlikely one. Bombardiers were well-trained in
map reading and target identification, and they had some schooling in navigation. Presumably they might serve as pilotage navigators, but I knew of no
instance in my operation in the 458th Bomb Group in which we had assigned
a rated bombardier as pilotage navigator.

Barger's description of the mission preliminaries was about the same as
that already given by other officers of Sincock's crew. He testified that he
could see a little over ninety degrees to each side of the aeroplane nose, about
ninety degrees above horizontal and about fifty degrees below from his seat
in the nose turret.

Krannawitter introduced into evidence three photos of the cloud formations on 4 March 1945. These photos were stipulated as having been
taken in the area where the 392nd Bomb Group flew on that mission day.
Krannawitter asked Barger if these looked like the clouds that Sincock's
ship had flown through. Barger said he supposed they would have looked
like that if his formation had been flying above them (the cloud photos had
probably been taken from a weather ship, flying up higher than the
bombers). Krannawitter then solicited from Barger the testimony that they
had not flown on top of the clouds, but through them. This seemed to
surprise Krannawitter, and I wondered if he had actually been listening to
the previous testimony. I also wondered who got the bright idea of intro-
ducing the photos in evidence. These pictures of cloud tops were not going
to snow any aircrewmen on the court board, they knew what flying through
high weather was like. The Trial Judge-Advocate may have just scored a
point for the defence. Maybe there was something to Sokarl's suppertime
psychiatric analysis.

Krannawitter asked Barger if he heard the command pilots of the formation give any announcements. Barger replied that he was on the intercom,
not on VHF, and heard only intra-ship conversations.

We got down to the nitty-gritty early in Barger's testimony. He said that when they came up over the hole in the clouds, Sincock asked him, 'Is it Freiburg?' Barger freely testified that he had identified the target city as Freiburg, Germany. The railroad, the river, the highways – all the check points matched. Zurich Lake was cloud-covered and could not be seen. Krannawitter asked if Barger would have identified this spot as Freiburg if Balides had not told him that they were in the vicinity of Freiburg. Barger said no, he would not.

Here, with two questions and their answers, Krannawitter had raised our hopes – then dashed them with the news that Balides had put forth the suggestion of their being over Freiburg. Was it, in fact, Balides, in his on-board darkroom who had initiated the delusion of the whole crew that they were about to bomb German territory?

Krannawitter next offered in evidence eleven photos taken by the camera of 392nd Bomb Group aeroplane number 650, the squadron deputy lead ship. It was stated that these were the actual photos of the bombing of Zurich by Sincock's squadron.

The view, due to the camera haze filter, might be clearer than that seen by the naked eye, and we agreed to that. Barger said that he had used the 1:500,000 Strasbourg map in making his erroneous identification of Freiburg. Krannawitter brought forth a Strasbourg map and also a 1:500,000 map of Zurich so that Barger could examine them side-by-side. On the Zurich map Mason, Foote, and I had drawn the course that we assumed was flown by Sincock's squadron, based on the strike photos and other evidence. Barger testified that he did not understand the assumed course as drawn.

Krannawitter asked him if the line drawn on the map was about the same as the actual course they had flown in crossing Zurich. Barger said he supposed it was. Krannawitter asked if the features shown on the Zurich map were the same as those he had used to identify the city, and Barger said they were.

That concluded Krannawitter's direct examination of Lieutenant Barger. Goldman stood to cross-examine.

Goldman asked Barger what a pilotage navigator did. The explanation was straightforward. Then Goldman asked whose primary responsibility it was to identify a target of opportunity. Barger said it was the primary responsibility of the pilotage navigator – score a point for our defence of Balides!

Goldman then got into a detailed discussion in which he asked Barger to identify the specific points on the maps that had caused him to identify their target as 'Freiburg'. Barger was about halfway through this procedure when Colonel Kearney, the Court Law Member, pointed out that the map being discussed had not been introduced into evidence, Krannawitter said he had intended to introduce it later.

The introduction of the maps, and all the attendant stipulations took a while, then Goldman was able to resume. He now asked Barger to identify landmarks similar to those he had seen on the map of Freiburg.

Krannawitter objected to the question on the ground that Sincock's aeroplane had not flown over Freiburg. This objection was sustained.

Goldman rephrased his question in terms of 'let's assume' then it passed muster. I found this procedure a bit silly and time-wasting. We all knew what Goldman and Barger were talking about, and from what I had seen of the legal personnel present, Goldman was the only one I would expect to know where he was if he looked out of the aeroplane window.

It came out in Barger's testimony that they had taken evasive action after they bombed the target. This had not, to my knowledge, been stated before. I wondered why they had taken evasive action. No testimony had been given that the Swiss fired on them.

Barger's testimony also established that there was no compass in the nose turret. Goldman asked, with a number of questions, whether Barger was certain at the time that they had attacked a legitimate target in Germany. Barger said he was and Goldman had no further questions.

But Krannawitter did:

'What made you first believe you were near Freiburg?' he asked.

' . . . the "Mickey" man's question, I believe, Sir.'

'And then what?'

'Then the navigator saying that we should be in the general area of Freiburg because that is where we were supposed to resume our withdrawal route.'

'And that was what you based your identification on. Is that not right?'

'Yes, Sir.'

Krannawitter couldn't give it up. No matter what anyone said, he had to get in the last word, hanging the responsibility for wrong identification of the target on Balides. I suppose that was the right thing for a Trial Judge-Advocate to do. After all, Balides was the only navigator on trial there.

But Goldman was not washed up yet. He stood to recross:

'What was the "Mickey" man's (Milrod's) question?'

'He said, " . . . Could it be Freiburg?"'

'But you positively identified the city from your pilotage map as being Freiburg. Isn't that so?'

'Yes Sir.'

Barger was dismissed from the witness stand. It was now nine forty-five in the evening. Colonel Stewart called a ten-minute recess. When we returned, First Lieutenant Alfred R. Williams was sworn in as a witness. He was the Bombardier on Sincock's crew.

Krannawitter went through the obligatory preliminaries, and then he asked Williams to tell how they had bombed Zurich. Williams told that the first indication he heard of a target of opportunity came from Milrod who said he could see a town ahead.

Krannawitter asked what Balides said about Milrod's comment. Williams testified that he had said nothing. Milrod had first said, 'Could it be Freiburg?' Balides had then responded, 'It should be Freiburg.'

Sincock then asked Barger, Williams said, to identify the city. Barger said that it was Freiburg. Sincock then told him, Williams said, to pick an aiming point, and drop the bombs.

Krannawitter had no more questions of Williams.

Goldman's cross-examination was brief:

'Where did your bombs actually strike?' Goldman said.

'I observed bombs strike on what I thought to be a railroad and I observed some of them striking on this road and some of them in a wood to the left.'

'How long was your bomb run?'

'Approximately sixty seconds.'

'Were you certain that the city you had bombed was a city in the bomb area?'

'Yes, Sir.'

As the results on the ground in Switzerland amply showed, none of the bombs dropped by Sincock's squadron hit a railroad. They hit streets and houses in the Milchbuck Quarter and, fortunately, about half of them landed in the woods described by Williams.

Sixty seconds is a very short time for a bomb run. Most well-executed bomb runs were twenty minutes long, or longer, and this gave the bombardier ample time to identify, synchronise, and drop the bombs. Sincock's squadron, as evidenced by the sixty seconds, must have dumped and departed.

Krannawitter, who seemed determined that we would get minimum sleep that night, decided to redirect again.

'Did you identify that town, or did you merely bomb on the command of the Pilot?'

'I bombed on the command of the Pilot, Sir.' And once again, Krannawitter, by picking the right phrase and the right inflection and asking the right question, had dumped the responsibility for this Swiss mess back on our defendants – Sincock this time.

Colonel James Stewart looked quickly around the courtroom. There didn't seem to be any legal eagle with his mouth open at that moment.

'You are excused,' Stewart said to Lieutenant Williams.

It was definitely getting on into the evening, but Krannawitter kept trotting out his witnesses. We had a gentleman's agreement that he could have the first day to present his testimony, and it looked like it might run into two days.

The prosecution called Captain Benjamin F. Foote, Jr, to the stand. By now I knew Foote, of course, having worked with him to see what sense we could make from the log and chart kept by Balides on the mission to Zurich.

Krannawitter went through his long preliminaries and established that Foote had been a rated navigator for nineteen months. He had spent seventeen of those months in England, and had flown a tour of thirty missions, ten of them as a lead navigator. He now worked in Eighth Air Force headquarters as Assistant to the Director of Intelligence. There his job was to analyse missions flown, seeking unusual situations which would be corrected in future operations. It seemed to me that the performance of Sincock's squadron over Zurich surely demonstrated the need for potential correction in future operations.

Foote testified that he held a B.S. in Chemistry from the University of Pittsburgh and also testified that he had analysed the navigation log and chart kept by Balides on 4 March 1945. In doing that analysis he had also made use of the log kept by Lieutenant Damerst, navigator of the deputy lead ship and had also used the Field Order setting up the mission.

Foote then referred to the map we had constructed and noted that Mason and I had collaborated in its compilation. Foote reiterated how the green line showed the briefed course, the black line showed the route according to Balides, and the red line showed what we jointly believed to have been the actual route flown.

Foote was then asked to explain why the black line had a break in it. He replied, correctly, that there was a lack of entries in the log which Balides kept, accompanied by a lack of charted positions. We could find no recording of positions from 9.51 a.m. through 10.09 a.m. The latter time was that of the 'fix' with transposed minutes. This lapse of performance didn't look very good for Balides. I thought of the first mission we had flown with our crazy instructor pilot. I said a silent prayer to thank God that my log and chart of that day were not on the exhibit list. I had considerable sympathy for Balides, stuffed in his dark room that day, getting confusing input from his fellow navigators while his aeroplane wandered all over the sky like a blind dog in a meat house.

Foote pointed out that we were uncertain, as Balides had been, about the probable positions of his formation during the searching and circling through the clouds. But Foote was kind enough to state that there had been precedent for the performance of Sincock's squadron over Zurich. He cited instances in which Eighth Air Force bombers, flying in conditions of weather like those of 4 March 1945, had bombed targets from fifty to one thousand miles away from the briefed target. These incidents, fortunately, did not always involve attacks on a neutral country.

I was appalled at Foote's statement. I could understand being fifty miles off course, but a thousand miles off course seemed to me like insanity. I could not imagine how it could happen.

Krannawitter asked Foote if he thought there had been error in the log kept by Balides.

'There was error in his log,' Foote said.

'Would you be able to state the degree of error? (Was it) minor, gross, or what type of error?'

Sokarl was up, smiling. Apparently he had digested his supper, and was ready to pick up his elephant goad again.

'I wonder whether or not error can be denominated into categories, or whether its outstanding characteristic is absence. It either is error, or it is not!' Max said.

Krannawitter turned a bit purple. 'I think this witness, an expert witness, would be competent to so testify!' he said.

Kearney interrupted the exchange: 'Are you proposing a question,' he said to Sokarl, 'or stating an objection?'

Sokarl smiled his most condescending smile – the one he probably used with small children. 'Stating an objection, if the Court please, to the question.'

'Overruled!' Kearney said.

'Put it this way,' Foote said, ' . . . on a mission of this kind the weather conditions were such that no one could turn in a perfect log. Grading the best log at 100, I would grade that log about 50!'

'Was the log of Lieutenant Balides kept up at all times?' Krannawitter wanted to know.

'No, it was not.' Foote had already testified to that. I had begun to see Krannawitter's method. Because the orders from on high said that navigators must keep up their logs at all times, Krannawitter would show negligence in failure so to do, and negligence was what he had to prove to get a conviction.

Krannawitter went on to examine in some detail the errors which Foote alleged, but this proved to be a line of questioning not entirely to the benefit of the prosecution.

'What did you say was the first error discovered in this log?'

'. . . an error in wind.'

'And what was the next error?'

'. . . a subsequent error in wind. Errors in drift began to show up.'

'And the third error?'

'. . . errors of omission, in the altitude, ground speed, true airspeed . . . that sort of thing.'

'The altitude and airspeed was off, was it?'

'It was not off! I said "errors of omission"!'

'Was there any reason for the airspeed to be inaccurately shown?'

'It was not inaccurately shown! In a good many places it wasn't shown. I said "errors of omission"!'

Apparently Krannawitter was not aware that there was an airspeed indicator in the aeroplane, and that all one had to do was to read it. The correction for true airspeed at flight altitude was simple and could be read directly off the E6-B Plotter which every navigator carried. Krannawitter did himself no good by appearing to badger his witness. Such was the performance envelope of the B-24 that indicated airspeeds of bombers flying formation usually stayed the same all day at any one flight altitude. The 'omission' in logging was not good performance, but it was far less than catastrophic.

Balides may have made errors in a high-stress situation, but Krannawitter was, possibly without realising it, trying to make him appear to be an utter idiot and Foote was not going along with the depiction.

We had agreed that, since Foote was such an impressive navigator, I would cross-examine him. I hoped, at least, not to forget that a B-24 had an airspeed indicator.

I asked Foote to tell how Balides had made the error in plotting his Mickey fix on his chart. Foote testified correctly that the co-ordinates were right as logged, but they were plotted wrongly on the chart.

'Would you say from your observation of navigator's logs and charts . . . that this mistake could happen very often?' I asked.

'I wouldn't say "very often". I would say "fairly often".'

I asked Foote if guess-work or logical assumption played a part in his work in reconstructing navigation events at Eighth Air Force and he agreed that it did.

'Would you say that a navigator doing his normal work . . . (uses) a series of logical assumptions from his best known information?'

'I would say that is true,' Foote said.

'When you were flying your operational tour as a navigator, isn't it true that on some of your missions what appeared to be a logical assumption in the air, on reconsideration on the ground often appeared not to be logical at all?'

'I would have to admit that,' Foote said.

Under questioning, Captain Foote reiterated that few of us knew how to compute a wind while we flew around in circles. I asked him once again to tell how Balides had transposed minutes. Then I asked Foote if this were a 'common' error.

Krannawitter was up to object, saying that I had already asked that question, but Corporal Palmer's record showed that I had not. Actually I had asked previously if such an error happened often.

The question was allowed.

'I would say that was a common error.' Foote said.

I thought that was a more convincing answer to have in the record than an error that happened 'fairly often'. I dismissed Captain Foote.

But, of course, Krannawitter was up again for redirect; it seemed to be his favourite exercise.

Krannawitter began by saying, 'Captain, I have only one question I wish to ask you,' and then proceeded to ask seven.

'Did Lieutenant Balides maintain a complete and accurate log and chart . . .'

'No . . .'

'Did he incorrectly determine (his) position . . . to be in the area of Freiburg?'

'He did determine his position to be in the area of Freiburg.'

'Was he correct . . .?'

'He was not.'

'. . .what . . . were the reasons?'

'. . . deficient log and chart . . . malfunctioning H2X equipment (and) no visual aid whatsoever.'

'He had a gee box, did he not?'

'The Germans (had a) severe counter-measure programme (and) jamming was evident.'

'As the (navigation equipment) was not (working), would that indicate to a navigator that he should be on his guard . . . ?'

'It would.'

'. . . shouldn't he be more careful?'

'He should.'

Sokarl elected to recross, though Goldman and I had both asked him to shut up so we could go home to bed. There was no repressing Sokarl.

In a long-winded and involved question, Sokarl wanted to know if, starting with the transposed fix, every position thereafter would not, *per se*, be in error. This was a dumb question, and Foote's answer put Sokarl in his place.

Foote pointed out that a navigator, having entered a condition of relative uncertainty, should do everything to remove the condition. He should not perpetuate a bad scene ad infinitum if he could avoid doing so. Sokarl dismissed Foote and sat down where he should have stayed in the first place.

Krannawitter now asked the Court to dismiss all the witnesses except Mason whom he intended to call to the stand again.

Sokarl asked that Colonel Barthel not be dismissed since (in accordance with my urging) we intended to call him also for the defence.

Colonel Stewart, having conferred with Kearney, granted these motions, and we were, thank God, finally adjourned and stood down at 10.40 p.m. It had been a hell of a long day.

I looked over at Sincock and Balides. They were worn to a frazzle from sitting silently all day and half the night, having their past mistakes aired like dirty laundry. Balides looked as if he might cry. Sincock was white-faced and thin lipped. It hurt me to look at them, but at least they were not in prison yet, though both were off flight duty – pay cut – and marked as pariahs among their fellow airmen.

But, the day was over, and tomorrow would be another day. So, we got to go back home for some well-earned sack time. At least, by putting in over-time, we had finished the interrogation of the last of the officers of Sincock's crew (except Sincock and Balides, that is).

It was difficult for me to get to sleep that night. I tossed and turned. As sometimes happened, when I was really tired, and wanted to sleep, I lay awake endlessly. I had often done it before a big mission with an early briefing scheduled. This night I needed all the sleep I could get. We were scheduled to start up again at 8.30 the next morning.

Finally I dozed off. I had dreams of bombs falling all over Switzerland. Heidi and her ancient grandfather were buried in the rubble, and all their cows were killed. The people of the 392nd Bomb Group, flying the biggest bombers in the world, were coming back over the farm for a second pass. I could hear their laughter echoing through the Alps.

CHAPTER 32

THE DEFENCE RESPONDS

Getting out of the sack to go to Ketteringham Hall on the morning of 2 June 1945 was no easy task. Goldman and I had breakfast together in the club at Horsham St Faith, and when we finished General Peck's big limousine was waiting for us out front.

The drive across Norwich in the beautiful June morning was magnificent. The sun came up early out of the North Sea. After long, black years peace had come again to Britain. Now we were anachronisms, unemployed warriors, here in 'This precious stone, set in the silver sea . . . this blessed plot, this earth, this realm, this England.'

We drove to Court across the green countryside, going to our assigned legalistic tasks, assigned to expunge past errors made in the heat and confusion of battle.

We got the usual brisk salutes from gate guards at Ketteringham Hall. They racked to attention even though the General's flag was covered on the front bumper of the Cadillac. The guards didn't bother to look inside. If Adolf Hitler had driven up in that car, he may have got the same salute we did.

We got to Court on time. Krannawitter was looking his usual natty best, and Sokarl was in fire-breathing form, as usual. The prosecution recalled Captain Albert L. Mason to the stand and he testified that he was the same Captain Mason who had previously testified. He certainly did look like the same one.

Mason recounted how he had examined the log kept by Lieutenant Balides on 4 March 1945, and also the log kept by Lieutenant Damerst in the ship flying deputy lead on the same day. Mason stated that Ben Foote and I had co-operated with him in that analysis. His testimony noted, correctly, that we had all three worked on the same composite map presented in the trial. He said that we worked in harmony, which was true. There was little doubt among us about the actual navigation events of that day when Switzerland was bombed. Mason went through our map in intricate detail and recited all the events of the mission as we believed them to have happened.

As Mason went on and on without interruption by Krannawitter, Colonel Stewart broke into his testimony. Corporal Dolly Palmer was having difficulties with such testimony as 'At this time an E.T.A. was entered in the log at some point. It is not shown in the log which of the points this expected time of arrival was for. Interrogation has shown that it was to be for the flak-free co-ordinates across the Rhine at about forty-eight degrees, fifteen minutes latitude . . .'

'Hold up there for just a minute, Captain,' Stewart said, 'This poor little lady over here is, ah, just snowed by some of this navigation testimony. Now let's just take it easy and give her time to get it all down on paper.'

And the President of the Court smiled at Corporal Palmer.

'You just let us know, Miss, if things get going too fast here. Just hold up your hand for time out, or something.'

Dolly Palmer blushed a deep crimson.

After a while Krannawitter led Mason into setting forth his damaging expert opinions:

' . . . will you tell the Court if he (Balides) maintained on this mission a complete and accurate log and chart?' Krannawitter asked.

'I would not say that he maintained a complete log; neither would I say that it was an accurate log.' Mason failed to describe the chart. Maybe that was just as well.

'Did he inaccurately and incorrectly determine the existing geographical position of this aircraft to be in the area of Freiburg?'

Sokarl was on his feet immediately, breathing fire – an old war-horse, leaping into the traces.

'I object to the question,' Sokarl trumpeted, 'It invades the province of the Court.'

'Sustained!' said Kearney.

I wondered why this objection was sustained when a previous action of the Law Member supported Krannawitter's objection based on the argument that Sincock's bomber was known not to have flown in the vicinity of Freiburg.

Krannawitter, meeting this rebuff, asked Mason whether Balides had kept a 'reasonable' log. Mason was of the opinion that the log was not entirely 'reasonable'. Furthermore, it had a break in continuity – bad news.

I found myself wondering whether 'reasonable' was the right word for anything people did who had volunteered for a career flying great, monstrous aeroplanes over Germany every day to drop high explosives. It was a sense of duty that sent us out, not reason. A reasonable person wouldn't have walked within five hundred feet of a B-24 bomber.

I stood to cross-examine my friend, Albert Mason. I asked if he had found it possible to reconstruct the path of Sincock's bomber during the searching turns through the clouds.

Mason said it had not been possible.

I asked if it were logical to assume that, if such an exercise were impossible on the ground with no time pressures, it would be impossible in the air during a mission.

Mason agreed with that view.

Then I got Mason to admit that the 'Mickey' fixes taken during the period of navigational confusion on this mission had little, if any, accuracy. By this I hoped to show that Balides had every right to be a little confused.

Finally, I got down to the question of the log and the chart. Both Foote and Mason had condemned the log kept by Balides, but they had not, for the record, put down his chart work.

'Would you say that it is possible to do accurate navigation without making use of a chart? – A chart of any description?'

'Do you include maps as a chart?' Mason asked me.

'Maps as a chart. Yes.'

'No. You cannot.'

'Would you say that . . . pressed for time . . . it would be entirely possible to do your navigation accurately and completely on a chart, putting all your information on that chart without referring to a log sheet?'

'It could be done,' Mason agreed.

I knew damn well it could because I had done it many times, filling in the log later to fulfil officious military rules. I released Mason from further testimony, and sat down.

Krannawitter, for a change, declined to redirect.

Now, for the first time, there were questions from the Court Board. Lieutenant-Colonel Walter C. Stroud elected to quiz Mason about how we had determined the red line on the chart, the one we believed to have been the actual track of Sincock's squadron.

Mason testified that a good deal of the information we had charted was confirmed by the log of Lieutenant Damerst, who had apparently been consistent in his work. No gaps were apparent, and he had made good use of his gee box in spite of German jamming.

I wondered once again why Damerst had not asked his pilot to get on the horn and say, 'What the hell, here? My navigator says we're over Switzerland, dammit!' But then, maybe the horn was out of order on that ship – it was such a totally screwed-up day anyway.

Sokarl, making use of the questioning of Colonel Stroud, stood to recross. He asked exactly the questions I had sat there wondering about. I had to admire Sokarl; he was sharp on his feet and paid attention to every nuance of testimony. I was getting a good object lesson in the essential differences between being a junior boy scout group navigation officer and a finely-honed, tough defence attorney.

' . . . I heard you say that this log of Lieutenant Damerst was . . . a good log. Is that correct?' Sokarl was smiling at Mason like a butcher smiles at a hog before slitting its throat.

Krannawitter was up, his trombone blowing: 'I object for the reason that the record does not show that there was any such question asked!'

'I'm asking if he made that statement,' Sokarl said.

Objection was overruled.

'Will you repeat?' Mason asked.

'That the log of Lieutenant Damerst, the wing navigator, was a good log?'

Mason gave a long paragraph of reasoning, but he climaxed it by saying ' . . . I would say it was a good log.'

Sokarl now went back to something previously established in the testimony: ' . . . is it not true that every navigator has been informed by proper official data that, when an international boundary is crossed, he will notify the pilot. Is that correct?'

'He should notify the pilot,' Mason said.

'And is it not true that it is also fundamental in dead-reckoning navigation that if a navigator finds himself five miles off course, it is his duty to inform the pilot?' Sokarl had learned his lessons well in our skull sessions, in spite of appearing to be bored.

'That is right,' Mason said.

'And would it not be the duty of the pilot so informed, if it were a wing ship, to so notify the pilot of the lead ship?'

Sokarl sounded as though he were narrating a horror movie.

'Yes.'

There followed a series of questions and answers, long and involved, in which Mason could not say for certain what he would have done had he been flying wing ship, and he could not say for certain that Damerst did not notify his pilot and that his pilot did not notify Sincock. Of course, he could not say that they did. Mason then put forth the weak excuse that Damerst's log did not specifically say that they were in Switzerland till after the bombs were dropped. He 'believed' that Damerst 'might have said' they were well south of some defined checkpoint after the bombing, but it was all pretty vague and conjectural.

First Lieutenant Max Sokarl had managed, by persuasive questioning to convey the broad but distinct implication that Damerst and his pilot had been the negligent ones on this mission, while Balides and Sincock were pure as the new-fallen snow. But there was an important problem with this performance, Damerst and his crew were not on trial, facing possible life imprisonment. Sincock and Balides were.

With the second testimony of Captain Albert Mason the prosecution rested its case.

Lieutenant Max Sokarl rose to speak: 'May it please the President, Members of the Court, I now intend to make a very short statement . . .'

Everyone acquainted with Sokarl, including the Members of the Court who had heard him for only one day, knew perfectly well that it was impossible for him to make a short statement. He spouted on and on. His message was that the rules permitted us, at this point in the trial, to make a plea of dismissal on the grounds of case not proven by the prosecution. And so on, and so on, and so forth . . .

But, Sokarl magnanimously informed the Court, he was not going to do that. Instead, he, and his young, innocent, defendants were going to rebut the case of the prosecution. We would show, Sokarl stated, that the whole charge was a gross fabrication – a waste of the Court's time to hear. Nonetheless, driven by patriotic duty and a sense of propriety, we would present our case, and the two innocent young lieutenants would now be asked individually to rise and state that they understood what Sokarl had said and state that they each individually agreed that there would be no such plea . . .

Colonel Kearney interrupted. He looked as though he had already heard enough bullshit for a month.

'That will be unnecessary at this time. Let's go ahead.'

Sokarl was disappointed that his dramatic soliloquy had been interrupted. But he went on, undaunted, ever the faithful old soldier.

'Now, if the Court please,' he said, and went on to tell what our testimony would be. He also described our intention to present stipulations, agreed to by the prosecution, as to what certain people would have testified had they been present. For, with the War in Europe ended, key people of the Eighth Air Force were already being returned to the States as a part of the plan to turn the might of the World's greatest aerial combat armada against the Japanese Empire.

Sokarl presented the first stipulation, which was that of the expected testimony of Major Morris R. Clark who was Acting Staff Weather Officer of Second Air Division on 4 March 1945. His expected testimony had to do with the actual state of the weather over Switzerland on the day of the Zurich bombing. The weather was described as very similar to that over southern Germany except that there were slightly larger breaks in the low and medium clouds.

Sokarl's stipulations were agreed to by the prosecution as each was presented.

The next stipulation was that of the expected testimony of Lieutenant Colonel Anthony T. Shogren, who was Staff Weather Officer of Second Air Division on 4 March 1945. His compiled weather data for that date was presented in complete and monumental detail.

The next long and involved stipulation dealt with the state of the electronic navigation equipment in aircraft 577 of the 392nd Bomb Group on 4 March 1945. The extensive notes, taken from the log of the 392nd Group Radar Officer, could be summarised by saying that, in that aeroplane on that day, the H2X (Mickey) radar set had failed.

We then called Lieutenant-Colonel Carl C. Barthel to testify on behalf of the defence. He admitted that he was that same Colonel Barthel who had testified for the prosecution.

Barthel testified that he had conducted his own, independent investigation of the incident of bombing Zurich. He said that he had not initially made use of, nor had he seen, the map which Foote, Mason, and I had prepared. Rather, he had used a probable route map made up by the late Captain Swangren of the 392nd Bomb Group. Swangren's map, Barthel said, agreed basically with the map which Foote, Mason, and I had compiled. Barthel said his purpose in carrying out this Division-level investigation was simply to try to make sure that no such untoward event happened again.

Colonel Barthel described the events of the Swiss mission from the viewpoint of Sincock's crew much as we had already heard them, but there were some interesting comments, viewpoints, and opinions which he had to add.

Barthel said that there were very few navigators who could cope with keeping the position of an aeroplane during a turn. However he forecast that the expected wider use of air position indicators would make such navigational performance possible in the future. I prided myself on being one of those navigators who could pretty well keep track of air position during a turn. The essential information was available. While the navigator did not have a rate-of-turn indicator at his station, he did have a watch. He could easily measure the elapsed time in the turn and that time, multiplied by true airspeed, gave the air distance travelled. The difference in compass headings taken at turn start and end gave the central angle of the turn; this angle, divided by 360 degrees, gave the portion of a full circle turned. Since the radius of a circle is equal to the circumference divided by two pi, it was simple to compute the turn radius. With a compass, the turn could then be laid out on the chart and the known wind could then be applied to the air position. I always carried a pencil-compass in addition to my navigation dividers – it often came in handy.

Thus, exercising the presumptuous and judgemental intolerance which is a characteristic of cocksure youth, I had little sympathy with those navigators who got lost in a turn. B-24 bombers, flying combat missions, could not make drastic turns and hold formation, their standard turns were even and easy to follow.

Barthel gave his opinion as to why Zurich was identified wrongly, and bombed. 'It (was) a collection of errors which normally negate each other. In this case they just backed each other up.'

In response to further questioning, Colonel Barthel gave the opinion that the transposition of latitude and longitude minutes Balides had made was an error normally of little consequence because it was subject to later correction. In this case, however, there were no subsequent fixes, due to jammed and failing navigation equipment. The problems, Barthel indicated, were the result of time pressures, fatigue, strain, and other human failings, common to all men. Barthel's testimony had been good for our cause, I thought, as we dismissed him from the stand. Krannawitter had no questions for him.

Jimmy Stewart broke into the proceedings at this point. 'It seems to me,' he said, 'that we could all benefit from a little break. It's 10.05 a.m. by my watch here – ah, subject to correction by all the learned navigators present – and I suggest we all come back here and start up at about 10.15.'

When we reconvened the defence put forth further stipulations. Among them was the expected testimony of Colonel Irvine A. Rendle, who commanded 96th Combat Wing, having taken over that job when General Peck moved up to head Second Division.

Rendle had flown an observation ship, a fighter, up over the Division attack line on the day of Sincock's mission to Zurich. His report of the weather and the problems it gave to bomber formations was dramatic. Rendle's opinion was that the dumping of bombs on Switzerland was 'the result of trying to accomplish an objective . . . beyond (our) capabilities, under existing complications'.

Sokarl then added a stipulation regarding the testimony of Brigadier-General Leon W. Johnson, commanding 14th Combat Wing. Johnson summarised his view by saying, 'I believe the aggressiveness displayed by this crew was commendable. They could have returned with their bomb load, under the weather conditions encountered, and not have been criticised.' This statement from their Combat Wing commander, a Medal of Honor winner, was about the most positive on behalf of Sincock and Balides that we had produced so far.

Sokarl then asked the Court to advise Sincock and Balides as to their rights in defence. Lieutenant-Colonel Kearney spoke for the Court:

' . . . Each of you has a right to do one of three things: You may take the stand and be sworn like any other witness . . . You may make an unsworn statement and it may be either oral or in writing . . . You (also) have a right to remain silent – to say nothing at all . . . Do you understand what I have just told you?'

Both understood and each stated that he wished to be sworn as a witness, which followed the advice we had given them.

Sincock took the stand first.

His account of the mission on 4 March 1945 was essentially the same story we had heard before but Sincock did add a few new twists. When he could not find his group formation north of Paris, Sincock said, he asked Balides to work up a series of intercept problems to try to catch up with the 392nd Group in the Division attack line. That effort must have been successful because they did find the Group and took over high squadron lead position from the deputy. There was conversation with the deputy ship pilot at that time which destroyed my surmise that the deputy lead pilot had not called Sincock to report that Damerst said they were over Switzerland because his VHF horn had failed.

Sincock testified that the deputy lead ship's flare equipment was non-functional. Therefore, when he got into proper Group position, Sincock ordered his engineer to begin firing the red-yellow flares that were assembly colours for the 392nd. It was these flares that attracted the diverse group of B-24 bombers that eventually made up Sincock's squadron.

Sincock testified further that not one, but several, big turns, possibly to the left and to the right, were flown, not to search, but to follow the lead squadron of the 392nd. Apparently the presumption that there was a single 360-degree turn, as recorded by Balides, was not so. The confusion, Sincock testified, came from his having told Balides, 'We are making a 360-degree turn.' The message should have been, Sincock said, 'Follow the pilot.'

This was interesting news. It would have been particularly enlightening for Foote, Mason, and me, trying to reconstruct where Sincock's lost squadron had gone through the clouds, but we had been so brilliant we neglected to get Sincock's version of what had happened. We just worked with the log and chart Balides had kept.

I began to get a more colourful picture of what had happened up there in the sky on the day we bombed Switzerland. The Second Air Division was in such foul weather it is surprising that anything was done right. The fact that there were no mid-air collisions was remarkable in itself. Pilot Sincock, like many another pilot that day, had woven an intricate and wild pattern through the sky, trying to keep up with his formation. These gyrations through the clouds had doubtless totally confused and unnerved not only Balides, but the entire navigation crew of the squadron lead ship.

It may have been that Sincock was trying, even without realising it, to protect his co-defendant. In describing the identifying of their target as 'Freiburg', Sincock testified that he recalled that identification to have been mutually agreed upon by Milrod and Barger. He did not mention Balides.

Sincock testified that Barger had called out, in order, on the horn for all on the ship to hear, all those features that he saw matching his map illustration of Freiburg. Sincock quoted Barger as saying, 'That town is Freiburg.'

Bombardier Williams asked, according to Sincock, 'Are you sure that is Freiburg?'

To this (Sincock said) Barger had replied, 'I am positive that is Freiburg.'

Sincock told Williams to drop his bombs, and the rest was history.

Sokarl asked Sincock if he would have ordered the bomb drop had he known the place was Zurich – a question more notable for dramatic effect than informative content.

'No, Sir. Certainly not,' Sincock replied.

It was Krannawitter's turn to question Lieutenant Sincock.

'(Did you know) that the gee equipment was not functioning properly . . .?' Krannawitter asked.

'Yes . . .'

' . . . (And) the Mickey equipment was only bringing in a limited amount of return . . .'

'Yes . . .'

Krannawitter asked if Milrod, reporting the 'fix' on Stuttgart, qualified his statement by saying the return was unreliable.

Sincock agreed that Milrod had made that fact apparent.

Colonel Allen Herzberg (left) awards the Distinguished Flying Cross to Captain Jackson Granholm at Horsham St Faith in 1945.

'Now,' Krannawitter pontificated, 'did you follow the navigation from that place (presumably near Stuttgart?) on out yourself, or did you rely strictly on your navigator?'

'I do not navigate the aeroplane.'

'And you were relying entirely on your navigator?'

'On the three navigators I have aboard. Yes, Sir.'

'And, in that instance, do you rely more on one particular navigator than the others?'

'No, Sir. It is the opinion of all the navigators, with the equipment and facilities they have available to them. When they arrive at a common decision, that decision is the one which I take!'

I suppose that Sincock meant this statement to be defensive of Balides and his position. I found it to be quite otherwise. I was happy that I didn't ride with Sincock, the lead ship rules and procedures made it quite clear that the dead-reckoning navigator was the lead navigator of the aircraft and the other two were his assistants. The navigational direction of the aircraft was his responsibility, and the buck stopped with him. It was not a committee decision of three navigators, and the pilot did not have a say in navigation, even though he was the aircraft commander.

I could hear, echoing in my mind, what the great Elmer Mottern would have replied to such an asinine statement. His blasphemous reply would have burned Sincock's ears. Mottern had once, during a mission, added to his legendary fame by telling Major Pappy Henson, flying Group command, exactly where to stuff his navigational opinion.

It seemed to me, not having been there and exercising expert hindsight, that Balides should have been tougher with his two assistants. When he got confusing input, he should have said that someone was full of it, and that they had better shape up.

The testimony established that Sincock did not have a map of Freiburg (or, surely, of Zurich). He could not see the ground well from the pilot's seat.

The rest of Krannawitter's questioning went back over now-familiar ground, and we had no further questions of Sincock. Since no Court member had questions, Lieutenant Sincock was dismissed by Colonel Stewart.

CHAPTER 33

THE VERDICT

We called to the stand Theodore Balides, First Lieutenant, Air Corps. As he stood up, Balides looked ill. His hands shook, his face was flushed, his step was halting. He was sworn in, and testified about his military career.

I began to sweat in sympathy while watching Balides. I could imagine myself in his position. It was not a reassuring vision. Could it be that we were actually sending this young man to life imprisonment, or at least to disgrace and discharge from the military? I hoped that Max Sokarl had known what he was doing when he set up this court martial for General Peck. With Sokarl's love of things theatrical it was quite possible that he had overlooked the real consequences of the potential result in human terms.

Lieutenant Sokarl, in a friendly, chatty, and laid-back mood, asked Balides to tell us his story of the mission to Switzerland from start to finish. He asked Balides to interpret as he chose without waiting for questions from his counsel.

Balides was nervous and fidgety on the stand. He told the story that had become so familiar to us by now, the story of how Sincock's impromptu squadron had become lost and bombed Zurich, but he added his own particular observations.

Balides told how, over the English Channel in their second aeroplane, there was a problem with the heater in his compartment.

'What heater?' I wondered. When those of us on Hayzlett's crew flew combat missions we forgot that the B-24 was allegedly equipped with heaters. When turned on they did nothing in the wind-tunnel of a nose compartment and usually filled the rest of the aeroplane with oily fumes. We depended on our cosy, electric-heated underwear for creature comfort in the stratosphere. In any event, Balides said that he had asked the flight engineer if he could fix the heater. The engineer accomplished this fix, but the procedure was an interruption and an unnerving disturbance for Balides who was under plenty of extra pressure to begin with.

It seemed to me that this squadron lead ship aeroplane which Sincock's crew flew that day had been a better candidate for the junk pile than for a bombing raid.

Balides also told how it was that, when they had arrived over the radio beacon of Buncher C-3 in France, the time had already passed for completion of Group assembly, but the Wing was scheduled to assemble on a triangular course west of Buncher C-3. Sincock had asked Balides to direct him into this Wing assembly area to see if they could find the 392nd Bomb Group.

That search for the Group was not successful, so they flew back again to Buncher C-3. From there they took off down the Division briefed line of flight to see if they could find Major Keilman and his group formation. Had they just gone home instead it would have been much simpler for them – they would not have been subject to criticism for such a move, and they would not be in the unholy mess they were now in.

As he testified, Balides spoke with halting syllables and breaking voice. Lieutenant Balides recalled that it was somewhere out east of Metz that they found the Group formation, but the exact location had been variously testified to by sundry people. Balides said that he must have been somewhere near the front line at about 9.14 a.m. because he remembered putting on his flak vest. He and Williams had a little ceremony in which each helped the other put on flak armour.

The flak armour exercise that Balides described sounded to me like a clever idea. I had never had anyone help me with mine, and I never wore it unless we were in really heavy flak already. The vest and helmet were too damn uncomfortable. Besides, like most young men in battle, I thought I was made of steel and probably enjoyed immortality.

Now, presumably, I wouldn't need my flak armour again to fly over Germany, but I built a little file in my mind for future use in case I needed to fly over Japan.

Balides told the same story of their flight path's twisting and turning that Sincock had described. Sokarl led him to the question of the transposed minute figures in charting his now-famous 'fix' on Stuttgart.

Balides admitted that he had indeed transposed the latitude and longitude minute figures, charting his position as some twenty-five miles south-east of where it should have been plotted, but he also said that this had never been mentioned to him during all the months of probing and investigation into why Second Air Division had bombed Switzerland. He said he had not known he had done it until the week previous to the trial when I had told him so. He had checked his chart and log and found that I was right. I felt guilty for having kept Balides in the dark for so long on this matter, though what difference it made I didn't know, really.

Balides told again the story of looking for a target of opportunity as they withdrew. He did not recall exactly what anyone had said, but thought it could be 'reasonable' that Milrod had said it 'might be' Freiburg. Balides was of the opinion that it would have been logical for all of them to think it was Freiburg. That was the only city of consequence within thirty miles of where they thought they were.

Balides said that Barger had been certain that they had not yet crossed the Rhine, for he could 'see it on the other side of the town'. (The Rhine does not flow through Zurich). Williams was also satisfied that the bomb run he made was an attack on Freiburg. Balides got gee fixes on withdrawal that showed him well south of course, but the cut of the gee lattice lines in this vicinity was so narrow that it was easy to be mistaken by quite a few miles.

It was not until late in the evening of 4 March 1945 that Colonel Lorin Johnson had called Sincock and Balides down to Group Operations and told them that they had bombed Zurich.

Sokarl noted that Balides had heard all the testimony and asked if there was anything that had been said that Balides wanted to rebut, or to comment on. Balides said there was. He said that Captain Albert Mason, in his testimony, had criticised his work for failure to compute winds on the way from France into Germany. Balides said that they had been constantly zigging and zagging on that route, avoiding the worst clouds, and trying to find the Wing formation. These constant manoeuvres had made it impossible for him to compute more winds.

As Balides offered these comments in his testimony, it was obvious that he had been deeply and personally hurt by the testimony that Mason had offered. His voice shook, and he was obviously disturbed. Yet, I had always found Mason to be matter-of-fact. He testified to nothing that he, Foote, and I had not agreed to in our navigational analysis. Certainly he had said nothing that remotely resembled a slur on the character of either defendant. Yet I could understand why Balides might be upset. Navigation, especially for a lead navigator, was a personal thing. To criticise one's navigation work was to criticise one's person in a very real sense. The sensitivity that Balides showed was understandable.

We turned Balides over for cross-examination by the Trial Judge-Advocate. Krannawitter jumped into the fray and led Balides over to our exhibit map. There he showed him the straight line drawn between his two gee fixes at 8.55 and 9.05 a.m. Since Balides had previously testified that it took ten minutes of straight and level flight to compute a good wind, Krannawitter wanted to know why there was no wind for this segment of the mission. Balides pointed out that the heading between the two fixes could have wandered all over the place, but since Foote, Mason, and I had only the two fixes, we had drawn a straight line between them.

Krannawitter went on, boring into the records Balides had kept – wanting to know why he had not got another wind after 8.03 a.m. He did a good job of picking the mission log and chart to pieces. It seemed obvious to me that Mason had coached him well, and Krannawitter was very impressive on the attack, in spite of Sokarl's guard-house psychiatric analyses. I figured that his questions alone might be strong enough to send Balides up the river.

At last Krannawitter got to his final question. Balides answered it, and was dismissed from the stand. He was sweating profusely and his hands were visibly shaking.

We then called Major Kenneth Paddock, Group Navigator of the 392nd, to the stand, this time to testify for the defence.

Goldman interrogated him.

Paddock was asked to evaluate the competency of Lieutenant Balides. Paddock stated that, in spite of some things that had been said at the trial, Balides was a good navigator. Paddock had evaluated his work on a number of missions. (I summoned up a vision of the past, of Elmer Mottern, when I was squadron navigator of the 752nd, calling me on the phone to report the sloppy performance of one of my men – 'What's that son-of-a-bitch think he's doin' up there, anyway?') Balides' work had been consistently good in Paddock's judgement.

Paddock also noted that Balides was 'aggressive' and 'positive' as a navigator. He was a decisive person, and in this sad instance he had just decided wrongly. It could happen to any of us. Paddock said that he would select Balides again as a lead navigator, if he had to do it over again. He still had confidence in him. Krannawitter declined to examine, and the Court had no questions.

Next we called to the stand Major Myron Keilman. He had flown Group Command of the 392nd on the day we bombed Switzerland, and not only was Keilman the Group Command Pilot on the fateful day of the bomb drop on Zurich, but he was also the Squadron Commanding Officer of both Sincock and Balides. These were his boys on trial.

Keilman was a kind, quiet man from the big sky state of Montana. One got the impression that he would have been as much at home on a horse as in a bomber. He was interrogated by Goldman.

Keilman described the responsibilities of a command pilot in keeping Group and Wing integrity during a mission, in supervising the flight, and making necessary decisions. Goldman asked Keilman's opinion of Lieutenant Sincock and Keilman described Sincock as a 'superior' pilot. He indicated that he was perfectly satisfied with Sincock's work as a lead pilot.

Keilman went on to describe Balides as 'an excellent officer', one who 'worked hard at his assigned duties'. Goldman asked Keilman if he could think of any specific incident which showed the particular qualifications of Balides.

Krannawitter was up at once, describing the question as 'far afield'.

Goldman purposely ignored Krannawitter's comment. 'I would like to recall to your mind,' he said to Keilman, 'the bombing of the Bielefeld viaduct. The 392nd was one of the few Groups of Second Air Division to attack the viaduct at Bielefeld.'

'Am I to understand that the counsel is testifying?' Krannawitter demanded with a sneer worthy of Sokarl.

'Overruled!' Kearney said, wearily.

Krannawitter sat down.

'Can you tell me who the navigator was on that mission and how he contributed to its success?' Goldman asked.

Krannawitter had a look on his face as though we were about to see Santa Claus actually come down the chimney.

Keilman went on, undaunted by Krannawitter's muttering, to tell how Balides, flying with him, had led them directly over the viaduct at Bielefeld with his gee-H set. Balides was the navigation hero of that day.

'No further questions. You may inquire.' Goldman said to Krannawitter.

'I don't wish to inquire.' Krannawitter said, sulking a bit.

Colonel James Stewart spoke up:

'Colonel,' he said to Major Keilman, giving him an instant promotion, 'During this mission of 4 March, did you receive over VHF or WT at any time information that some other unit or units of the force had abandoned the mission?'

'I did,' Keilman replied.

'Thank you,' Stewart said.

That being the end of Keilman's testimony, he was dismissed.

Sokarl presented yet another stipulation. This related to the statement of Colonel Lorin L. Johnson, Commanding Officer of the 392nd Bomb Group. Johnson had been ordered back to the States and was not able to appear in person to testify.

While Johnson had signed the charges against Sincock and Balides, he wrote his belief that what had happened to them on 4 March 1945 could have happened to any combat crew. He characterised the past performance of Sincock and Balides as showing devotion to duty, ambition and patriotism. They were, he said, men of unquestionable character and their performance had been excellent.

Johnson stated that he had told his men that any bomb on a railroad track in Germany was a good bomb.

Krannawitter took a good deal of the glory out of Johnson's statement by saying, ' . . . in these stipulations we are merely stipulating that, if the witnesses were called here, that would be their testimony – not that these facts are true!' Krannawitter's comment went unchallenged into the trial record and it seemed to me that it may have made all our stipulations not worth the paper they were written on. In my unlearned opinion, we had really offered little else in the way of defence.

I was also worried about the content of the stipulation of Colonel Lorin Johnson. If that was his statement, why had he signed the accusation against Sincock and Balides? Had high command sat on someone's head? Had Johnson been ordered to make his accusation, 'or else'? Was General Spaatz determined that someone would be punished for this Swiss screw-up? Were Sincock and Balides going up the river?

The thought occurred to me that maybe we were all taking part in a big charade. Maybe it was all cut and dried, and Sincock and Balides were the sacrificial victims. Maybe they were 'guilty' no matter what Sokarl, Goldman, and I did.

In the American Military Cemetery at Cambridge were six thousand and thirty-two graves of men killed in aerial combat in Second Air Division. Now that the Third Reich had surrendered, there would be no more airmen buried there. No more American young men would die from German flak or fighter fire. But Lieutenants Sincock and Balides might become the final casualties among combat crews of the B-24 Division. If we convicted them here, today, their lives would be taken from them just as surely as if they were shot down.

Sokarl informed the Court that the Defence would rest. Krannawitter offered no rebuttal.

Colonel Stewart, noting that the clock read 12.30 p.m., called a recess for lunch and reminded us to be back at 1.30.

The ladies of the Ketteringham Hall lunch room were once again overwhelmed by the presence of the famous Colonel James Stewart in their midst. He, however, was calm about the whole matter, pretending that the English waitresses acted totally silly every day. They did exercise an amount of decorum and British cool. It was only about once every thirty seconds that their inane twittering reminded us that we had a public figure present.

We went back into Court at 1.30. Krannawitter made a closing argument for the prosecution that was remarkably free of vindictiveness. In essence he said, 'You've heard the facts, gentlemen. Make your decision fairly.' It could have been far worse.

Sokarl, summing up for the defence, was not going to miss the opportunity for some outstanding theatrics: He referred to ' . . . these innocent young men, the pride of our nation, caught up in the web of relentless fate.' There were tears in his eyes as he put his arms around the two accused, as though to shelter them should the sky fall, and told how, in these few short weeks he had become fast friends with them, had shared some of their travail and suffering, and was moved by their plight. To hear this sad story you might presume that Sokarl was the one who could be sent up the river if found guilty.

Then, in a voice intoned like the closing bars of a Beethoven symphony, he told the court that they had to – they must – see that justice was done here. And justice, of course, demanded that these two innocents be set free!

Flak damage to the left rudder.

The members of the court martial board filed grimly out to deliberate. It was their duty to vote in the manner prescribed in Articles of War 31 and 43 of the United States of America.

We went out on the porch to enjoy the sunny afternoon of East Anglia, and to sweat on behalf of our clients.

'What do you think?' I asked Goldman.

'Looks pretty good to me,' he said.

'It's a shoo-in,' Sokarl said.

I looked at Lieutenant Max Sokarl – he was perspiring. For the first time since I had known him, I saw him look worried. Having seen this haunted look on the face of Max Sokarl, he of the carefree life – the archetypical military bon vivant – the ultimate personification of perpetual cool – I was mightily concerned for these two men we had tried to defend. I could envision my name written down in military history as the guy who screwed up the defence of Lieutenants Sincock and Balides. I could see them both going to military prison with no chance of pardon – ever. I wondered weirdly if some ironmonger's shop in Norwich might have big sledge hammers – I could give them these as going-away presents for a lifetime to be spent on the Federal rock pile.

In almost too short a time, at 2.15 p.m. we were summoned back into the Court. I looked at Balides. I was sure he would faint at any moment. I looked at Sincock; he was pale, stiff and quiet.

I looked at Lieutenant-Colonel Kearney. His face was like granite.

Then I looked at Colonel Stewart. He looked human. He smiled at me. Was there hope?

Kearney read the Court's verdict in stentorian tones:

'The Court finds the accused Sincock: Of the specification of the charge: Not Guilty. Of the charge: Not Guilty. The Court finds the accused Balides: Of the specification of the charge: Not Guilty. Of the charge: Not Guilty.'

The two lieutenants were up and over at the defence table, thanking us. I looked as they shook hands with Max Sokarl. Once again he had tears in his eyes.

Colonel Stewart was kind enough to come over and offer congratulations to each of them.

After a few minutes, we all left the courtroom and went our separate ways. I have never seen Sincock nor Balides again.

CHAPTER 34

FINAL DAYS

The War was over in Europe, Bomb groups of Eighth U.S. Army Air Force awaited orders to go home. Air-crews were to fly their bombers west across the Atlantic. Ground personnel would be assigned to troop ships. Those of us at the 458th Bombardment Group (H), Horsham St Faith, sweated out our turn in the departure line.

I walked out along the perimeter track of the airfield at Horsham St Faith. The grass was green and the pastoral surroundings pleasant in the English spring. No more were our combat air-crews roused from fitful sleep by the awakening to life of great, growling, twin-row radial engines sounding in the pre-dawn darkness. No more did long lines of dreadful war machines parade into take-off lines at the main runway. Our missions were over. We were relegated to the status of dinosaurs – great death-dealing pteranodons with nothing left to destroy. The training programme for the group's navigators had gone well, thanks primarily to the expertise of our squadron navigators. I'd been so tied up with the trial of Sincock and Balides that I had contributed little to the effort.

The navigators of the 458th were well checked out on transoceanic navigation. After the trauma of combat flying, this retraining was a relaxing exercise. Those men who had flown their missions as wing navigators, playing follow-the-leader, were now to get a chance to do their own thing. It was not intended that we fly the ocean in formation. Each bomber would find its way home alone.

These retreaded skills of navigation over water were imparted to every navigator in the group except one. The Group Navigation Officer had been too busy with a huge court martial to take part in the training. However, I intended to fly back to the States as a passenger. All the staff, command, and honcho flight-rated people – those who had no regular crew assignment – would go as passengers. A B-24 could easily carry ten extra people and their baggage in addition to the crew; it could carry twenty extra if comfort was no criterion.

I had been in England for well over a year. During that time I had accumulated many of those useless things with which people surround themselves, so now I went through the process of throwing a lot of these things away. In addition to my flight bag and navigation brief case, I would be allowed to take my G.I. foot-locker. In that monstrous receptacle I packed all my books and a few clothes. The books were the most important of my acquired British possessions.

As Group Navigator I was responsible for all of the navigation equipment assigned to the 458th. Included in such equipment were all the navigators' hack watches and chronometers. Each navigator needed his hack watch, and he was supposed to maintain two chronometers in his aeroplane. These became especially important during transoceanic flights. During our time in England, I had inherited from Major Elmer Mottern the custom of issuing timepieces to those who were authorised to have them. Navigation hack watches were particularly popular among pilots who were not authorised to have them and I was hard-nosed about the watch issuance. Somehow I especially enjoyed turning down some officious major who would wander into my office demanding that I give him a hack watch.

To fly the ocean, each navigator needed a bubble octant in working order. This instrument was the airborne navigation equivalent of a shipboard sextant. It was used for shooting celestial navigation fixes but we never used octants in combat navigation. Although each navigator was supposed to keep and maintain his own in good condition, when it was time to go home, about half the navigators in the Group could not find their octants. These had been lost, left in pubs, given to girlfriends, and otherwise forgotten and neglected. So I set up a little business in my office, checking out and issuing bubble octants to those navigators who had lost, misplaced or damaged theirs. I also had a trade-in service for broken octants.

The Group Supply Officer, as a part of tidying up to leave, asked me to sign as responsible for all those watches, octants, and other pieces of navigation equipment which the Group had been issued since day one. I did this with some misgivings – I had visions of later receiving a bill for several million dollars from the U.S. Federal Government, military division.

One day Lieutenant-Colonel Walter Williamson came into my office. He wanted to have a confidential talk on the subject of a career in the military. In brief, he said that we could all recognise that the War would end soon. Japan didn't have a chance now that Germany had collapsed, and what he wanted from me was a promise to stay on – to become regular Army.

Williamson spoke highly about my performance and I was considerably flattered. Doubtless he intended me to be. I had always liked Walter Williamson a great deal, and I respected him as an officer, a gentleman, and an excellent person. But somehow I couldn't see myself as permanent Army so I told him I'd think about it.

Irving Goldman was busy with his regular job as Group Radar Officer. He also had a lot to do to get ready to go back home, but Goldman and I made time to get together when we could. We talked about the court martial which had dealt with the bombing of Zurich, and what a unique experience it was.

We did not see Max Sokarl. He was apparently busy doing whatever one does as an aide-de-camp to keep his Commanding General happy. In fact, we did not actually know whether Sokarl was still at Ketteringham Hall, or on his way back to the States with General Peck.

Goldman and I concurred that the court martial of Sincock and Balides had been Sokarl's show from start to finish. He was the one who had planned, organised, and executed it. At least he was the prime mover in everything we got involved in connected with that Court.

I thought back to the trial, and Sokarl's remarkable performance throughout. I thought of the tears in his eyes when he told the Court about the probable fates of Sincock and Balides should they be convicted. It seemed obvious that Sokarl really cared. But did he? When you had come to know him as well as I did, you had a different plausible explanation: Max was able to get so carried away with his own oratory that he cried at the beauty of its very effectiveness. Possibly the only thing that Sokarl really believed in was whatever he was saying at the moment.

Whatever it was that motivated Sokarl, one thing was certain. He was able to sweep up people's emotions with his speeches, carry them along with him, and capture their full attention, imagination, and even their willing co-operation. He had demonstrated this in the big trial just as thoroughly as he had in heisting the Wendover bus.

Meanwhile Valerie Forde's vaudeville troupe was back at the Norwich Hippodrome Theatre. So I went downtown to watch Valerie roll herself up in the curtain and skid on her butt across the stage. Her act was just as charming as ever.

I waited at the stage door for Valerie.

'It's you again, Yank,' she said, 'I thought you'd gone home.'

'Not yet. How about lunch tomorrow?'

'You remember me then?'

'Who could forget you? No one else on stage rolls up in the curtain.'

'Noon here then, is it? How simply utter!'

And Valerie and I had lunch at the same tea room where we'd lunched before and then we strolled the green lawns around the cathedral.

B-24 *Briney Marlin* comes in to land on three engines.

'How about the Officer's Club at Horsham after the show tonight?' I asked her. 'We're having a party. Even Limeys are invited. Can you come?'

'Can I bring my two friends from the dance act?'

'Sure, the more the merrier!'

I recruited two friends from the Group staff. We met Valerie and her show-girl chums at the theatre door late in the evening and we all crowded into the cab for the air-base.

The English showgirls had never seen a big military air-base before and they were fascinated. We borrowed a colonel's jeep and took them out along the flight line, through the hangars, and around all the perimeter roads.

'I had no idea they were so big!' Valerie said, looking at a row of B-24s. The night mechanics were warming up engines and kicking tyres. It was quite a show.

We went back to the endless party at the club. We danced, talked, and bought drinks for our English girlfriends. It was apparent that they were rarely entertained well.

At about one-thirty a.m. some officious idiot decided that it was time for all visitors to leave the base. We called a cab and loaded Valerie and her friends into it.

'Come with us, Yank,' Valerie said, 'We'll go downtown and dance all night. Come have breakfast with me!'

'Sorry, I can't. Duty calls, you know, and all that stuff. But you'll get there safely.'

'All right then,' she said. I was astonished when I looked at her. Her eyes were all misty. What was bothering her?

'See you soon, Love,' she said, 'Ta Ta!' And off she went into the dark morning.

But Valerie was mistaken. I never saw her again.

The next morning we loaded up, taxied out to the runway, and took off, headed for home.

CHAPTER 35

GOING HOME

Twenty of us, with our luggage, rode our B-24 out of Horsham St Faith. Of these twenty, ten were the regular crew of the aeroplane, and ten were passengers, of which I was one.

We flew to Valley in Anglesey, Wales. The airfield there was a staging area for American bombers flying west across the Atlantic. Because so many of us were headed home, the airfield got the nickname of 'Happy Valley'.

We hung around Valley for two days. As a passenger, I had nothing to do except eat at the officers' mess and enjoy the Welsh scenery. At about three o'clock one morning a G.I. woke me and insisted it was time for us to go. I took my luggage, walked out to the flight line, and found no one else at our aeroplane, so I put the luggage on board, crawled into the tunnel under the flight deck, wrapped a casualty blanket around myself, and went back to sleep. Shortly after dawn the rest of the passengers and crew showed up, and we took off, heading south-west for the Azores.

Since I was already in the ship's nose, I climbed into the nose turret and rode there all the way to the Azores, enjoying the ocean scenery below on a sunny day over the Atlantic. Occasionally I would open the turret doors to ask the navigator if he was really on course. Doubtless he appreciated the interest.

The weather in the Azores was beautiful and balmy, but weather in Newfoundland, our next scheduled stop, was bad, so we were held up for about six days, waiting for Newfoundland to clear up. At the Azores we were kept on the air-base. The Allies leased the use of the field from the Portuguese government, but the rest of the place was neutral.

Finally the weather pundits determined that the Newfoundland weather was good enough for us to find the place, so we went out to our bomber and boarded. I was comfortably resting in the waist compartment when a jeep drove up – it was Captain Harry Black, Group Training Officer of the 458th. Black was flying co-pilot in another ship, and their navigator had turned up sick – in the hospital with pneumonia. Understandably, Black wanted to go home, but the ranking authorities of the base would not clear his ship for take-off without a navigator aboard. He wanted me to go with him.

Now the fat was in the fire. I hadn't trained myself in the transoceanic classes, though I'd made sure everybody else was trained. Also, the briefing on how to find Gander Lake Airport in Newfoundland was finished. Everybody was on board the other bombers, engines cranking, lining up for take-off.

I had my duty to do. I went with Black in his jeep, got the weather report, a Mercator, a gnomonic chart, a map of Newfoundland, the allegedly correct time, and went out to the aeroplane, ready to go.

Then I found out the identity of the navigator who rested in the hospital, too sick to travel. Every bomb group had a few goof-offs. Our missing patient was that navigator of the 458th about whom I had the most foul-up reports. His aeroplane indicated it. None of the instruments were calibrated, and the compass had never been swung or checked. A great beginning to a transoceanic flight!

However his octant was on board, and apparently working. Also his sun compass was in place in the astrodome, I was not daunted and told the pilots to roll it when ready.

Though I had not put myself through transoceanic navigation training, I had a few tricks up my sleeve. After all, I was the Group Navigator – not paid to be a complete dummy, and because I hadn't been to the morning briefing, I hadn't heard the word passed out there – the word that told us that, as combat navigators, we were too dumb to know how to fly great circle courses. We should go to Newfoundland flying rhumb line constant heading, the briefers said. That way no one would get confused.

Not knowing these things, I laid out a great circle course on my gnomonic chart and transferred it to my transoceanic Mercator. Then, using the winds given out at the weather briefing, I laid out on the chart my dead-reckoning positions all the way to Newfoundland. One thing about celestial navigation, done by hand, is that each position line begins at an assumed position, and corrects it. My pre-computed dead-reckoning positions were going to be good enough for that purpose all the way across. With this approach, I could devote maximum time to shooting sun lines and taking radio bearings. In other words, I could get more real fixes if I precomputed my dead-reckoning. The day was 21 June 1945 – the summer solstice. The sun held its same declination all day, so I didn't have to look it up in my Air Almanac.

We took off and climbed out. Everyone else had left a half hour previously. The navigation on the way across worked beautifully. The pilots were nervous, however, because I kept giving them different headings every twenty minutes or so in order to stay on the great circle track.

In my spare time at Horsham St Faith, instead of devoting efforts to drinking and wenching, I had read navigation books for relaxation. Rather than making Jack a dull boy, this spare time boning-up now paid off. In ship navigation, which I had studied, there is a procedure for taking a noon fix on the sun. This method was not taught in Army aerial navigation schools, so most flyboys were unaware of it. With only the sun visible it is usually possible to get lines of position only, but when the sun crosses your meridian, you can fix position at local apparent noon if your timing is good.

I convinced the pilots to hold steady, and I shot the sun every thirty seconds for fifteen minutes. Its point of highest elevation was our local noon. We were right on course and on time. We hit the coast of Newfoundland at the expected place and time.

I tuned into the Gander radio beacon, and began to take bearings. Also I gave the pilots a five-degree right correction so I would be sure I knew on which side of the airport we approached. We came abreast of Gander to the north exactly at the estimated time of arrival, flew into the traffic pattern, and landed.

We had beaten nearly everybody else to Gander from the Azores. There was a big weather low over the western Atlantic and we had skirted the northern edge of the bad weather everyone else flew through. Not only that, our great circle route was sixty miles shorter, and the low gave us a tail wind all the way. Luck had flown with me.

The next day the weather over eastern North America was bad. We were given the choice of hanging around for better weather, or going home. We chose to go. The flight to Windsor Locks, Connecticut, was uneventful. We navigated through a lot of clouds, but we were used to that from flying combat in Europe. It was the last flight I was ever to make as aircraft navigator.

I got out of the aeroplane in Connecticut with my luggage. I put my engineering boots – the boots I wore on every combat mission over Europe – down on the concrete ramp. There I left them, forgetting them as I went off in a jeep to find quarters. It was a symbolic forgetting.

We were given a month's leave, and train tickets to go home. Having flown in the toughest aerial combat known to history, we were now returned to the railroads for quiet travel. The trip back to Washington State through the American summer was a worthwhile homecoming.

After a month at home I was assigned to the air-base at Sioux Falls, South Dakota. The place was overcrowded with airmen returned from Europe looking for something to do. I volunteered to stay with the 458th Bomb Group which was scheduled into March Field in Riverside, California to retrain in B-29 bombers. I looked forward to it. The B-29 had a pressure-cabin, suitable for shirt-sleeve flying. The navigator had a big, comfortable desk up in the greenhouse nose. It was a limousine compared to a B-24.

My orders were cut for March Field when the *Enola Gay* dropped on Hiroshima. The War was over in Japan. Given the choice, I elected to go home and become a professional civilian.

That fall my high-school girlfriend and I were married and I went back to the University of Washington to resume my studies.

After a time I graduated in Physics and got a job in the Physical Research Lab of the Boeing Company. It was the first of a number of positions in aerospace, electronics, and related technology which have occupied me ever since.

Sometimes I spend time in reminiscing about how it was in the Eighth U.S. Army Air Force. It was an adventure not to be repeated, but one that it would be a shame to have missed.

Sometimes news came to me of old friends of the 458th:

God called a surprising number of World War II combat airmen in slightly-belated events of civilian life – as though He had forgotten to take them during the days of aerial warfare, and had second thoughts. Our flight engineer-top gunner, Lynne Griefenstein, died in an auto accident shortly after he came home from combat. Lynne had been a tower of strength and a solid member of our crew. I have no doubt that he saved all our lives when we iced up in the thunderstorm over El Paso and he probably did the same when our turbosuperchargers failed north of Hannover.

At the end of October, 1984, I got a letter from Dee Gniewkowski. She told me that Eddie had died, suddenly, from a stroke. That news made me sad. Eddie Gniewkowski and I had been good friends, and had endured much together in the nose compartments of B-24 bombers. The news of Eddie's departure set me wondering where the other people of my original crew were.

I knew that Bob Stoesser, our original co-pilot, had stayed on in active duty, for he had come to visit me in Seattle once, wearing his natty blue Air Force uniform. A letter to the Air Force Locator service brought me the news that Bob had also gone to the great flight line in the sky.

I found Bob Hayzlett, our quiet, competent pilot, living in retirement in Grass Valley, California. I drive by to visit with him when I can.

I keep in touch with Weldon Sheltraw, our superb radio operator. He lives in Hemlock, Michigan. We write to each other at times.

That magnificent tail turret gunner, Brownie Harvath, lives in Rio Linda, California. Brownie flew many miles with us through unfriendly skies, riding alone, freezing in his rearward-facing turret, protecting our tender buns from German fighter attack.

Dominic Giordano, waist gunner, is a retired printer living in Melrose

Sergeant Brownie Harvath, tail gunner on Lt Robert Hayzlett's crew, had his records confused in the military archives. Here in March of 1991, he is awarded the Distinguished Flying Cross by Major-General Michael D. Pavich at McClellan AFB.

Park, Illinois. Dom was the most unfailingly happy man on our crew, always ready to cheer up anyone, even in the worst of times.

Carsie Foley started flying with us in the ball turret. He was the smallest man on our crew, and I remember him looking like a grade school student in his flight togs. I found Carsie living in Lexington, Kentucky. Some time later Brownie Harvath called to tell me that Carsie had left us.

Our faithful gunner, Clair Stahl, has also gone to the flight line in the sky. Clair lived in Alliance, Ohio.

Bert Kemp, who became our radar officer when we entered the electronic age of aerial warfare, lived in Ashton, Illinois. He sometimes visited other crew members until his recent death from a brain tumour.

I haven't been able to locate Frank Shepherd who flew regularly as our pilotage navigator, riding the nose turret.

There are others I remember often, and with nostalgia:

Clear across the continent, in November 1954, a strange incident took place at the Institute of Living in Hartford, Connecticut. The Institute is one of the most noted private organisations in the country set up to deal with the problems of mental illness.

Max M. Sokarl, a well-known attorney of New London, Connecticut, appeared at the Institute, asking to have himself admitted for examination and diagnosis. After several days the Institute staff could find no specific problems from which Sokarl might suffer, and he was so advised. However, the Institute doctors asked him to stay on for a few more days, to relax and to chat further with them.

In mid afternoon of Thursday, 25 November 1954 – Thanksgiving Day – a duty nurse noticed that Max Sokarl was missing from his quarters. She searched the area but could find him nowhere.

Across the street in a three-storey apartment building Mr William Moran, a resident of the third floor, noticed someone climbing the fire escape outside his apartment. He opened the window and asked the man what he was doing.

'Looking for the painter!' was the answer.

'Oh,' the tenant said, and shut the window.

A few moments later a body hurtled from the roof to the sidewalk below. Moran called the police.

Detective William M. O'Brien and Police Sergeant Robert J. Daley found Max Sokarl, drastically injured, lying on the sidewalk. They rushed him to the hospital where he died a short time later.

Irving Goldman, our tower of legal strength in the trial of Sincock and Balides, went home to become a judge in upstate New York. His court dealt with family matters. I can think of no one better than Goldman to preside in such a court, for he always showed genuine concern and compassion for people and their problems.

Air Force Locator service informed me that Elmer Mottern, toughest navigator in the Eighth Army Air Force, had gone on to his reward, which I found hard to believe. Elmer had always seemed too rugged to die.

In winter-time I am sometimes able to arrange happy meetings with the ever-smiling Chuck Booth and retired General Jim Isbell. Chuck and Big Jim are often to be found enjoying the sunshine in the California low desert where they can escape from the winter-time chills of home. We sit around the table and tell old war stories. Some of the stories are scary enough without making them more outlandish every year.

In October of 1987 the 458th Heavy Bomb Group held its first-ever reunion at Wright-Patterson Air Force Base, Dayton, Ohio. I flew out of Los Angeles on TWA to Cincinnati, leased a car, and drove north to Dayton. A lot of old friends were there. Many people were glad to greet Jim Isbell again. He had been a popular commander – tough but always fair and well-organised. I was the only one in attendance from our original combat crew, but I met with many other ancient airmen of fond remembrance.

I exchanged war stories at Dayton with old office mate, Fred Vacek, Group Bombardier. We had not seen each other since Fred finished his mission tour and went home from England. A few months after the Dayton reunion, Fred died.

Today, as I write the final sentences of this book, the young flyers of the United States Eighth Army Air Force have become old men. They begin to resemble the blue-suited ancients of the Grand Army of the Republic who sat on the sunny porch of their retirement home as my English-born grand-mother walked past with me, a small child at the time, understanding nothing of the Civil War that had given us such veterans.

Today we have a new breed of blue-suited military people in the United States Air Force. No longer are there huge formations of aeroplanes – Today's American military aircraft are few in number and overwhelming in performance and capability.

The B-24 was a big bomber for its day, larger than anything the Germans or Italians could fly, and during World War II the United States built over eighteen thousand of them. No one in his right mind could imagine that World War II would ever have started if the United States had eighteen thousand B-24 bombers before the War began.

The majority of the people alive today in England and the United States of America do not personally remember World War II. Those vast aerial armadas of the United States Eighth Army Air Force are history. Also becoming history are the airmen – combat veterans of that European air war of long ago.

INDEX